# THE FORMAL FRENCH

# THE FORMAL FRENCH

BY

## W. L. WILEY

HARVARD UNIVERSITY PRESS · CAMBRIDGE

MCMLXVII

Distributed in Great Britain by Oxford University Press, London

Library of Congress Card Number 67-17322
Printed in the United States of America

FOR MY GRANDDAUGHTER

COSBY FORD WILEY

# PREFACE

*The Formal French* has as its purpose the examination of a basic aspect of French nature: namely, a tendency toward formalism in its varied manifestations and an inherent respect for rigid rules, particularly when they are written down. The Frenchman is likely to have formalistic inclinations in any age or time, but the primary era of formalism in France embraced a little more than two centuries, from the first part of the sixteenth century to around the middle of the eighteenth. *The Formal French* will be concerned for the most part with literature and literary criticism, but will have a look also at the other arts, manners, architecture, entrees and ceremonials, and gardens. A selection of engravings from the period will be included in the book, in the belief that they will add flavor and give visual confirmation of the ideas presented.

Over thirty years of experience with the people of France, both in times of peace and in times of war, have been the inspiration of this book. The source material has been the literature, criticism, and memoirs of the sixteenth, seventeenth, and eighteenth centuries; much of this substantive background is not new, but the philosophical and critical approach, may be. All translations of French prose or poetry in the text are my own; several excerpts from original sources have been put in the notes, with the spellings and accentuations of the editions employed. It is hoped that this work will fit easily into the world of scholarship, since in its composition every effort has been made toward accuracy of research and legitimacy of interpretation. It is hoped, in addition, that the book will have appeal for the general reader who has an interest in the culture and civilization of France.

If there is any bias in my critical judgment, it might be toward the Great Classicists of the School of 1660 who were formalistic in the best sense of the word. Nevertheless, there has been a conscious endeavor to avoid equating formalism with perfection or correctness. In the Quarrel of the Ancients and Moderns, *The Formal French* might well evidence a preference for the Ancients and a consequent disapproval of Descartes and his influence on literature.

I am indebted to many of the personnel of the Bibliothèque Nationale in Paris, especially to mademoiselle Bernadette de Sagey of the Cabinet des Estampes, for assistance with books, manuscripts, and engravings. To the Research Council of the University of North Carolina I must give my thanks for travel grants during the Summers of 1961 and 1963. I am grateful to my colleagues in the Department of Romance Languages at the University of North Carolina for their helpful advice along the way; in particular, I owe a debt of gratitude to Alfred Garvin Engstrom, Alumni Distinguished Professor of French, for looking at portions of the manuscript with his exact critical eye. Finally, my appreciation is due my wife, Dorothy Ford Wiley, for her encouragement, for reading certain chapters as they were being formed, and for keeping quiet at the proper times.

*The Formal French* is being dedicated to a little girl who is now five years old, and who has just learned to call me *grand-père*.

W. L. W.

Chapel Hill, North Carolina
March 21, 1966

# CONTENTS

# ILLUSTRATIONS

# THE FORMAL FRENCH

# THE GENERAL PICTURE

THE FRENCH are, by nature and tradition, inclined toward formalism. This tendency has found expression in almost all phases of life in France: in art and architecture, in the French language and literature, and in social and political institutions. One of the reasons that the Reformation received final rejection in France was the fact that the French, even in matters of religion, preferred to Calvinistic simplicity a ceremonial and formalized ritual such as that symbolized by the Church of Rome. Nowhere has the well-measured cadence and the ordered beat of a military parade received greater acclaim than in Paris, particularly in the stylized setting of the Champs-Elysées with the majesty of the Place de la Concorde at one end of the Avenue and that of the Arc de Triomphe at the other. When to the pomp and circumstance of France's men-at-arms on parade is added the solemnity of the *pompes funèbres* for a national hero—such as was done for Marshal Joffre in 1931—the external manifestations of the formalistic French are to be seen at their best, and the people of Paris in attentive homage jam her streets, squares, and bridges from the Invalides to the cathedral of Notre Dame. The French have through the years, possibly to a larger degree than any other nation in Europe, had a great respect for order, measure, ritual, regularity, and form.

A rather strange paradox is the fact that France, particularly in the environs of Paris, has been willing for more than a century to welcome within her boundaries almost any informal movement in art and letters that chose to flourish there. This apparent contradiction is no real indication of a declining respect for form and proper procedure. The French can at the same time be liberal and formalistic, a quality of dualism that has been most manifest since the eighteenth century. A Montesquieu, for example, might well lay down in his *Esprit des lois* the basic rules for a democracy, but the French have never been willing in any complete sense to follow them. Montesquieu's concepts fitted more easily into the governmental framework of a young and informal nation like the United States. A Chateaubriand at the end of the eighteenth century might visit the New World and sing a song of praise for its natural grandeur and simplicity; yet Chateaubriand felt that Napoleon, in his ritualized setting and self-created imperialism, was a more impressive figure than George Washington. France, then, during the past two centuries has listened to and sometimes nestled to her bosom the *libertins*, the Cartesians, the *philosophes* and the physiocrats; the anarchists, Bonapartists, and the royalists; Lord Byron, Heinrich Heine, and Edgar Allan Poe; the realists, the symbolists, the cubists, the dadaists, the surrealists, and the existentialists; and such "informalists" as Van Gogh, Picasso, James Joyce, and Gertrude Stein. None of these disparate ideologies and assorted personalities would have felt ill at ease on French soil. But the French themselves, in the depth of their well-cadenced souls, are more comfortable even today when encompassed by the formalized dignity and authoritanianism of a Charles de Gaulle.

A primary illustration of French formalism is the French language itself, with its wealth of polysyllables, its exactitude and clarity, and its emphasis on the *mot juste*. A respected and established man of letters like Georges Duhamel can thus—as he did in the newspaper *Le Figaro* in 1961—dismiss English as a mere "langue commerciale." Understandably, there has been resentment during the last few years, on the part of sober defenders of the purity of the French language, at the progressive incursion into it of English words, especially slangy monosyllables. The French never like, even in affairs of daily living, a monosyllable when a polysyllabic construction can be found to take its place. The process of "quick freezing" came into French as "congélation ultra-rapide" and a "permanent wave" for a feminine coiffure was first "ondulation indéfrisable." A "bicycle path" is a "piste cyclable," "stainless steel" is "acier inoxydable," and any grain that can be used for bread is a "céréale panifiable"—the latter a good example of formalized compression where English demands a longer phrase.

The language of the military might be expected in France to observe the rigors of form, and it does. A person "subject to draft" is "mobilisable," the process of going "through channels" is to proceed "par la voie hiérarchique," and a "military transfer" is a "mutation."* Travelers in French railway coaches have long been familiar with the politely formal French version of "don't lean out the window": "Messieurs et Mesdames sont instammant priés de ne pas se pencher dehors." This admonition in very recent years have been shortened, possibly due to the influence of English. But a three-year-old at the Gare du Nord (August 18, 1963), in his legitimate excitement over the arrival from London of the Golden Arrow, does not tell his mother to look at the train or the engine: he says, "Maman, look at the *locomotive*." Formalism begins early, as is further indicated on a crowded Opéra bus when a little Boy Scout bows rigidly to his grandmother and shakes her hand before getting off. Correctness

---

* All these examples of military language have been taken from the French subtitles attached to an American motion picture, *The Young Lions*.

of phrasing is even to be discovered in the new Mont Blanc tunnel, where there was a sign during its construction which said that visitors were "*formellement* forbidden" to penetrate it without being properly accompanied. At the French racetracks, too, the rigors of the linguistic amenities are observed. The winner of the Grand Steeplechase de Paris at Auteuil in 1965 did not get a monetary prize and a "cup": he received 300,000 francs and an "objet d'art." A French thoroughbred may well bear the name of the Renaissance warrior, Anne de Montmorency; or a horse may be called, in a lofty mixture of French and Spanish breeding, Le Cid. In the more mundane matter of changing money to make a wager at the hippodrome of Longchamp, there may be some question as to the number of francs received; in that case a complaint is not "made"—it is "formulated." The nuclear arsenal of the United States contains weapons with simple earthly names like Honest John and Minute Man, or bearing the godlike monosyllable, Thor; France, in a nice combination of respect for Roman history and the power of woman, has a rocket named Bérénice.

The classical and conservative spirit of the Frenchman is seared when he sees his language—and the language, *mon Dieu,* of Racine and of Voltaire—invaded by a series of lowly words from English, especially from American English. He has long been accustomed to English terms of sport like "un gentleman-jockey" or "un set" in tennis instead of "une manche," but the situation has become much more generalized. Commercial material stored in a warehouse might now be "les stocks," and a superb performer in either an intellectual or sportive field is "un crack." The great English train robbery of 1963 was described as "un hold-up," and a band of young musicians in the same year was called, in what must be a linguistic nadir, "les sloppers." French purists and intellectuals have spoken out strongly against the corruption of their language by this popular brand of English, and with some justification. A magazine of the broad circulation of *Paris-Match* has carried articles decrying the tendency; yet *Paris-Match* itself is one of the worst offenders in mixing English and French. The issue of May 2, 1964 carried, among other hybridizations, "le rush des vacanciers" and "quelques gadgets amusants."* The French sometimes forget that English has a long history of borrowed words from the land of France: savoir-faire, surveillance, chaise-longue, a propos, to name a few. The formal Frenchman is not too much impressed by such limited improvement of a commercial language. His attitude simply is that the English and Americans show some elements of savoir-faire in seeking to smooth out their unpolished tongue.

The French have traditionally, in their seldom unbiased analysis, been rather critical of the irregular languages and cultural deficiencies of other nations. As early as 1521, Pierre Fabri said that three basic languages came out of the Tower of Babel—Hebrew, Greek, Latin—and that French has had the responsibility of carrying on the spirit of this legacy of speech from the Biblical past.[1] A bit later in the sixteenth century, Ronsard and Du Bellay, the leaders of the poetic school of the Pléiade, had much to say about what they considered the trivialities of the Italian language. This showed marked lack of appreciation, in view of the many borrowings of poetic form and of critical concept the Pléiade made from the Italians. Du Bellay used the Petrarchan sonnet freely, then objected to the "Petrarchists" in France. Ronsard said in his "Au Lecteur," a preface to the reader which preceded the first four books of his *Odes* in 1550, that he was going down an "unknown path" with Pindar and Horace, and would not try to please any courtiers with a "sonnet Pétrarquisé" or "some triviality of love." Ronsard

---

* A further addition might be made to this "franglais:" a French writer on contract bridge in the summer of 1965 described a technique by which one's opponents might be "squeezés."

gave additional evidence of his preference for the formalistic, non-Italian path when he took up the matter of epithets in his *Abrégé de l'art poétique* of 1565: epithets should have a Roman dignity and not be idly strung along as in an Italian combination like "alma, bella, angelica e fortunata dona." Ronsard paid his respects to the Spaniards in his advice to the reader which prefaced his unfinished epic, *La Franciade*, in 1573: writers who practice the epic should have conceptions that are lofty and noble, and "not monstrous and pretentious like those of the Spaniards."[2]

With their developing confidence in measure and formalistic control, the French continued into the seventeenth century their feelings of artistic, linguistic, and cultural superiority over other nations. Jules de la Mesnardière in his *Poétique* of 1639 made an interesting survey of some of the neighbors of France. In an attempt at describing national characteristics, he catalogued the French, the Spanish, and the English. The French were found to be, among other things, "courteous, bold, inconstant, polite, fickle in love." The Spanish were "presumptuous, tyrannical, politically astute, somber, ridiculous in love." The English were "faithless, lazy, brave, cruel, property-conscious, hostile to strangers, arrogant, and self-interested."[3] La Mesnardière was not totally unobservant in this critical survey; nor did he give the French a blanket coating of whitewash. As for Spanish writers, he upbraided Lope de Vega, who had a "spirit of great intelligence," for not obeying the rules he set out for the other poets of his nation.

A peak of respect for the formal and regular was reached in France in the second half of the seventeenth century, during the golden years of Louis XIV. France at this time was the dominant nation in Europe, politically as well as artistically, and French critics were disparaging of other countries in matters of language, literature, and many of the arts. Much of the expression of self-admiration and confidence took place in the 1670's, when the French language, with its measured periods and exactitude, was well on the way to becoming an instrument of international diplomacy and culture. The grammarian Gilles Ménage said in an epistle dedicating his *Observations sur la langue française* of 1672 to the sophisticated gentleman, the chevalier de Méré: "Indeed, Monsieur, since the establishment of the Académie Française, our language is not only the most beautiful and the most rich of all living languages, it is also the most restrained and most modest." And, in further exuberance and pride, Ménage assured Méré that since the conquests of "our King," "it [the French language] has become today the principal study of all foreigners."[4] At about the same time, Le Père Bouhours, the Jesuit father whose critical opinions were so well-known in his day, published a series of delightful imaginary conversations between a certain Ariste and one Eugène, who are strolling along the seashore in Belgium. Ariste remarks that it is wonderful to know languages, since they enable a person to go anywhere in the world without an interpreter. Eugène admits the validity of Ariste's statement, but adds: "All your arguments will not give me any desire to learn Flemish." The reply to this reservation is: "Already French is spoken in all the courts of Europe. Every foreigner who has any wit at all prides himself on knowing French. Those who hate us as a nation love our language." The continuing discussion between Ariste and Eugène brings out the fact that there is something "noble" and "august" about French that lifts it "infinitely" above Spanish and Italian. Spanish is too bombastic; indeed, there is nothing more "pompous than Castilian." On the other hand, Italian is too much like burlesque, and too "frolicsome" with its diminutives. French is the dignified golden mean between Spanish and Italian, and possesses a "grandeur tempered by reason" as a result of an "order" that is natural. French is smooth, subtle, and capable of both clarity and tenderness; any awkwardness of phrasing is the result of foreign importation, like, said Bouhours, "the jargon of some German recently arrived in Orléans."[5]

In the same year (1674) that Boileau, the lawgiver of the French classical school, was rebuking those writers "beyond the Pyrenees" who ignored the rules and lacked the measured cadences of the French, Le Père René Rapin in his *Réflexions sur la poétique d'Aristote* was making a similar criticism of the Spanish, as well as of the Italians and the English. It is necessary, he said, to know measure and restriction, and to "finish things where they should be finished," something that Horace and Vergil understood. There must be a "subjection of the creative urge to the rules of art," a concept that "Italian and Spanish poets have comprehended almost not at all." As for "the English our neighbors," they are rough and insular, and "separated from the rest of men"; therefore, "in their plays they are fond of blood, in keeping with the nature of their temperament." The French, on the other hand, are more "human," and a "sophisticated sentiment" is legitimate for "our tragedies," although they have commenced to degenerate and lose gravity by imitation of the Spaniards.[6]

During the eighteenth century, the French underwent, as is well known, considerable intellectual and literary influence from England. However, at least until past the middle of the century, Voltaire and other critics carried on an attack against the English for their lack of formalism and recognition of the rules. The abbé Raynal in his *Nouvelles littéraires* (1747-1755) was very caustic in regard to the English theatre. He spoke about it to the duchesse de Saxe-Gotha as follows: "You are acquainted, Madame, with the English theatre: it is without manners, without decency, without any rules; these islanders are naturally so somber, so sad, so melancholy that the roughest, boldest, most exaggerated scenes are never too much to distract them and affect their emotions." Raynal regretted that the French in recent years had shown the bad taste to copy English tragedy; he regretted equally that for "Roman loftiness and grandeur" in French plays there had been substituted "Spanish bombast."[7] Clearly, many French critics well into the eighteenth century resisted the overthrow of formalistic regulations in literature and art, and were opposed to all types of foreign invasions.

The age of French formalism, then, embraced a little more than two centuries, the period from a few decades before 1550 to around 1750. These temporal limits must necessarily be a bit pliable and susceptible to occasional stretching in both directions. In any case, the centuries of France's primary allegiance to form and regularity have as their base the civilization and culture of classical antiquity. The French, in their inclination toward the formal and regular and polysyllabic, looked back to Greece and Rome. A full chorus of critical voices from the early sixteenth century on—and in many instances totally unappreciative of Italy as an intermediate connection—called out the names of Homer, Plato, Aristotle, Horace, and Vergil. The late fifteenth century in France, it is true, was not without its writers who admired the Romans. Some of the school of poets who have since been called the "great rhetoricians" took pride in being known as the "French Ovid" or the "French Seneca." However, these writers indulged in poetic acrobatics in their verse, and in rhetorical excesses in their prose, with the possible exception of the best of the group, Jean Lemaire de Belges. They confused late Latin grammarians with the noble Romans of the Augustan era, and their writings possessed the flamboyance of the other arts of the declining fifteenth century. The direct and well-ordered road to the past was not to be traveled by the French before the sixteenth century, the era of the Renaissance, when the critical signposts began to point to the ancient glories of Greece and Rome.

With the progressive rejection of things medieval that was
discernible during the reign of Francis I (1515-1547), the
very form of language, criticism, art, and living in France
took on the appearance of antiquity—frequently an antiquity that was classical but with an Italian interpretation. The
King himself with his retinue liked to visit the "nymph" that
guarded the fountain that gave the name to his palace of
Fontainebleau, and the imported Italian artist, Niccolò dell'
Abbate, drew a sketch of one of the meetings. A composer of
verses ceased to be a "rhymester" and became a "poet"; a
treatise on the writing of verse was no longer a "second
rhetoric" (a "full rhetoric" in medieval terminology treated
both prose and poetry, and the last one of these was that of
Pierre Fabri in 1521), but a "poetics" or an "art of poetry"
in the manner of Aristotle or Horace. Translation of Greek
and Roman material was in high favor during the first part of
the sixteenth century, and helped to fix the form and mold
of the ancients in French. A good poet like Clément Marot
rendered two books of Vergil's *Aeneid* into rhyming couplets, Melin de Saint-Gelais translated the plays of Terence,
and Charles Fontaine put ten of Ovid's *Heroides* into French
—to cite a few examples. Thomas Sebillet in his *Art poétique of* 1548 was high in his praise of translators, an opinion
not shared by Du Bellay a year later in his *Défense et illustration de la langue française*. Du Bellay favored the pillaging
of the ancients but not the mechanics of direct translation.
There was general agreement among the critics that Greek
and Roman forms should be adopted in France, and Du
Bellay himself recommended the abandonment of medieval
poetic genres as "just so many groceries." The five-act form
of the Roman tragedy of Seneca thus became the model for
French tragedy for more than two centuries, along with an
inclusion of a good deal of formalized Senecan bombast. The
epistle and elegy were borrowed from Ovid, Propertius, and
Tibullus; the epigram from Martial; the satire from Horace;

the ode from Pindar (the peak of stylized formalism), Anacreon, and Horace; the epic from Homer, who was known as the "first captain of the Muses," and from Vergil. It goes without saying that the French were not always successful, particularly in the epic, when they copied the form and literary manners of the ancients; nevertheless, the formalized basis of French creative efforts was, as the Renaissance progressed, Greek and Roman.

Most of the critics paid homage to the antique past. Sebillet was one of the first to speak, in Plato's terms, of the poet's "divine fury," and to say that "the poet is born, the orator is made." In the cult of Plato that came into France from the Platonic Academies in Florence and the commentaries of Marsilio Ficino, Sebillet, like many Frenchmen, did not realize that Plato's "frenzied" poet was put no higher than an "inspired" lover or soothsayer. At any rate, Sebillet mentioned inspiration, in an added interpretation to Plato's meaning, as the quality that distinguishes a poet from a rhymester. With encouragement from Francis I many poets have blossomed, and it was not a fantastic hope that poetry would soon be as advanced, according to Sebillet, as it was "under Caesar Augustus." The "style and the eloquence," said Sebillet, of today's writers came from the ancients; they were the "swans" who have left their "plumes" (or pens) to a later creative age. At about the same time, Antoine Fouquelin in his *Rhétorique française*—a real treatise on rhetoric and not a collection of rhyme schemes—used "plumes" in a slightly different sense. According to Fouquelin, the French language was "improperly garnished with everything it needs" and has had to borrow its "plumes" from the ancients. The "plumes" in question were rhetorical "tropes and figures," all primary instruments of formalism. A grammarian of the period, Louis Meigret, was a trifle more optimistic concerning the classically based French tongue in his *Traité de la grammaire française* of 1550. He made a strong claim: "Now the fact is that today our language is so enriched by the utilization of and contact with the Greek and Latin languages that there is no art or science so difficult and subtle that French can not treat it amply and elegantly." Unlike Fouquelin, Meigret felt that French had already evolved from its ancestral roots into a linguistic mechanism of form, clarity, precision, and measure.[8]

Du Bellay also favored the "plumes" of antiquity for bringing ornamentation to French, but recommended the botanical device of "grafting" in order to make a new and improved plant; French would attain beauty and stylized perfection by the grafting onto it of a stalk of Latin just as Latin was improved by the grafting of Greek. Ronsard, who was very much of the same critical mind as Du Bellay, advised the French to saturate themselves in Greek and Latin fragrances but make of them the "honey" of French. Vergil, the great master of figures and periphrases, was for Ronsard the source of "venerable majesty." Like Ronsard, Jacques Peletier du Mans in his *Art poétique* of 1555 praised Vergil's use of words. Vergil, to Peletier's way of thinking, employed the same vocabulary as other Romans but "in a fashion more proper, more gracious, and more suitable," which made his writings shine forth "in a certain form and a certain majesty like the moon among the stars." Here is something of an anticipation of Pascal's remark on the precision of style: all writers, like players of court tennis, make use of the same linguistic "ball"; the masters of craftsmanship and form simply place the ball better. Pierre de Laudun d'Aigaliers in his *Art poétique français* of 1597 repeated in many ways the doctrines of the Pléiade and of Peletier on the correct manner of borrowing from the ancients. It was "lèse-majesté," according to Laudun, for a Frenchman not to compose in his own language, though he was privileged to use Greek and Roman material—in the familiar simile—"as the honeybee uses the flowers." Vauquelin de la Fresnaye, in his *Art po-*

*étique* published in 1605 (though written a bit earlier), grounded much of his criticism on Horace's *Ars poetica*. Vauquelin, in the matter of adding words to the language (a poet's privilege, according to Horace), admitted that he had relied largely on Greek and Latin, but suggested that such additions might well be mixed with words "commonly used." On the other hand, in Vauquelin's opinion the Muses prefer a speech that is "measured," and for a poet to acquire full and precise mastery of his profession, "it is necessary to go sailing on the Greek and Roman sea," preferably with Vergil as a navigator.[9]

The formalized legacy to France from the ancients continued to be recognized by critics in the seventeenth century. Pierre de Deimier, in his lengthy *Académie de l'art poétique* of 1610, claimed to have read all the great masters of poetic art from antiquity, and concluded from them that poetry must have "measure," since "the human spirit is delighted by that which is measured, ornamented, and harmonious." François de la Mothe le Vayer in his advice to French orators in 1637, *Considérations sur l'éloquence française de ce temps*, was a believer in the necessity of dignity and formalized arrangement in prose. As a background, said Le Vayer, it is a good thing for a public speaker to know Greek, and it is imperative for the seeker of true eloquence to steep himself in the orations of Cicero. An orator may be allowed some latitude of composition, but he must remember to keep the "greatest order possible in everything that he writes." A mass of materials, argued Le Vayer in a more visual comparison, will not make a palace unless arranged with the "symmetry" that architecture demands. La Mesnardière in his *Poétique* of 1639 emphasized the social position of the lofty and formal literary genres, and denied (in disagreement with the Italian critic, Castelvetro) that poetry is destined "for the pleasure of a stupid populace." Poetry is "majestic" and the measured cadences of a "pompous and sublime tragedy" are beyond the appreciation of the rabble, in the opinion of La Mesnardière. Another phase of cultivated and mannered formalism before 1650—also beyond the perceptive powers of the people—was the vogue of fashionable hellenism, represented in many ways by the genteel chevalier de Méré. Greek heroes like Alexander the Great could thus be clothed with a precise and courtly gallantry. Formal words were added to the French language to designate certain attributes of a refurbished antiquity. Guardians of literary style such as Vaugelas, Louis Guez de Balzac, and Jean Chapelain discussed terms like "sériosité" and "urbanité." "Sériosité" was supposed to be applicable to the Greeks, while "urbanité" (a word that may have been invented by Chapelain) was of Roman origin and had Roman implications.[10]

The high level of French formalism in all of its manifestations was reached at the court of Louis XIV, in the golden age of French classicism, which was sometimes called, for literature and literary criticism, the school of 1660. The lawgiver of the school was Boileau, who modeled his *Art poétique* of 1674 after that of a most sophisticated and correct Roman, Quintus Horatius Flaccus. Boileau was himself a fine example in modern Gaul of Roman urbanity. He was supported in his dignified allegiance to Rome by Le Père Bouhours who said in his *Doutes sur la langue Française*, also of 1674, that it was a sin against Cicero and Horace (and the "rule of good sense") to invent "useless words." However, if a new word was to be added to the French language, it should be derived "in some fashion from Latin" or from one of the modern languages that "have the Roman tongue for their mother." The background of the Frenchman's present-day antipathy toward English words that slip into his language clearly goes back several centuries. Boileau and Bonhours were supported in their classical formalism by Le Père Rapin, who went farther back than they and started everything with Aristotle. Rapin, in his *Réflexions sur la poétique d'Aristote* (of 1674, too), said that Aristotle's *Poetics* was "nature controlled by method, and good sense reduced to principles." Perfection could be reached, according to Rapin, only through adherence to the Aristotelian rules, and those who ignored them have wandered off along rocky paths of irregularity.[11]

The eighteenth century saw the decline of formalism as a controlling concept in French art, literature, and criticism. In the last years of Louis XIV, Versailles became sad, and the Moderns backed by the argumentative processes of the Cartesian method pushed aside most of the defenses of a formal Ancient like Boileau. Novelty was in the air, the moral excesses of the Regency (1715-1723) sought to obliterate the memory of the somber religiosity of madame de Maintenon, and nobody cared much about Homer and the Muses. Paris was a teeming city, gambling was rife at the Court, and everybody was going to be rich through the speculative schemes of the Scotsman, John Law. There were many who preferred the disheveled informality of an English garden to the rigid designs of Le Nôtre. Importations of furniture, painted screens, and objets d'art from the Far East added a flavor of the fantastic and asymmetrical to French life, despite royal edicts against the bringing into France of exotic "chinoiseries." On the other hand, the mannered ceremonials of the court of Louis XV went along their formalistic way, and the Aristotelian unities remained practically intact in tragedy. A critic like Charles Batteux in *Les beaux arts réduits à un même principe* of 1746 said he had read all the rules up to his time, but that the regulation that really impressed him was "the principle of imitation established for the fine arts by the Greek philosopher"—namely, Aristotle.[12] Though Aristotle and Horace remained names to conjure with throughout the eighteenth century, after 1750 the ideas of informal (and very disparate) *philosophes* like Diderot and Rousseau were in the ascendancy. The movement of measured formalism, based on the philosophical and cultural legacy of Greece and Rome, had come to a close.

Even in the primary years of French formalism, there was some disagreement among the French as to how close an attachment should be maintained with classical antiquity. In 1540, the fine classical scholar and printer Etienne Dolet published a treatise on translation, *La manière de traduire d'une langue en autre*. In it he defended the worthiness of his own language but recognized some of its imperfections. A translator would at times have to use Latinisms for exact shadings of meaning, "for it is well known that the Greek and Roman tongues are richer in expressions than the French." However, in an elaboration of opinion, Dolet minimized Latinisms and stated that for the translator "the best procedure is to use ordinary words." Many fine Latinists of the Renaissance, including such scholarly men of letters as Rabelais and Montaigne, objected to the ready insertion into French of too many formal and learned words of recent Latin extraction. Rabelais (and other good scholars) called the process "Latin verbosination" or, in the hands of inept and emptily formal users, *écorcher le latin*, "the murdering of Latin." Rabelais and Montaigne both blamed such pompous and formalistic display on the pedagogues, especially the professors of the Sorbonne, though it would be difficult to find a more delightful Latin verbosinator than Rabelais himself. And, too, Rabelais ignored in his criticism the strong propensity for Latin- and Greek-based polysyllables that has been native to the French throughout the ages.[13]

Some of the objections to the overdose of Latin in the French language came from the Latin-trained pedagogues themselves. Barthélemy Aneau, a professor in a *collège* in Lyons, attacked Du Bellay soon after the appearance of the *Défense* in 1549 for Du Bellay's too great a deification of things Greek and Roman. Aneau, in a pamphlet called the *Quintil Horatian* (a paradoxical homage to Horace), accused Du Bellay of trying to induce everybody to "Greekize and Latinize" and of vituperating "our native form of poetry." Aneau had a good point in suggesting that the classically inspired and formalistic critics of the Renaissance ignored the long history of the French language and literature of the Middle Ages, and the natural development through popular usage of Latin, classical and Vulgar, into a vernacular that became French. Aneau, then, berated Du Bellay for his formalistic vocabulary—though Aneau's style is just as formalized and Latinized as Du Bellay's—and for "murdering this poor Latin language without any pity." Aneau's own respect for form and the rigors thereof was shown when he translated a book of emblems of Alciati (Lyon, 1549) from Latin into French. The Latin descriptions were rendered into French with the same number of syllables as in the original text, because "the ancients did it this way." According to examples furnished by Aneau, Vergil translated Homer with this fixity of form and Horace did the same for Pindar. As for the emblems, Aneau stated that he had arranged them in "celestial" and "terrestrial" classifications in order that his work "might be presented in more beautiful form to the eye of the reader," since "things well-arranged are more attractive than when scattered about, and more pleasing when well-ordered than when they are confused."[14]

By the middle of the seventeenth century, few Frenchmen, even those who were confirmed classicists, doubted the polish, excellence, or exactitude of their own language. No question remained as to whether French possessed the proper "dictions" or "vocables" to render any desired shading of meaning. It was a linguistic instrument suitable for a royal proclamation, or the formal edicts of the law court, or the stylized alexandrines of a tragic hero. Somewhat surprisingly and unnecessarily, therefore, Desmarets de Saint-Sorlin brought out in 1675 a pamphlet, *La défense de la poésie et de la langue française*, in which he decried the use of Latin in

the land of France. Saint-Sorlin lamented those Frenchmen who, in their intoxication with Latin, have "lost the love
and respect that they owe their native land" and "never cease
to berate our language." Latin, for Saint-Sorlin, was dead and
could exhibit only a "breath of life in the schools." A confirmed Modern, he asserted that the French should "stop
dipping into antique fountains" and should remember that
"we speak a language more noble and more beautiful than the
sad Latin that is dragged out of a tomb."[15] Saint-Sorlin was
spanking a dead horse; more than a century earlier the best
critics had sought to rally French writers to the use of their
own language. The Moderns also objected to the employ-
ment of Latin in inscriptions, the priority of Homer, and
the deification of antiquity in general. They saw their cause
triumphant by the middle of the eighteenth century; but
they could not remove from the French language an innate
quality of formalism that had its roots in antiquity.

The mold of more than two centuries of formalism in
France was established primarily by the ruling kings and
their courts. Francis I, who had a good knowledge of Latin
and an interest in poetic composition, first set up a royal
"court," a term that had previously been applied to legal
bodies. His theory, too, was that a court should be a "cour
des dames," with an appropriate ceremonial attention that an
expanse of feminine charm demanded. Many biographies of
the first of the Valois-Angoulême monarchs have revealed
that Francis' interest in women was on many occasions more
carnal than formal. Nevertheless, the ritualistic framework
for ladies' participation in life at the French Court was
established by Francis I. His concern for languages—it might
be said in passing that his sister, Marguerite de Navarre, was
one of the best linguists at the Court—led him to establish
in 1530 the Collège de France, under the direction of the
fine Greek scholar, Guillaume Budé. The royal library at the

*1.* Cardinal Richelieu

2. Assemblée des Académiciens

3. The Forty Immortals

great chateau of Blois became the basis for one of the world's great collections of books, the present-day Bibliothèque Nationale in Paris. Francis was called by Brantôme, before the end of the sixteenth century, "the father and true restorer of arts and letters," and the classical foundation of French formalism was laid during his enlightened reign.

At the death of Francis I in 1547, his second son (his eldest son, the Dauphin François, had died in 1536 after becoming overheated in a game of *jeu de paume*) came to the throne and ruled as Henry II. Henry was tall and dark, a superb athlete and soldier, though not the intellectual or patron of the arts and letters that his father was. However, the most formal school of lyric poets that France was ever to know, the Pléiade, flourished during Henry's reign. Court procedure became more and more ritualized, and feminine participation therein achieved greater complexity under the direction of Henry's queen, Catherine de' Medici (the clever daughter of Lorenzo de' Medici and for almost half a century the most powerful woman in France), who was subtly assisted by the King's favorite, Diane de Poitiers. Catherine brought into vogue the presentation several times a week at the palace of Fontainebleau of precise and correct evenings of music. She also introduced as Court entertainment the Italian ballet, and some of these were lavish spectacles of ritualized music and dance. The first example of that well-ordered literary genre in imitation of Aristotle and Seneca, classical tragedy—it was called *Cléopâtre captive* and was written by a member of the Pléiade, Etienne Jodelle—was performed before Henry II in 1552. Unfortunately, after the death of Henry II in 1559 Catherine de' Medici forbade the representation of Renaissance tragedy at the Court, since she thought it might be symptomatic of bad luck and bring further misfortune to the Valois house. She never forgot that Henry had died while indulging in a formalistic and chivalric display of simulated combat: in full knightly regalia he was riding at the barrier against a captain of the guards when a broken lance penetrated (possibly because of Henry's bravado in leaving his visor open) into the royal brain.

After the death of Henry II, the man with the black beard, three of his and Catherine's sons ruled successively as King of France—Francis II (1559-1560), Charles IX (1560-1574), and Henry III (1574-1589). All were weaklings in comparison with their father and grandfather, and the three of them were pretty well dominated by their mother. It was a period of unrest in France, marked by warfare between the Catholics and Protestants, and a general objection to the powers of the Queen Mother. Nevertheless, under the last of the Valois monarchs the natural formalistic processes of the French continued to function. There came into being an academy of poetry and music, an ancestor of that most formal and sedate assemblage founded in the seventeenth century, the Académie Française. Ronsard tried to glorify the reign of Charles IX by a most pompous, pretentious, unsuccessful, and not-to-be finished literary effort, the epic poem of *La Franciade*. Henry III, "by the grace of his mother King of France" (the phrase of the sober chonicler, Pierre de l'Estoile), established a new chivalric body, the Order of the Holy Ghost, the ceremonials of which were ritualistic and impressive. The foppish Henry III managed to make the ultimate gesture in regal and formalistic procedure: he saved his throne from the ambitious duc de Guise by having the royal guards stab the duke to death in 1588. Henry III was destined himself to die by an assassin's hand in 1589, and thus end the Valois dynasty.

The first of the Bourbons, the tough and soldierly Henry IV, was no patron of formalism. He was too busy fighting battles, unifying his kingdom, winning the affection of the people of Paris, hunting the stag or surrounding his unwashed body with the charms of Gabrielle d' Estrées to bother very much with courtly ritual. For dramatic entertainment, he preferred a lusty and bawdy farce to the stilted tragedies of the time or to an insipid pastoral—though it was said that Henry IV liked to have read to him, of all things, the interminable pastoral novel, the *Astrée*, when he was sick. Basically, Henry IV brought to France that quality most admired by the French, a sense of order—in government, in finance, in roads, even in religion. On this solid foundation of governmental order and national unity later manifestations of formalism and sophistication could develop in seventeenth-century literature and art. One of the important early formalists, François de Malherbe, was welcomed to Paris during the regime of Henry IV—Malherbe, who in Boileau's famous couplet brought to the French language for the first time a sense of "proper cadence." Henry IV, like his immediate predecessor on the French throne, was killed by an assassin; while riding in a carriage through the streets of Paris that he loved, he was stabbed to death by one Ravaillac. The year was 1610.

The son of Henry IV continued the Bourbon line and ruled as Louis XIII. He lacked the dynamism and physical skills of his father, but was a well-intentioned though not brilliant king. Under him were continued the policies that have caused the seventeenth century in France to be designated by the contemporary historian, Pierre Gaxotte, as "an epoch of order, of discipline." Most of Louis XIII's plans and efforts were dwarfed by the activities of his minister of state, the master formalist and superb man of order, Cardinal Richelieu. Richelieu had his dignified and austere hand in everything, and successfully. The master technician in affairs of state, he found time outside the council chamber to organize in 1635 that disciplinary and controlling body for language and literature, the Académie Française, today called with mixed feelings the "Forty Immortals." He built his own theatre, and lent his support to the most formalized of literary genres, classical tragedy. He gave pensions to men

of art and letters, and sat (or stood) for one of the famous
portraits of the period, done by Philippe de Champaigne and
now hanging in the Louvre (Figure 1). In it can be seen
symbolized the disciplined intellectualism and the crimson-
tinted correctness of an epoch, since Richelieu combined a
spirit of external display with an "imperious need for order
and clarity." La Mothe le Vayer described him in 1637 as
the master of "divine eloquence" and his discourses as "im-
mortal." Le Père Le Moyne later in 1671 called Richelieu the
"grand Armand, the honor of our history." This incredible
man, whose awesome formalism allowed few men to get
close to him, died in 1642, one year before Louis XIII, who
liked to dance in ballets but who was no match for his prime
minister, Armand Duplessis, cardinal de Richelieu.[16]

Louis XIV, the son of Louis XIII and Anne of Austria,
represented the ultimate in formalism covered with regal
robes. His portrait by Hippolyte Rigaud caught the mood—
the uplifted chin, the haughty mien, and the right hand held
high on the staff of authority. Louis' palace of Versailles,
with its regularity of façade and balance of wing, its chiseled
expanse of gardens and a fountain dedicated to the mother of
Apollo, its gallery of mirrors and ceiling shining with the
sun's radiance, bore witness to the rigid and formal majesty
of the Roi Soleil. Versailles was no place for the shimmering
convolutions of the great Italian artist, Bernini, whose plans
for the construction of the palace were rejected. The affairs
of the nation during the minority of Louis XIV were directed chiefly by another cardinal, Mazarin, who was clever
in maintaining the policies of Richelieu, had difficulty with
the great nobles around him, and was more astute than formal. But he had his formal moments, which he showed in his
construction of a superbly ornate hall (now the Galerie Ma-
zarine of the Bibliothèque Nationale) to house his collection
of art. After his marriage to Marie-Thérèse of Spain in 1660,
Louis XIV took personal control of the affairs of the nation,

and dispensed with prime ministers. He was the state and he looked the part; his court was the model for all Europe, and the rigorous and formalistic etiquette thereof demanded the daily bowing and scraping of thousands of the noblest families of France. It was the age of French Classicism, of the *grands classiques*, whose names still shine forth with a proper sheen in any catalogue of the great moments of European culture: Molière, Boileau, Racine, La Fontaine, Bossuet, Mignard, Rigaud, Le Brun, Le Nôtre, Le Vau, madame de Sevigné, Mansart—and the list is far from complete. Louis in his own lifetime was compared to Caesar Augustus, "that Roman emperor who was so famous."[17] The era was over by the early 1690's when Louis was getting old and a bit tired. While it lasted—and it was a legitimate and normal cultural cycle of some thirty years—it reflected French formalism at its best.

With the Moderns becoming victorious in the Quarrel of the Ancients and Moderns the Age of Louis XIV ended even before his death in 1715. After the excesses of the Regency, the Sun King's great-grandson who had come to the throne as Louis XV began his active rule in 1723. It has been customary to speak of Louis XV's regime as frivolous rather than formal, and in many respects the empty frivolity was there. But Paris during his reign reflected well-conceived plans of urbanism, and a continuing architecture of dignity and form. In matters of state, Cardinal Fleury, who was prime minister from 1726 to 1742, brought an element of order out of the chaos of the Regent's policies. The art of the period might be called *exquis;* yet there was a touch of pink formalism in the paintings of Boucher. The Opéra had an audience, and there were fine actors at the Comédie Française, performing Voltairean tragedies that had novelties in them but which were Racinian at heart. In spite of the pompous panorama of Versailles, however, Louis XV was a sensual weakling with no real desire to rule. He reached the peak of his career

at the battle of Fontenoy in 1745, where his presence was a
symbol of proper regality and military form. With ensuing
decline of health, he listened more and more to his trivial
bourgeoise, madame de Pompadour, whose critical taste was
prettified rather than dignified. After the middle of the eighteenth century, France drifted inevitably toward that most
informal of all political and social spectacles—revolution.

Formalism, whether in language, art, literature, or government, is not necessarily a good thing. Nor is it a quality which
is the sole monopoly of the French, though by inclination
and classical heritage it is something that the French take to
naturally. During the more than two centuries of primary
French formalism, much that was said and written was nothing except empty bombast. But it was also the period of
French Classicism, and the majestic couplets of Jean Racine.

The great organization of the French merchant marine
has been traditionally called the "Compagnie Générale
Transatlantique," which becomes in English, simply and officially, the "French Line." The pride of the French Line is
the magnificent ship, the S.S. *France*, superbly modern and
contemporary in décor. In the cabins, directions for the use
of life belts are given in French and English, as well as in
Spanish. The English version reads: "Pull the two ends
across your chest and fasten the tapes very tightly." The
French version is: "Réunissez les deux extrémités sur la
poitrine et fixez-les solidement au moyen des cordons."

# LANGUAGE AND STYLE

THE FRENCH have long been proud of the form and structure of their language, and their ultimate derogation of any clumsy or inexact expression is: "it is not French." The offending word or phrase is thus banished to the provinces or the benighted foreign land whence it came. Or, during the precise centuries of French formalism a current word might never have attained highest social acceptance, and have been relegated by the critical arbiters to "the people." For more than two centuries, the measured and correct language in France was that spoken at "the Court," where the technical details were worked out by scholars and critics usually on royal pensions. With the great centralization of government and greater spirit of nationalism that came in during the reign of Francis I, provincial noblemen lost much of their powers and the Court was centered around Paris and its environs. The Parisian dialect, or that of the Ile-de-France, became the basis for the language of the Court. For their part, the writers and the classically motivated scholars living on the King's largesse unearthed the Greek and Roman ancestry of the royal standard of speech. Courtly language became more restrained, and gentlemen at the Court were encouraged to become a trifle more erudite. Formalism was properly the vogue, and formalism in language was definitely "French."

The French language of the fifteenth century was not an undeveloped tongue, and a poet like François Villon showed that in skilled hands it could bring immortality. Or a prose chronicler like Froissart could use it for a readable account of incidents in his nation's history. However, by 1500 the language of France—more exactly, the language of northern France since by this time the language and literature of the south had ceased to be important in Gaul—had proliferated in all directions and its vocabulary was more extensive than that of modern French. Many of the words in it were entirely popular and bore too greatly the mark of their contact with the people. The language of scholars and of the Church was still Latin, and many writers (Erasmus, for example) continued to believe in the sixteenth century that Latin was the only language for civilized and international communication. A Neo-Latin poet like Johannes Secundus had an appreciative and extensive audience for his erotic verses. In any case, in order for French to compete with Latin at the scholarly and sophisticated level, the vernacular needed pruning, codifying, standardizing, and formalizing. Accents came into existence to aid in pronunciation, and efforts were made—many of them futile—at greater exactitude in spelling. Formalism, for better or for worse, began to cut its linguistic way.

The Frenchman's pride in his language and its possibilities was asserted in varied fashion as the sixteenth century progressed. With attempted precision and exact measurement, the physical mechanism necessary for spoken French was defined. The tongue by itself was not enough; altogether "nine instruments" were needed: the tongue, the palate, the gullet, two lips, and four teeth. From this combination would result "the rounded speech that is French." The specific four teeth required were not indicated, but the theory as a whole was supposed to go back to a Latin treatise. Also, many Frenchmen began to be proud not only of their language's origin in

Latin, but of its ability to compete with Latin just as Latin had competed with Greek. Before 1550, it was claimed by learned and formal critics that French had reached such a stage of perfection "that strangers will no longer call us barbarians." One of Du Bellay's favorite claims in his defense of his native tongue was that French was not by nature crude, imperfect, and "barbarous"; it required only proper embellishment and ornamentation to render it illustrious like its classical forebears. General cognizance was taken, too, of the effect of royalty on the regular development of the French language, and the linguistic historian Claude Fauchet said in 1581: "languages are reinforced according as the princes who use them increase in power." French formalism in language, then, became more and more a symbol of the strength of the monarch.[1]

Many thought that the most pompous and impressive language was used by the orators rather than the poets. The primary model for oratory was Cicero, supported by Seneca and Quintilian, and the three Ciceronian levels of language and style (the high, the middle, and the low) were copied by the French. Oratory was something of a legacy from the Middle Ages, though the sermons and funeral orations of Bossuet late in the seventeenth century showed that the courtly world still liked to listen to a well-rounded and formalistic period. Pierre Fabri spoke in 1521 of the three manners of speech: the "high and grave," the "middle," and the "low." The first was to be used "when one speaks of theology, the seven liberal arts, the activities of princes, and the *chose publique*"—the last a direct rendition of Cicero's *res publica*. The loftiest of the Ciceronian levels would most naturally be a base for later formalism in prose. Fabri gave an example of "lofty terms" and "lofty material" to be employed in proper address to a king: "Sire, you are our sovereign king much feared and respected throughout the universal world because of the very splendid and rigorous battles in which you have victoriously triumphed over your enemies." Fabri early discovered an attribute to the French language: the most sordid and depraved idea can be clothed by it in the most sophisticated terminology. Fabri stated that French was very fertile in "honorable and proper terms," and "things that are improper are supposed to be expressed by circumlocution." For Fabri, the insertion of diminutives weakened the dignified language of the orators, "the quite eloquent orators adorned with fine intelligence and depth of knowledge," who were so important to the welfare of the state. They normally avoided the "frivolous" words which slip into speech when the "rules" are ignored.

Rhetorical figures, the "colors of rhetoric," were the legitimate tools of oratory and the formal tactics of persuasion. Proper phrases were reserved for various ranks and classes. There was, for illustration, a correct method of paying homage to womankind in what was a "generalized praise": "The excellent beauty of women, who are angelic of face, burning and piercing in regard, and gracious in speech, brings delightful enjoyment to man." If the orator were in a different mood, he might with possibly greater formalism launch forth at woman a "generalized vituperation": "The beauty of woman intoxicated by fiery libidinousness, corruptive of every virtue and attractive to every sin, brings a miserable destruction to man." A tinge of this second apostrophe, which is reminiscent of the *Querelle de la Femme* that was continuing in the sixteenth century, might be noted in some general advice to the orator after he has "clothed naked materials with the colors of rhetoric": despite embellishment a sentence must have a basic mold of structure and order, wherein more worthy things go before the less worthy, "like man before woman, the honorable before the humble, day before night," and similar examples of precedence.[2]

The "fine French orators," who were to be preferred to

the poets in the modeling of correct French, would be discovered in a variety of places—"in the splendid imperial, royal, princely, and seignioral courts, in great councils of state, parlements, and embassies, in *conciles,* in assemblies of wise and loftily discursive men, in sermons and predications, in consulates, syndicates, and the political operations of governments." By this collection of responsible and dignified orators the French language would be better defended and ornamented than by the "subtle juggling of the greater part of poets," the weakness of which class was recognized when they were rejected from the "Platonic republic." Even in the matter of translation—and Cicero would be the most appropriate Roman writer of prose to be put into French—care should be taken to use "oratorical and resounding words," so that the listener's ears might be delighted as well as his soul. However, the "splendor of words" would be of little effect unless they were arranged in proper "order" and "collocation." Good judgment would avoid in French prose a "fricassee" of Greek and Latin words, which would form a "superfluous mixture" indulged in only by "pompous little fools." The poets, according to the defenders of oratory, were addicted to periphrases which were not suitable for "prose didascolique." The designation of the Roman poet Horace as the "Latin Pindar" would thus be a "superfluous transnomination." But proper pronunciation and the addition of accents, in accordance with the correct ideas of men of learning, would cause either prose or poetry to be clearer and more easily read. A grammarian around 1550 made a contribution to formalized language by designating the three French accents (acute, circumflex, and grave) that were to become standard; he based them on musical tones and hoped they would add a little logic to French spelling.[3]

Oratory, rhetoric (the "art of elegant and correct speech"), and grammar thus played their part in the Renaissance. The mouth of a child should be formed by a grammarian, so that the child "may pronounce all sounds roundly and perfectly, and not vomit words forth from his stomach like a drunkard." The tropes and figures of rhetoric were admitted by sober critics to be appropriate to both prose and poetry, and their solid source was placed in classical antiquity, which had produced Demosthenes and Cicero. Allegory, enigma, hyperbole, metonomy, synecdoche, anaphora, epistrophe, epanalepsis, and other figures all had their proper place—even "addubitation," which was the rhetorical question of a "man perplexed and in doubt." The formal and sometimes pompous figures of rhetoric penetrated the whole of Renaissance writing, and Rabelais' warlike monk in *Gargantua*, Frère Jean, could claim when he was fuming and swearing in the heat of battle that he was not blaspheming but only making use of the "colors of rhetoric."[4]

Prose of the seventeenth century became simpler, and the free-running sentences of Rabelais or Montaigne were curbed a bit by the letter writer, Louis Guez de Balzac, the popularizer of antiquity and reformer of French prose. Balzac was a proponent of a somewhat more rigid structure of phrase which resulted in the periodic sentence. French prose started to take on a characteristic that has distinguished the best French writing ever since, namely, clarity. *Clarté* came to be a word to conjure with, and even the masters of oratory and eloquence proclaimed it as essential to their profession, wherein, they began to say, the first demand was to be intelligible. The periods should be neatly balanced, and neither be too short nor too long; a period that was too short resembled "the speech of an asthmatic." Thoughts were to be well conceived, couched in eloquent language, and the realization kept in mind that the "three perfections of an orator are to instruct, to please, and to move"—and here is to be noted a foretaste of a later dictum of Racine and Boileau. Words were the clothing that became an ornamentation, even though words were constantly shifting and renewing like the leaves on a tree, "according to the statement of the Latin poet."* Foreign words smacked of the "barbaric," but eloquence at times permitted a touch of the barbarous just as medicine might contain a dash of poison, music a false note, and a beautiful lady wear a contrasting *mouche*. Too fastidious a choice of terms could never lead to dignified magnificence, but would resemble the prissiness of a man picking imaginary hairs off his clothes. The first oratorical effervescences might well be like a frothy new wine and need some aging: or, exuberant first words could require deletion or replacement by more dignified forms. The orator should not assume that every phenomenon of nature was to be designated by a frank and earthy word. It would be his responsibility to see that no subject in his hands was treated in "an impolite sense." Formal and correct language was inevitably an attribute of eloquence.[5]

Figures of speech were still recognized in the first half of the seventeenth century as a necessary part of the orator's or prose writer's ammunition, but they were to be kept under proper control. Exaggerated hyperboles, strained metaphors, and violent antitheses, in the manner of some of the Greek rhetoricians, were to be avoided. For illustration, to say that something was "lighter than the shadow of cork" would be overdoing it, even in Greek. It would be perfectly correct in French to call the lower part (*bas*) or root (*racine*) of a mountain its foot (*pied*), but it would not be acceptable to say that the foot of a man was his root. The rhetorician Gorgias introduced into the Greek language many "antithetical dictions" as a novelty; they would be just as barbarous in French as they were in Greek. On the other hand, Greek was a very good thing to know. Many cultivated ladies and gentlemen, who had been touched "by the atmosphere of the Court," were considered to have an excellent and correct speech. An acquaintance with the formalized

* Horace.

structure of Greek, however, would do them no harm. The very rigors of Greek conjugations and declensions, which were more complicated than their Latin equivalents, would have a good effect on any linguistic carelessness. The finest and most eloquent French speech, in any event, was not too bombastic or "stormy," nor too studied and complicated, but possessed a natural dignity that "shone forth with a pure and radiant fire."[6]

By the seventeenth century there was objection to the artificial and formalistic device of putting rhyme in prose. The Romans were blamed for it, and Claude Fauchet said late in the sixteenth century that certain Latin word combinations, inside a line or sentence, were responsible for the development of rhyme: for example, *gestorum tuorum* and *hora novissima, tempora pessima*. Whatever may have been the origin of the practice, the inclusion of a rhyme pattern in the interior of a prose sentence was universally condemned. The staunch Malherbe, the "tyrant of words and syllables," spoke out against it early in the seventeenth century because it gave a prose period an empty poetic ring. A little later in 1637 it was said that nothing was "more vicious in an oration than to slip into it unexpectedly a few lines of verse," even though the procedure went as far back as the Greek orator Isocrates. Vaugelas, the great protagonist of usage as the arbiter of language, also objected to the insertion of verse into a passage of prose, particularly any array of words that sounded like an alexandrine couplet. Ménage later, in a typical argument among formalists, accused Vaugelas of not "keeping his own precepts," and of slipping rhymes into his prose. Scipion Dupleix in his analysis in 1651 of the French language and its purity agreed with Vaugelas, and placed further responsibility on the Romans by quoting an internal rhyme from Cicero (*sollicitudine . . . valetudine*). Bouhours said later in the century that French had avoided juxtaposing in its periods words with the same sounds (like *ruisseaux d'eaux*) or "combinations that approach rhyme." There was general agreement among French formalistic critics that prose and poetry had a different form and rhythm, each one dignified and distinctive.[7]

During the more than two centuries of French formalism the language of poetry received more discussion and analysis than did that of prose. Very early in the sixteenth century—and critics continued to talk about them for several decades—attention began to be focused on the famous Roman formalistic divisions for linguistic creativity: invention, disposition, elocution, memory, and pronunciation. These five divisions were for the Romans primarily applied to rhetoric and oratory, but the French sought to fit them also into measurements of poetry. Du Bellay took them up in his defense of the French language, and Ronsard in his *Abrégé d'un art poétique* of 1565 sought to give them some definition and application. Invention was probably the most important concept. For Ronsard, invention was "the fine natural quality of the imagination conceiving the ideas and forms of all things" in order to "represent, describe, and imitate them" without creating "the forms of monsters." Ronsard's idea of invention would keep creativity in formalistic balance, in obedience to the Aristotelian or Horatian concept of the golden mean. Disposition was the "elegant and perfect collocation and order of the things invented," all embellished by the "antique treasure found underground" in the ancient soil of Greece and Rome. Elocution was, in the mind of Ronsard, "the proper splendor of words well-chosen and ornamented with brief and solemn maxims," which would make verses gleam like precious stones decorously mounted on "some nobleman's fingers." Elocution would mean equipping and arraying, in best Homeric fashion, all gods and goddesses in correct "clothes, chariots, and horses." Ronsard did not feel it necessary to give much treatment to the last two of the five Roman divisions, memory and pronunciation; nor did Laudun d'Aigaliers in his art of poetry of 1597, although Laudun made some additions to the general critical theories of the Pléiade. However, on invention and kindred matters Ronsard and Laudun were just about of the same mind. For Laudun, invention involved the proper "conception of the ideas and forms of everything celestial and terrestrial." Disposition was the correct "ordering and arranging of the things invented," and elocution concerned the "fine choice and elegance of words, grave maxims, and comparisons," with the certain elimination of "gross and crude expressions." Poetry in Renaissance critical opinion was formalistic and upper-stratum, and made no pretenses of talking the language of the people.[8]

The question of the five Roman divisions did not occupy the seventeenth century a great deal, but the question of rhyme in poetry did. This problem, in fact, received considerable attention during the whole formalistic era in France. Rhyme was definitely an attribute of French formalism, but many Frenchmen, ignoring the theory of Fauchet, wondered how it got into their metrical scheme of things. It posed a problem for the translating into French of the unrhymed hexameters of Vergil or the limping elegiacs of Ovid. The usual form of verse in the sixteenth century for rendering Latin or Greek into French was the ten-syllable rhyming couplet; or in the seventeenth century the twelve-syllable couplet, the alexandrine. Rhyme went through the eighteenth century as rather a mechanistic device, when poetry was generally regarded as something artificial, irrational, and the Cartesians would have gladly destroyed it. The nineteenth century revived poetry, but would have liked to break a number of its formalized rules; and in the latter part of the nineteenth century the fine poet Paul Verlaine lamented the flaws of rhyme and said it was a cheap jewel that sounded "hollow." All of which in contemporary French poetry has led to a slackening of formal rule, the uneven line, and the general release of free verse.[9]

But as the sixteenth century began French poetry was already a "measured language" and had inherited from the "great rhetoricians" a set of rhyme schemes so complicated that the writing of verse could well be an exercise in metrical acrobatics. The Romans, as has already been said, were given credit for inadvertently creating rhyme. No matter who invented it, said Jacques Peletier du Mans in 1555, rhyme should be welcomed in France as a "formal beauty of poetry." The sixteenth century abandoned for the most part of the florid excrescences of late-fifteenth-century rhyme—the coronated, equivocal, and leonine—and sought to make French poetry formal without being flamboyant. The eight-syllable couplet was not much in vogue because it recalled too easily the earthy medieval farces, but the ten-syllable and twelve-syllable couplets were strongly in favor. Both had a measured and formal cadence, with a well-marked cesura in the interior. The less formal nine-or eleven-syllable verse, with its slight offbeat and underemphasis, would not have full acceptance before the pastel shadings of the symbolists of the 1880's. The Pléiade recommended the alexandrine for the most lofty poetry but never had much success with it. And before 1600 Vauquelin de la Fresnaye, in his praise of the magnificent expanse of the epic, said it could be done in either ten-syllable or twelve-syllable verses, the latter the equivalent of the "grave hexameters" of Vergil. The whole poem should flow along majestically and "as sweetly as the water from the Castalian spring."* Unfortunately, no French poet was able to create such a gentle and noble current. By 1610 Pierre de Deimier was saying that rhyme was "proper to French poetry," and that the perfect poem should have seven qualities— "invention, clarity, measure or the just

---

* The Castalian spring, with its powers of inspiration and rejuvenation, is sacred to Apollo at Delphi.

quantity of syllables appropriate to the verse, richness of rhyme, elegance and sweetness of words, loftiness of language, and value and propriety of theme." Deimier laid down here a fine and formal code; he thought, along with it, that some verse forms had little grace and were "contrary to the nature of our language." A slight divergence of opinion was expressed in 1639 by La Mesnardière, who said that rhyme was of a "subsidiary beauty" and a "sort of rouge" applied by languages inferior to Greek and Latin. Gilles Ménage in his examination in 1650 of the origins of the French language gave a short history of the alexandrine, and attached its name to the twelfth-century narrative poem on Alexander the Great. Ménage pointed out that this couplet was now being used more and more, and that it was "majestic and difficult." He was to live to see the triumph of the alexandrine in the formal majesty of Corneille's tragedies, and in the smooth sophistication of those of Racine. On into the eighteenth century, in the hands of a skillful manipulator like Voltaire, the alexandrine was a precise instrument of poetry. Only after the middle of the century, when there was a growing admiration in France for Shakespeare's unrhymed iambics, did the alexandrine (and rhyme in general) come under strong attack. The classical alexandrine, with its alternating masculine and feminine couplets and its even cadences, marked the very peak of formalistic perfection in French poetry.[10]

There was a movement in the sixteenth century to do away with rhyme in French verse and substitute for it the classical system of long and short syllables, and feet. Probably the most important person connected with this operation was Jean-Antoine de Baïf, the experimenter of the Pléiade and popularizer in France of the Ovidian love-tale. Baïf advocated and tried to write what he (and others) called "measured verses." Part of the philosophy behind such a scholarly and formalized endeavor came from the Pléiade's general derogation of medieval French poetry, which Du Bellay dismissed as obsolete material belonging to the Round Table. Another objection to the French system of rhyme was made by the rigid and formalistic critics who thought that it was too easy for untutored rhymesters and versifiers to write poetry. With the help of rhyme, poetic composition too readily became the property of the rabble. The dramatist Jacques de la Taille published in 1573 a little treatise which he called *La manière de faire des vers en français comme en grec et en latin*. In his announcement to the reader, La Taille said that his reason for doing the pamphlet was that he had become "disgusted with our rhyme through seeing it used by both the trained and untrained." According to him, a crowd of "slaves and imitators" had thrust themselves into the midst of the most learned men of the day, which had made it necessary for erudite composers to "climb up to Parnassus on the road carved out by the Greeks and Romans." La Taille maintained that French words had quantity—that is, long and short syllables—just as did Latin. He drew up a list of words with the long and short (and "common") syllables marked. In it he showed, at least, a knowledge of Latin etymology, a preliminary condition that La Taille felt was necessary to a quantitative poet. An interesting part of his treatise was his listing of several French words that made "feet": a spondee (two longs), *seigneur;* an iambus (a short and a long), *devoir;* a trochee (a long and a short), *homme;* a dactyl (a long and two shorts), *inciter*—and so on. In a triumph of understatement, he admitted that there were many who might scan French words in a different manner from the one suggested, and that the whole process of writing poetry in the "measured" language was difficult.[11]

Baïf actually wrote some measured verses which were published in 1574; in the collection were poems to the Queen Mother (Catherine de' Medici) and to the King of Poland (later, Henry III of France). Baïf created a new and com-

plicated spelling in order to make his quantitative verses easier to read—a supposed long *o*, for illustration, was designated by the Greek omega—and to improve the "clean and
pure language of the French." He composed some lines
which he designated as "dactylic heroic hexameters," of
around sixteen syllables and without rhyme, and some "iam-
bic trimeters." Baïf stated that he was not minimizing or
"subverting" the splendid French poetry that had been written in rhyme, but that he hoped his efforts at quantitative
versification would put two poetries in vogue in France.
Jean Passerat, a clever poet (in standard fashion) and professor of Latin eloquence at the Collège de France after 1572,
wrote at least two odes which were "rhymed in the French
manner, and measured according to the manner of the Greeks
and Latins." Most linguistic analysts of the seventeenth century believed that all these stilted and formalistic efforts to
imitate classical poetry were ill-adapted to French. One
phrasing of the idea was that Latin "measure" simply did not
harmonize with the "sweetness of the French language." Another very accurate, and still quite acceptable, distinction was
made between Latin and French poetry: Latin poetry, particularly in the splendid dactyls of Vergil, was admirable because of the rhythm of its beat; French poetry, on the other
hand, attained its effect by having "all the syllables . . .
counted in the verses," without any diversity of cadence.
Yet even in the eighteenth century it was claimed that
French had long and short syllables which, in the hands of
good versifiers, would produce "on an attentive and trained
ear the same result as Latin poetry." French was capable of a
"rapid cadence, a gentle cadence, and a harsh cadence"—all
with examples; but the recognition of differences would not
be "without difficulty" for many persons.[12]

The vocabulary of French formalism, whether in verse or
prose, aroused some interesting and heated interchanges. As

a generality, the scholars and upper classes in the budding
Renaissance leaned toward a learned and formally Latin-
based language, while the people and noncourtly citizens
preferred a simpler and more naturally evolved tongue. The
arguments began to acquire a great deal of heat around 1550,
and a number of them were directed at the classically minded
Pléiade, many of whose members had as schoolboys written
for their homework parallel poems in Greek, Latin, and
French. The erudite Pléiade was accused of ignoring the tra-
ditions of the French language, of putting strange words
into it, and of "vituperating" the poetic legacy of the Middle
Ages. Du Bellay was attacked on this score, and Ronsard
was accused of very arrogantly priding himself on bringing
the "Greek and Latin lyre into France because he has made
us gape at those clumsy and strange words, strophe and
antistrophe." Ronsard could indeed produce some formalized monstrosities; one of the worst was a bit of praise in
1565 "to the Majesty of the Queen of England," wherein
he lavished admiration on Elizabeth I for her "prudente
gynécocratie."[13]

The Pléiade poets were charged with overdoing periphrases, and with some justification, though they probably
never called a calf a "son of a cow." Du Bellay and Ronsard
both thought that circumlocutions, preferably of a classical
and formal extraction, added flavor to the language. Du Bellay recommended antonomasia which would make of Jupiter "the fulminating father" and of Diana "the virgin who
hunts." Ronsard, too, felt that figured language was a good
thing if it were done after the manner of the master of such
devices, Vergil, who called bread "the gift from the laboratory of Ceres" and wine "the goblets of Bacchus." Such locutions would be fine in French if they were done "without
the extravagance of a frenetic." Ronsard had a very sane
theory on the transfer of classical words and phrases into
French: Latin should not be distorted to fit into the French

language, but it was all right to create "boldly words in imitation of the Greeks and Latins," provided that the creations were "gracious and pleasant to the ear." This was an excellent concept, though it did not always restrict Ronsard in his construction of formalistic polysyllables. Even more than Ronsard, Du Bellay hammered away at the notion that without imitation of the Greeks and Romans the French language would lack "enlightenment" and "excellence." The poet therefore should not be afraid to "innovate a few terms" so that his work would be "enriched and decorated with proper words, interesting epithets, and solemn maxims." The venerable majesty of antiquity should be pillaged, not to put whitewash on an old wall but to make something new as did the bee (a favorite figure in Renaissance criticism) which had sipped the fragrant essences of flowers.[14]

Amadis Jamin, a satellite of the Pléiade and secretary of the Royal Chamber, said that Ronsard did resemble the bee that took its "profit from all flowers to make its honey." Jamin very likely had in mind the first lines of Ronsard's epic, La Franciade, which reflects a formalized phrasing and Vergilian copying at its best:

> Muse, the honor of the summits of Parnasse,
> Guide my tongue and sing to me the race
> Of French kings descended from Francion
> The child of Hector and Trojan of nation, . . .

Here is a fine and dignified beginning for an epic, and also an echo of the Aeneid's opening, Arma virumque cano. . . . Unfortunately, Ronsard could not keep a sane formalism very far into his poem, as is witnessed by his description, still in the first book, of the lamentation of Jupiter over the destruction of Troy through the stratagem of the horse, which disgorged into the city "a million Argive ruffians." Incidentally, the French normally used Jupiter rather than the more logical Zeus to designate the king of the gods, possibly because Zeus was a monosyllable and considered harsh in sound. At

any rate, out of the horse came the Greek chieftains in
veiled and circumlocuted verbal disguises:

> There raged two tigers without any mercy,
> The great son of Atreus and the little one, too,
> Eager for blood: the flesh-devouring son of Tydeus
> And the arrogant descendant of the son of Aeacus:
> There raged the Ithacan under the weight of the great shield,
> Which was not his, shining like a lightning flash. . .

A mythological dictionary and genealogical chart would be
needed to straighten out the names of these warriors: the
"great son of Atreus and the little one" were Agamemnon
and Menelaus; the "son of Tydeus" was the brave Diomedes;
the "arrogant descendant of the son of Aeacus" was Ajax,
the son of Telamon, who was the son of Aeacus; the "Itha-
can" was Ulysses, who had claimed the shield and armor of
Achilles. Such pompous and formalistic complications,
though imitative of the ancients, were certainly one of the
reasons that the *Franciade* was not successful and remained
unfinished. But intricate and overblown epithets—Aristotle
was known as the "son of Nicomachus" and Horace as
"the harp-player of Calabria"—continued to be employed
throughout the sixteenth century. Vauquelin de la Fresnaye
asked the Muses to leave Mount Cithaeron (Ronsard, according to report, has already persuaded them to abandon
Mount Helicon) and to allow "the singing fountain of Hippocrene to teach its songs to our listening waters." In a
slightly different concept, poets were reminded by Vauquelin that the Muses could not be forced to pour out "their
Pegasian floods" (Pegasus had kicked the rock to make the
fountain of Hippocrene) against their will.[15]

By the beginning of the seventeenth century, there was
under way in France the trend toward clarity in poetry as
well as in prose, and toward the rejection of the obscurely
formal epithet supposed to make a sentence gleam. Much exaggerated and high-flown language was blamed on the Ital-

ians, and the Huguenot narrative poet Guillaume du Bartas was given credit for "stuffing and padding" his lines. Deimier in 1610 made a plea for "clairté" of word and concept in writing, and said that Du Bartas' repetitive *ba-battant* and *flot-flottant* violated "the simple structure of our language," and that Du Bartas, in seeking to fit the right number of syllables into a verse, "had no respect for the principles of grammar." A reaction against too far-fetched mythological allusions set in, and Malherbe, the blunt lawgiver of the first quarter of the century, issued his famous dictum that poetry should be simple enough to be understood by the porters and carriers of hay. Malherbe's theory might be designated as one of formalistic simplicity. He was adamantine in his adherence to rule; but he wanted to make the mechanics of the rule as simple and clear as possible. There were those, like Mathurin Régnier and Théophile de Viau, who disagreed with him and asserted that they composed in confusion. And nobody put forth any concentrated effort, in keeping with Malherbe's dictum, toward making poetry attractive to the crude and uneducated. Nevertheless, there were definite forces concerned with pruning and purifying the somewhat ornate and bombastic language of the late sixteenth century. A more rigorous formalism came into play.[16]

During the reign of Louis XIII the primary guides for the French language became clarity and usage. Usage was the usage of the Court, which was automatically assumed to be the arbiter of "good French." The language of the Court was supplemented by that of the salons which were under the control of women. The most famous salon, that of madame de Rambouillet, did much to refine the manners and speech left over from Henry IV's rough court, but the general influence of such salons as the Hôtel de Rambouillet was toward preciosity and prettified formalism. If the frequenters of madame de Rambouillet's famous house on the rue Saint Thomas du Louvre (just across the square from the palace) really called a chair a "convenience for conversation" or a mirror "the counselor of the graces," it probably had little effect upon such serious linguistic minds as those of Malherbe, Balzac, Vaugelas, and the pompous Jean Chapelain. Nevertheless, women by this time had won the *Querelle de la Femme*, and were receiving a more proper treatment and a formal courtly adulation. The language of the farces had been cleaned up so that delicate feminine ears would not be shocked when ladies sat in a box at the theatre. It must have been easy to pay a little homage to an attractive, intelligent, and virtuous woman like Catherine de Rambouillet. Even Malherbe took time out from his vigorous protection of the purity of the French language to make three anagrams on her given name; the one that she liked the best was Arthénice.[17]

The language of the Court was the correct language. The provinces were simply outside the linguistic pale, and everything uncouth or "not French" was blamed on them. The Renaissance had found some values in the dialects, but the seventeenth century began the tradition of considering the provinces as a land of provincialisms and uncooked birds. One of Malherbe's primary projects was to "de-gasconize" the standard French speech. Another opinion was to the effect that "Provençal and Gascon usage" would allow certain expressions, but "those who speak good French" would employ a different phrasing. Vaugelas, the great protagonist of courtly usage, said in 1647 that "provincials" could correct their speech by being around the Court, and that a man in the Court's aura should not "allow himself to be corrupted by the contagion of the provinces in spending too long a sojourn there." In so doing, he would inevitably add to his vocabulary many words that were not French. Comment was made in 1651 concerning the damage that was done to the language by those areas that were "far-distant from the Court." It was observed, too, that the correct and precise

pronunciation of French was difficult, not only for foreigners but also for "the greater number of provincials," especially those from Gascony, Languedoc, Lyon, and Pro-
vence.[18]

The regulated language of the Court was admired generally in the seventeenth century, but not universally. Ronsard had already stated that the way to honor in letters in
France was through a "langage courtisan" since there was
only one king. For Ronsard, the royal language was not immediately the best but it had the value of official and formalistic imprint. The magic cachet, *par le roi*, was stamped on
it. The case for the Court's being the standard of linguistic
usage was stated firmly in the seventeenth century by Vaugelas, who said that *usage* meant "the manner of speech of the
sanest part of the Court, in conformity with the manner of
writing of the sanest part of the authors of the time." The
Court included for Vaugelas "women as well as men," and
several enlightened persons residing in the city that was the
seat of the prince's court—which would obviously be Paris.
Also, to the speech of the Court should be added the legacy
of the best Greek and Roman authors, "the spoils of which
are a part of the richness of our language, possibly the part
that is most pompous and most magnificent." Vaugelas would
go only to the "sanest" portion of the Court for good usage;
as for the "people," they were the "master only of bad form."
The grammarian and historian, Scipion Dupleix, some four
years later in 1651 disagreed with Vaugelas on several of his
points: "good usage" was admirable and would, in its formalistic precision, eliminate "barbarous words" and "vicious
phrases." However, as for copying the language of "the
sanest part of the Court," where was it to be found? Dupleix
maintained that he had formed his own style on that of those
who had the "highest reputation for elegance, politeness,
and purity of language," both at the Court and in the Academy. If "courtly usage" meant the approval of *courtisans*

("women as well as men") on the question of choosing words, then the whole idea was absurd. The ladies and gentlemen of the Court might well be consulted on matters of politeness, fashions in dress, or dancing; but not on the "elegance of terms," wherein their knowledge of rules and their reasoning powers would be limited.[19]

The Court, quite naturally, continued to exercise its control over both language and manners as the century went into its second half. Boileau paid homage to the king's entourage as a symbol of the humanity that one should know. The rigorous forms and ceremonials of the Court became even more formalistic, and the language thereof reached the ultimate in classic dignity. That fashionable gentleman, the chevalier de Méré, said in 1668 that the Court had "made progress in wit and gallantry," and in the precise mechanics of conversation, a device so important to the rituals of polite society. For best results in the oral use of words, it was necessary, he said, to be instructed in the "manners of the Court." Bouhours a few years later lamented the fact that he was a provincial and could not know the delicacies of language "reserved for those who haunt the Court." In any case, Bouhours claimed that he had studied hard, knew his Vauge-las, had frequented many "courts of Europe," and was knowledgeable in the classics. Therefore, he felt free to query the learned gentlemen of the French Academy about certain words in the first of his linguistic loves, French.[20]

The words approved or disapproved of by the formalists, as classic French came into being, brought on some vigorous arguments. An examination of a few of them might reveal something about the Frenchman's nature and linguistic philosophy. In many cases conflict arose when classical ancestry and courtly usage were opposed to each other, and when learned authorities sought to resist a general trend. As far back as the early years of the sixteenth century, for example, objection was made to "the incorrigible error of saying in French four score and twelve where one ought to say ninety-two." Many later critics have agreed with this opinion, but, as every elementary student of French today knows, *quatre-vingts* and *quatre-vingt-dix* won out over the Latinized *octante* and *nonante*. But the popular term was seldom victorious over the learned one in the formal language, and a poet like Ronsard pleaded for the use of "beautiful and magnificent words" instead of the vulgar and trivial. The Renaissance, spearheaded by the Pléiade, liked the "ornament of the polished tongue."[21]

Vaugelas, in something like six hundred pages of analysis, sought in 1647 to make a list of the proper and correct words, which was based on upper-class usage and not on that of the "dregs of the people." The "gross mistakes" of the untutored and provincial were to be ignored, but an expression employed by Malherbe or the cardinal du Perron (who had brought Malherbe to Henry IV's notice) would automatically receive consideration. The "satirical, comical, and burlesque" were all ruled out as being unworthy of belonging to a proper vocabulary. Some of the words that gained Vaugelas' approval (he did not put them in any alphabetical order) were: *vénération, souveraineté, soumission* (which had displaced *submission,* in use twenty years earlier), *insidieux* ("not purely Latin," but supported by Malherbe), *demoiselle (damoiselle* was "no longer written"), *sériosité* (it might one day be accepted, thought Vaugelas—he was wrong), and *Cléopâtre* (instead of *Cleopatra*). Some of the words and phrases condemned by Vaugelas were: *invectiver* (not in "good usage"), *nonante,* and so on (simply "not French"), *chez Platon* for *dans Platon* ("insupportable" —but it is in modern French), *compagnée* ("barbarous"— it is no longer in French), and *élever les yeux** ("not French"). Though some of Vaugelas' predictions did not come true, he was amazingly accurate in setting the basic

---

* The modern form would be *lever les yeux,* "to lift one's eyes."

and correct form of modern French. He himself admitted
the difficulties involved in "establishing a certain rule for the
perfection of our language."[22]

One of the words that caused a rather amusing contro-
versy among the linguistic formalists of the seventeenth century was *poitrine*, "breast" or "bosom." Vaugelas insisted
that it had fallen into disuse because of *poitrine de veau*,
"breast of veal," which smacked too much of the butcher
shop. He conceded that it was a silly nicety to abandon such
a good word, but the fashions of usage, "the life and soul of
words," were not predictable. Dupleix, who thought that
Vaugelas was too rigorous in the "polishing of style," came
up in 1651 with a defense of *poitrine* and similar solid French
words. Vaugelas was wrong, according to Dupleix, in giving
a coarse "breast of veal" connotation to *poitrine*. The same
thing could be done "by a dirty mind," said Dupleix, to a
good Latin-based word like *face* by making it be both the
face and the rear of the human anatomy—which was done
by Rostand in *Cyrano de Bergerac* when he had Cyrano
slap a heckler, then turn him around and boot him off the
stage. In 1672, Ménage took up *poitrine* and *face* again,
which he claimed had fallen into disrepute because of lowly
combinations, like *poitrine de mouton* and *face du grand
Turc*. It was ridiculous, to Ménage's way of thinking, for
superdelicate writers to avoid the words because of their use
in certain popular phrases. On the other hand, Ménage advised against the use of *face* in amorous verses, "when one
might be speaking of the visage of one's beloved." Both
*poitrine* and *face* have remained in the French language.[23]

Dupleix lashed out at Vaugelas and others for being such
"refiners of style" that they were taking the meat and bone
out of the language. In a pompous and pretentious epistle to
the architect Claude Perrault, Dupleix waxed formalistic
while defending natural simplicity. Perrault was called in for
support as being one "who, possessing in a lofty degree the

knowledge of the principal languages along with being an encyclopedia of sciences, would not be able to approve of the grammatical bizarreness with which certain spelling-book critics and refiners of style enervate and infeeble our language under the pretense of polishing it and purifying it; and they even destroy it by the extraction of several terms of strong and energetic expression." For Dupleix, language should not be hindered in its development by too much obedience to grammar, courtly usage, and women. A writer should be allowed to pick the words he likes, if the resulting composition might be "without barbarism, without impropriety, and without solecism." If the women around the Court were to be the arbiters of language, Dupleix argued with prime inconsistency, they should be instructed in the "rules of grammar" and the "precepts of rhetoric"—and also "versed in the Latin language, even in Greek"; and where would women be found who could meet these conditions? As for specific words, Dupleix condemned rightly *esclavitude*, which he said Vaugelas wanted to put "in esteem"; *invectiver* (not in "good usage"—Vaugelas' opinion too); *exactitude* (a "monster," but usage demanded it); *sériosité* (in agreement with Vaugelas); *recouvert* (he wrongly supported *recouvré*); and *demoiselle* (opposed by "scholars," blamed on the "coquettishness of women"—but it stayed). Dupleix favored words like *ambitionner* and *matinal*, which have remained in the language; but his judgment and linguistic intuition were not so sound as those of Vaugelas. Ménage, who was primarily an etymologist, had several misses to his credit in his predictions: *précipitamment*, favored by Vaugelas and a standard word today, was considered "abominable"; *Henri Second* was preferred to *Henri Deux* (he was wrong); and *Arsenac* was mistakenly supported instead of *Arsenal*. Menage offered objection to the accepted present-day *plaît-il?* (I beg your pardon?): he thought the full formalistic extension *que vous plaît-il?* would be better.[24]

In the 1670's the good critic Bouhours had several things to say about proper words in his noble language. Among other things, as a sophisticated Jesuit father he admitted that women talked well, possibly because French was well-suited to expressing "the most tender sentiments of the heart." He did not like *obscurcissement* and *enivrement,** words which he said had recently come into the language (and they have stayed); *urbanité* he had doubts about, though Louis Guez de Balzac used it (this fine Latinism remained); *hautesse* (which has been replaced by *hauteur*) "put him in pain"; and "the word *religionaire* is not French" (his opinion has been confirmed). He thought that *sériosité* was no longer "fashionable," though he admitted that the problem of making a substantive out of an adjective was a difficult one; and it was a violation of Ciceronian and Horatian good sense to make up useless words. No word, however beautiful in construction and sound, could do anything "against usage." In a bit of formalistic hair-splitting, Bouhours conceded that he would accept "effusion of blood," "effusion of bile," and possibly 'effusion of colors" (for a sunset), but he could not understand "effusion of anger." Bouhours included several words that usage allowed to have varied meanings: *glorieux* might be good or bad according to "the tone"— Voiture said he always felt "glorieux" when he received a letter from madame de Rambouillet; *libertin*, which could mean an "impious man" or a "man who hates constraint"; and *renaissance*, which could be employed "without scruple" in both a literal and figurative meaning—as, for the latter, "la renaissance des beaux arts." It should be indicated that here is one of the earliest uses of "renaissance" in the modern critical sense.[25]

As it was for Vaugelas, word order was important for Bouhours, and his recommendation for a more logical posi-

---

* "Darkening" (or "black-out") and "intoxication," for some reason linked together by Bouhours!

tion of object pronouns became the normal rule for modern French. All in all, Bouhours continued to believe in the major principle of Vaugelas: usage disciplined by formalized regulation. Bouhours, therefore, was afraid that Dupleix' *Liberté dans la langue française* might become the "rule for the Court and the style of good authors." Bouhours, as a prime French formalist, would have been opposed to any such deviation from standards. The result of the debates between the linguistic codifiers of the seventeenth century was the fixation of the basic form of French, a form that was to remain essentially unchanged down to the present time. The eighteenth century was satisfied with the order and precision of the language and did very little tinkering with the mechanics of its structure.[26]

Style and language are inevitably intertwined, and the lines of separation between the two are not always easy to draw, whether a composition be written in French, English, or Russian. It was natural, then, during the centuries of formalism in France for many of the critics who analyzed the structure of the language to lend their attention, in addition, to the intricacies of literary style. This was in the best classical tradition, since Aristotle in the second part of his *Poetics* had probed both into the makeup of words and into their proper use for the most effective phrasing. As for the French in their formalistic period, they found at least one important link between language and style in a favorite word and concept: *clarté*. They believed, with growing certainty from around 1550 to past 1700, that the individual word should have an exact connotation and that the stylistic sum-total should have a clarity of meaning. Not that a great critic like Boileau failed to discover other nuances of style than ease of comprehension; nor did critical precepts remove from many French writers of the sixteenth and seventeenth centuries their innate pomposity and turgidity. But the blending of lan-

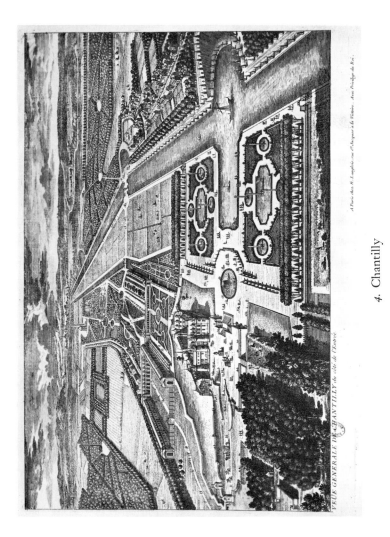

VEUE GENERALE DE CHANTILLY du côté de l'Entrée

A Paris chez R. Lançlois, rue S.Jacques à la Victoire. Avec Privilège du Roi.

4. Chantilly

LA MAISON DE VAUX LE VICOMTE apparienoit à Monsieur Fouquet du temps de sa surintendance, le sieur le Veau en fut l'Architecte, elle fut commencée en 1653 ce a esté mise dans la perfection ou elle est avec une promptitude et une dispence extraordinaire. Elle appartient presentement à Madame Fouquet fait par Perelle.
A PARIS Chés N. Langlois rue s'Iaeque à la Victoire Avec Priuilege du Roy.

5. Vaux-le-Vicomte

6. Vaux-le-Vicomte

guage and style in discernible formalistic progress can be observed in some of the great composers from the sixteenth to the eighteenth century: compare, for example, the unbridled excesses of Rabelais and Du Bartas with the lucidity of Racine and Voltaire.

Words and style went hand in hand, but style among the French formalists was more than the sum-total of all the words and the mere obedience to the correct processes of grammar. The French for two centuries, from the Pléiade to Buffon, had a lot to say on the question of style. Du Bellay in 1549 said that a writer should focus the "point of his style" on the Greeks and Romans so that it might be better tempered and sharpened. On this question Du Bellay agreed with Sebillet, who had said the year before that "style and eloquence" came from the ancients. Ronsard, in his turn, advised digging in the "ashes of antiquity" before writing in French; after such delving a versifier would come nearer to being a poet who could speak with proper thunder from the top of a mountain. If his heroes died it would be from a dignified and "mortal" wound; his captains would be courageous, and the "splendor of their armor would glow in the light of the sun." In regard to the more mundane machinery of style, Ronsard disapproved of forced transposition of words. It would be a violation of the best form to say: "To Orléans from Paris the King to sleep went." Herein would be a foretaste of monsieur Jourdain's struggles with the word order of his love letter to the beautiful marquise in Molière's *Le bourgeois gentilhomme*. Back in the Renaissance, Peletier du Mans was in agreement with Ronsard concerning the formal dignity of poetic images: an army in movement would not be a "swarm of flies"; two valiant combatants would not be a pair of "peasants' mongrels," but a "lion" against a "bull"; and a weak man against a strong man would not be a mouse against a cat, but rather a "powerless dove" in combat with a "rapacious eagle."[27]

Claude Fauchet in his study in 1581 on the origin of French said that Gallic poets had carried French poetry so high that "they have surpassed already all those who have written in verse since the time of Augustus, the Italians not excepted and even less the Spaniards." After this immodest statement, Fauchet gave a long discussion of the rhythmic, metric, and stylistic devices that made French so superior to other tongues, and so attractive to other nations. Vauquelin de la Fresnaye at about the same time was making the same lavish claims for French, of which he said inaccurately Italian and Spanish were "vassals" through attachment to "our Catalan and Provençal." For Vauquelin, France had lifted her language toward the heights of perfection, "and soon surpassed the vulgar tongues of Europe." He offered the following explanation in support of this rather immoderate assertion: because of the variety and exactitude of words and style the Frenchman could express anything "in his own native French." Vauquelin gave the poet and dramatist Robert Garnier a good deal of credit through his "sweet and grave style" for the fact that "our language has surpassed today the boldest of the others." And Laudun d'Aigaliers in 1597, in anticipation of Vaugelas, stated that the first ornament of French poetry was clarity.[28]

While supporting clarity and rejecting obscurity in French poetic style, Pierre de Deimier in 1610 added the suggestion that poetry needed also the formalizing "ornament of reason." To the claim that poets have the right to "say everything," Deimier would give the interpretation of "everything honorable and reasonable." Early in the seventeenth century there came into French poetic theory the sober doctrine of reason—a universalized, non-Cartesian reason—that was to receive its culmination in the celebrated admonition of Boileau, "love reason." One of Malherbe's objections to the poetic efforts of Desportes and Régnier was that they were exaggerated and irrational. Thus Malherbe,

the precise literalist, objected to Régnier's stylistic conceit
of France's rising into the upper airs to make a complaint to
Jupiter; Malherbe said that he had been living in France for
fifty years and had never noticed that "she had changed her
place." In matters of language and style, words like purity,
clarity, logic, and cleanness were important to such men as
Malherbe, Balzac, and Vaugelas. The story has been told
many times of the dying Malherbe's saying that he would
defend until death "the purity of the French language."
Vaugelas made a distinction between purity and cleanness or
neatness (*netteté*): purity concerned individual, nonbarbaric
words and their meaning; *netteté* had to do with the proper
arrangement of words so that they would "contribute to
the clarity of expression." A neatness of style would not be
attained in a sentence that was full of double meanings, in-
flations, and ambiguities.[29]

The French had no restraint during their more than two
centuries of formalism in lambasting what were considered
the linguistic and stylistic excesses of their neighbors. The
primary targets were the Italians and the Spaniards, in woe-
ful lack of appreciation on the part of the French for borrowings from the cultures of Italy and Spain. As has been
seen, the French felt that their language was superior to
other modern languages; they also believed that it was used
more logically and correctly, with less bombast of style. The
Spanish romance of chivalry, the *Amadis de Gaula*, which
was popular during the sixteenth century in Des Essarts'
translation, was criticized for its exaggerations—though Vauquelin de la Fresnaye claimed that the *Amadis* had first been
"rhymed in the old Picard dialect" and later taken over by
the Spaniards. Deimier, in his discussion of clarity, insisted
that the subject of a poem should be made clear and not
muddled with confused and fantastic arguments, as had been
the case with "certain Spanish poets and some Italians." Malherbe esteemed a number of ancient classical poets, very few

of the "ancient" French poets, and practically none of the Italians. The Italians were criticized for their abundance of diminutives, though the French had certainly used plenty of them during the Renaissance. Bouhours asserted, however, that the seventeenth century had seen the disappearance of exaggerated diminutives from French and that the dignified French style of the 1670's was a golden mean between the frivolous burlesque of the Italians and the inflated pomposity of the Spaniards. There was something noble and august about French writing, said Bouhours, that gave it majesty; while "nothing could be more pompous than Castilian," which attaches grandiose names to small things. The Manzanares River in Madrid, for example, has such a grand name that one might think it the "largest river in the world" when in reality it is only a "small brook which is most often dry." In contrast to the Italian and Spanish modes of writing, thought Bouhours, French has exhibited a "reasonable grandeur."[30]

Despite French claims to sedateness and formal correctness of style, the pompous and emptily formalistic was frequently discernible in French compositions up to 1650. It happened in both prose and verse, and it was visible during the Renaissance in several of the Pindaric odes of Ronsard, which sought to pay homage to royalty. Some of Malherbe's odes, particularly one in 1611 dedicated to Marie de' Medici on her regency, had about them a stiff rigidity if not pomposity. The sound and fury of words was probably more obvious in prose than in poetry. Antoine Fouquelin illustrated this in his treatise on rhetoric of 1555, dedicated to "Madame Marie, Reine d'Ecosse," the foreign princess betrothed to the Dauphin (who was to be the pitiful Francis II) and later known in English history as Mary, Queen of Scots. Fouquelin said that his work was being offered to "a princess born and divinely predestined according to the common hope not only for the amplification and advancement of our language but also for the illustration and honor of all knowledge." All of which was a trifle florid for a little thirteen-year-old girl whose native speech was not French, but Fouquelin liked resounding phrases; and they were appropriate to royalty. He also liked rhetorical figures, notably metonymy, and thought that one of the finest examples of it was in a hymn of Ronsard's wherein bread was called "the favorable present from Ceres" and wine "the beneficial liquor from the genteel Bacchus."[31]

One of the most pompous, if not the most pompous, pieces of seventeenth-century French prose was a preface of the grammarian Dupleix and it was all about himself: "I do not doubt that those who will consider the fifty years I have devoted to bringing out into the light of day various works of excellent, lofty, and serious argumentation, will find it strange that I am producing and revealing today observations on the French language which are only bagatelles of grammar. For what appearance is there that a mind which has woven by obstinate endeavor the history of the Gauls and of France from the flood down to the present time; and of Rome from its foundation down to the empire of Charlemagne; who has made a commentary for the Institutes of Justinian, and has put in Latin verse the rules and maxims of both civil and canon law; . . . who has demonstrated in his metaphysics the immortality of the rational soul, the nature and properties of angels and intelligences; who has contemplated the first, eternal, and true object of contemplation, God the creator, preserver, and sovereign lord of all things: what likelihood is there that this same intelligence after the contemplation of so many sublime, celestial, and divine objects, might have precipitated himself suddenly, as though through a fall of Phaëthon,* into these lower regions in order

---

* Phaëthon, the son of Apollo, drove the Sun-god's chariot across the sky, lost control, and fell to earth, struck with one of Jupiter's thunderbolts. Phaëthon was a favorite subject for painters of the period.

to captivate himself with such abject occupations as the principles of grammar!" Dupleix did write the books listed in the above apostrophe to himself; both the list and the apostrophe have been cut just about in half.[32]

La Mesnardière, who wrote a volume of poetry and two tragedies in addition to his poetics in 1639, sought in his criticism to explain levels of formalistic style as they fitted varying social classes. "For if it is not reasonable," he said, "that a merchant speak like a prince, accepted literary usage prevents him from doing it; and this majestic air and absolutism of terms which suit potentates would be completely ridiculous in the mouth of a bourgeois." Even a prince's style of speech, including expressions of sentiment, should be changed a trifle in keeping with the rank of the person addressed. According to La Mesnardière, if a prince were enamored of an "ordinary woman whose great beauty is her principal ornamentation, his respects will be expressed as extreme civilities rather than as formal adorations." Also, if a man of position were telling about a shipwreck in which he had lost his friend, his son, or his mistress, he would not launch forth into a description of a storm "as though, in using this splendid subject, he wished to compete for the Prix de l'Eloquence." Tragedy, that noblest of French literary genres of the seventeenth century, should always "speak majestically" without "lowly terms" and "popular expressions." La Mesnardière illustrated the point from his own tragedy, Alinde, in which a queen wondered about the faithfulness of a lover for whom she had given up two kingdoms:

> By what art, oh just gods, can a woman in love
> Be rid of a malady that in herself she creates!
> And how can a mortal be the conqueror
> Of an immortal serpent ever renewed in her heart?

For La Mesnardíere the above couplets made a "formal and intelligible declaration," suitable for the revelation of the emotional crisis in a queen's soul. It must be conceded that, in their formalized dignity, they accomplished their mission rather well.[33]

The complete codification of formalistic style came in the second half of the seventeenth century. Le Père Le Moyne, who published in 1671 an epic called *Saint Louis, ou la sainte couronne reconquise* (in eighteen books, and 235 four-column folio pages), prefaced it with a lengthy dissertation on the subject. Le Moyne agreed with "the late Malherbe" that epic poetry should be heroic, and not low and vulgar. All poetry should be "elevated," as symbolized by Pegasus, the horse with wings; and not in the manner of certain ladies who were grand only because of "the height of their shoes." Poetry should have ornamentation, pomp, and adornment, but not the adornment of the village bride who had rouge on her cheeks while at the same time there was dirt on her brow. Poets were born for the satisfaction and honor of mankind, and not to amuse some "perfume-dealers" and "makers of stews." It is too bad that the briskness of Le Moyne's criticism did not carry over into his interminable epic, though in it Louis IX finally brought back the holy crown from the land of the Saracens, where it had been protected by two proper guards—a lion and a giant.[34]

The chevalier de Méré in his *Conversations* that began to appear in 1668 spoke of the formalized rules that should regulate style in genteel conversation. By this time the lofty words of classical formalism were coming more and more into critical use—words like good sense, judgment, verisimilitude, the amenities, and taste. Méré agreed that the first rule of correct conversation was that of good usage, which created in a gentleman proper speech through social contacts rather than study; but he felt that "there are other rules which go farther and which are derived from good sense and long experience." He thought that there was a "language of the heart as well as a language of the mind"—wherein he would seem to have borrowed from Pascal's famous statement, "the

heart has its reasons which the reason does not comprehend."
Méré did not like the "flowery style" of the salon poet and
favorite discourser of madame de Rambouillet, Vincent Voiture, who was accused of mixing the "flowers of rhetoric"
with nature's flora. For Méré, the perfection of style came
through "keeping in mind the large things and not neglect-
ing the small ones." In his opinion, Voiture showed stylistic
neglect when he indulged in careless metonymies and mixed
Julius Caesar up with the Greeks. The chevalier was a strong
proponent of the amenities (the *bienséances*), which would
be a great attribute of both courtly and literary formalism.
It was important not to be shocking in word or deed, and
"to be irritating to no one." Alceste in Molière's *Le
misanthrope* was, therefore, ridiculous because he violated
accepted social and conversational formalities. On another
slant and in a combination of formalism and snobbism, Méré
rejected certain words in conversation "when they are affected by people one does not like." In Méré's mind, "conversation is the greatest use that is made of the power of
speech," and every effort should be put forth to render it
agreeable. The "manners of the Court" would be of primary
guidance, although, "as far as the Maisons Royales are concerned, conversations in them are very much interrupted—
people go there less to talk than to be seen." This rather
wry opinion is reminiscent of the duc de La Rochefoucauld's
sage reflection on conversation, made at about the same
time: "What makes so few persons pleasant in conversation
is that they are thinking about what they intend to say
rather than about what is being said." Méré had a balanced
formalism: he advised an elegant but unaffected conversational style, and the golden mean of something in between
the "too little" and the "too much." Madame de Sévigné,
the famous letter writer and commentator on society of her
time, had a word to say in 1675 concerning the speech of a
lady from the provinces: "Madame de Quintin is at Dinan;

her style is as inflated as her person: . . . a lady of some provincial social position is quite a dangerous thing, especially
when she has, according to her way of thinking, taken on the
air of the Court."[35]

By the 1670's it was pretty generally agreed that there was
dignity and maturity of style in French. Even Desmarets de
Saint-Sorlin, who objected to any deification of classical antiquity, admitted in 1670 that France was in a mature era,
with the fruit and riches of past ages at her feet. The sweetness and measured quality of her heroic verses, he said, show
a "continuing force and clarity." The prime critics and meas-
urers of the formalized classical style were, in addition to
Boileau, Bouhours and Rapin. Bouhours said in 1671 that
Ronsard was the first to drive "barbarism out of France"
and to inspire in our fathers a "taste for letters"; Voiture
taught us that "easy and delicate manner of writing" presently in vogue, an opinion at variance with that of the
chevalier de Méré. For Bouhours, Voiture's apparent negligence and repetition of words was a "hidden artifice," but
there could be an unpleasant effect from too many synonyms,
such as would come from putting "contentment" and "satisfaction" in the same phrase. Bouhours expended some fifty
pages on style—the "exactitude," the "politeness," and the
"perfection" of style. In his concept, as in that of Vaugelas,
one of the great secrets of correct style was the proper arrangement of words, without which beautiful phrases would
be lost. Bouhours answered those who criticized his great
emphasis on exactitude: "Exactitude correctly understood is
in the creations of the mind, as in works of art and architecture, a certain proper and regular quality which blends well
into the idea of the august and magnificent." Polishing of
words and retouching of structure would always be in
order after the first fire of inspiration, "but to give to a work
the turn and form which the noblest works possess, it is necessary to have in one's head an idea of perfection and the

rules which lead to it." Neither Horace nor Boileau could have phrased better the concept of classical formalism. But, said Bouhours, the overdoing of Horace's labor of the file would take away too much substance and result in compositions that were "dry" and "unnatural"—and emptily formalistic. Rapin was also a classical formalist and purist. He felt that style should be natural and clear, without forced transpositions, and with metaphors well under control. Ronsard and Du Bartas brought into French too many big words, and ended up by making the language "barbarous"—and here is another dissenting opinion on Ronsard. The freethinker Théophile de Viau in the opinion of Rapin had too much "affectation" and became puerile; but Malherbe came along and joined "purity and grandeur of style." Rapin believed that there was a "mysterious order in poetry," which few moderns would ever know.[36]

Toward the end of the century, the uninhibited poet Urbain Chevreau (but whose editor said in 1697 that he succeeded in "uniting the good taste of the moderns with that of the ancients"), in a letter to a lady excused her for "negligence" in verse composition: the excuse was given because the lady was in grief over the death of her brother and as a result ignored many of "the rules of art." The formalistic concepts of style thus went on through the Quarrel of the Ancients and Moderns, and made their way into the eighteenth century. Charles Batteux, in his treatise of 1746 on the fine arts, suggested that for the training of the taste one should read Sophocles until an appreciation was gained of the grandeur of his style and characterization. Batteux then gave a formalistic if perhaps limited definition of good taste: "good taste is an habitual love of order." This concept would scarcely have satisfied a complicated classicist like Voltaire, who had a good deal to say about taste, style, and measure. The best-known commentary on style in the eighteenth century was that of the naturalist Buffon who gave his celebrated *Discours sur le style* on the occasion of his reception into the French Academy in 1753. The most quoted statement from this discourse is his conclusion that only those things that are well-written will endure: the material face of the earth will change but "style is man himself." It is sometimes forgotten that Buffon began his remarks with a formalistic definition: "Style is nothing but the order and movement which a writer gives to his thoughts."[37]

# THE QUESTION OF
# THE BAROQUE

NO INQUIRY into French formalism could possibly ignore the baroque, however pleasant it might be to stay out of critical waters already darkened and muddied. Baroque as a descriptive term in the arts, especially for painting, has been in use for more than a half a century; "baroque" architecture has had a long period of application, and the same could be said for "baroque" sculpture and for "baroque" music. The baroque in literature, more specifically "baroque" poetry, was first discovered in Germany, and then applied to the literatures of Italy and Spain. The "baroque" in French literature, as it has been employed by critics both inside and outside France, is of more recent vintage and goes back about thirty years. In its generally accepted connotation, baroque would be opposed to the regular, the direct, the measured, the formal, the classical, and the restrained. By most of its proponents, therefore, it would be considered the antithesis of formalism.

There is no easy definition of the baroque, although everybody seems to agree that it came from the Portuguese or Spanish *barroco*, a word in the parlance of jewelers meaning an "irregular pearl." As for *baroque* in French, it was not there during the Renaissance, according to E. Huguet's authoritative dictionary of the French language of the sixteenth century; the word appeared in France during the seventeenth century and was listed in Furetière's dictionary of 1690, still referring to pearls "which are not perfectly round." Saint-Simon in his memoirs of 1711 employed baroque in reference to any strange or "shocking idea." The 1776 supplement to the *Encyclopédie* applied the term to music "the harmony of which is confused." Quatremère de Quincy in his *Encyclopédie méthodique* of 1788 said that the baroque, in its associations with architecture, indicated "a nuance of the bizarre," and he blamed such Italian designers as Borromini and Guarini for it. The Littré dictionary of the nineteenth century stated that baroque was descriptive of something "of a shocking strangeness"; and J. -K. Huysmans in his novel *En route* lamented the appearance of the church of Notre Dame des Victoires in Paris with the remark: "It is ugly enough to cause one to weep, it is pretentious, it is baroque." The dictionary of the French Academy as recently as 1932 said baroque meant "of a bizarre irregularity," and Paul Robert in his *Dictionnaire alphabétique* of 1953 gave exactly the same definition.[1]

Very few of these limiting and derogatory concepts would be accepted by a confirmed *baroquiste*, who would prefer to take his lead from German criticism of the second half of the nineteenth century, specifically from H. Wölflinn's *Renaissance und Barock* of 1888. This important work, though its primary concern was painting and the visual arts, gave impetus all over Europe to "baroque" as a general critical term. The French, deterred by their own formal natures and by the classical criticism of scholars like Emile Faguet and Gustave Lanson, were the last to apply it to literature. But in the last few decades, many French critics —and foreign critics of French letters—have been most assiduous in defining the baroque and then finding manifestations of it in French literature of the sixteenth and seventeenth centuries. As recently as 1945 there was a slight timidity in the application of the word, a feeling which caused it to be put in quotation marks—as, for example, "our 'baroque' poets of the sixteenth and seventeenth centuries." By 1953 a dedicated advocate of the baroque in French, Jean Rousset, was using the term with complete confidence, although he admitted that it had not received acceptance in France "without certain reticences." In 1955 Marcel Raymond dedicated a study of the baroque in French literature to Rousset, whom he called the "master pilot in Baroquie." In theory, then, "Baroquie" should by now be a land with well-marked boundaries, with well-charted channels leading into its harbors, and a well-defined position on the map of letters.[2]

Nothing could be farther from the case. The most ardent proponents of the baroque are confusing when they seek to explain it, and in disagreement as to when it occurred in the literary history of France. To grasp the meaning of the baroque in French letters is something like grabbing hold of a handful of mercury: little puddles of it run off in all directions. Some of the attributes that have been ascribed in recent years to the baroque are "change, inconstancy, trompe l'oeil and adornment, funereal spectacle, the transciency of life, the world in instability"; it would further be symbolized by "Circe, metamorphosis, the peacock, and ostentation." Disguise, magic, and dissimulation would also belong to the baroque, and, says Rousset, "water in movement takes us to the heart of the baroque": a baroque façade would be a Renaissance façade reflected "in agitated water," with columns twisted and everything vibrating with the rhythm of the waves. The linear quality of the Renaissance would be illustrated by the fountains, say, of the Villa d'Este outside Rome, where the water is quite static and rises and falls in simple jets; the diffusion of the baroque would be denoted

by the Trevi fountain in Rome where the water is scattered
and shimmers in many peacock fans. The Trevi would reflect the spirit of the architect and sculptor Bernini, who "is
the heart of the baroque." Tears would belong to the baroque, since they depict internal storms and frustrations. In a
more lugubrious vein, the macabre, death and the images of
death (open graves, skeletons, and such things) would be a
part of the baroque. Another phase would be shift and
changes in matter or the weather—bubbles, flame, sleet, and
snow. As for language and literary style, exaggeration, antithesis, asyndeton, braggadocio, oxymoron, hyperbole, and
similar figures would be baroque. In the minds of some of its
protagonists, the baroque would be linked with the Gothic,
the Counter Reformation, the age of discovery, as well as
"panpsychism, pandynamism, and pantheism."[3]

All of which is a bit confusing, and it leaves a rather
nebulous picture of the baroque. An effort at clarifying it
and its critical implications was made by Helmut Hatzfeld in
1962: "Motifs like vanity, death, instability, movement,
change, mask, disguise, illusion, dissimulation, conflict, ostentation, melancholy, solitude, scruple, honour, generosity, de-
tachment, chastity, sanctity, grace, duty-passion and vir-
tue-*raison-d'Etat* tension, suffering, love as lure and danger,
seduction, sin, atonement, . . . may duly be called baroque.
Devices like chiaroscuro, impressionism, ambiguity, vacilla-
tion, prismatic presentation, suspense, mirage, pompous gestures, metamorphoses, casuistry, reconciliation, *bienséance* in
feeling and language, paradoxical relations between fatality
and providence, ascetic retreat, and cosmic speculation may
likewise be called baroque." Also, Hatzfeld would put in
the category of baroque "symbols of motion and emotion
(flame, wave, dance, storm, echo, cloud, reed, foam, fountain, snowflake, soap bubble), symbols of eroticism and
change (faun, peacock, Proteus, Calypso, Alcina, Hylas,
Ariadne), symbols of sin and earthly limitation (prison, lab-

yrinth, grave, graveyard, ruins)." Even with this added
mapping, it is still difficult to know what are the territorial
limits of Baroquie.[4]

If a workable definition for the baroque in French literature is hard to find, the period of the "baroque movement"
in France is equally illusory, if not protean. The literary
phases have been started as early as Rabelais and carried on
beyond 1670 to Jean Racine. In the opinion of Raymond,
the baroque age in France went from 1550 to 1650, since
this period was "that of a cultural condition or rather of
crisis in cultural condition wherein works of baroque form
and content have been able naturally to take their birth."
Raymond would not insist that these undefined "works of
baroque form and content" actually "flourished" during the
century that he has designated; nor would he agree with
Rousset that the baroque period in France extended to 1670,
which Raymond would call, in more standard fashion, the
"age of classicism"; to his mind the classic age of the 1660's
was "post-baroque," though his statements are somewhat
contradictory on this point. For Rousset, who is more in-
sistent that Raymond, the years between 1580 and 1625
would be "pre-baroque," while those from 1625 to 1665
were "full-baroque." This would be getting pretty close to
Molière and Racine; and, in fact, in 1963 the claim was made
that "the universe of Racine is the universe of the seventeenth-century baroque." But Rousset would consider Racine the opposite of the baroque, since his characters are
detached from time and are not "changing beings." From
another angle, the balanced *baroquiste*, Victor L. Tapié
(the same balance might be seen in A. Cioranesco's *El Barroco*, though he is primarily concerned with Spanish manifestations), said in 1961 that several of the pre-1650 "baroque" poets—poets who were "irregular, moody, nostalgic,
imaginative"—might one day be claimed by the "manner-
ists." Here would be noted a further borrowing for literary

criticism of a word more normally used in the world of the visual arts. In confirmation of Tapié's opinion, Hatzfeld has suggested that writers like Agrippa d'Aubigné, Montaigne, Saint François de Sales, Rotrou, and Corneille should be designated as manneristic and not baroque. The epithet of baroque should be applied to an author "only if he offers in a controlled, dignified, grave style his attempt at coming to terms with his interior inquietude." From this conclusion, it would seem logical that a "baroque" writer would not indulge in exaggeration, antithesis, oxymoron, stormy diffusion, or any linguistic contortions; he would, paradoxically, write as a dignified and controlled formalist.[5]

Many of the protagonists and critics of the baroque in France are not unconscious of the difficulties of their position. Tapié has said that, while the baroque was flourishing in Italy (especially in architecture), France "continued to nourish a predilection for classical prescriptions, harmonious and severe, and to pretend that her national spirit, distinguished by clarity and logic, was repugnant to the fantasies and exuberances of Italian art." Eugenio d'Ors saw the baroque in all periods of a nation's culture, as a revolt against the limitations of order. In partial agreement with this theory, Henri Focillon offered the opinion that in any evolution of an artistic concept there are three periods: the experimental, the mature or equilibrated, and the period of exuberance and fantasy. For Focillon the third period would be that of the baroque, but his position would not be acceptable to most of those critics who argue for the baroque in French literature. Where, according to Focillon's ideas of progression, would the first part of the seventeenth century (the age of Louis XIII) be put? Tapié avoids any application of Focillon's theory to French writers by deciding that it "applies to the history of plastic arts with more felicity than to that of literature." Tapié then makes the reign of Louis XIII, for better or for worse, the "predecessor" rather than the "successor" in the chronology of the baroque. It could not matter too much, since for Tapié the baroque is that which "sang of glory, force, joy, liberty, the conquest of God through faith and sacrifice lucidly accepted."[6]

An historian and present-day Academician like Pierre Ga-xotte thought that the French in the seventeenth century resisted the arrival of the baroque from Italy just as they resisted Spanish and Italian mysticism. To Gaxotte's way of thinking, "it is precisely its quality of the oratorical and redundant, of theatrical gesticulation, of trompe l'oeil, of swollen and inflated form, of useless complication, that makes the baroque repugnant to the spirit of the French." Gaxotte, it must be said, was speaking of Italian art and architecture rather than of literature. There was general agreement that the development of the baroque in the arts of the countries of Western Europe was in many ways an evolution of the Gothic, or a "transmutation of Gothic form." Germany, then, went from the Gothic to the baroque, with no classic interlude except for Goethe. France "missed the period of great baroque art, but on the other hand alone possessed in the seventeenth century a great classic art," according to Raymond. There would be no great quarrel with this conclusion, and Raymond concedes that many baroque writers have been revealed only by a "retrospective illumination." Then he lists, as though they were on equal levels of acceptance, four critical "universals"—Renaissance, Classicisme, Romantisme, Baroquisme. It is doubtful that such a term as "baroquism" could ever become popular.[7]

The sponsors of the baroque would tend to deny, for continued complication, that regularity is a part of classicism or formalism, and that irregularity or absence of clarity is sufficient to make the baroque. Nevertheless, in the transfer of the Wölflinn terminology from painting to literature, the *baroquistes* have in general accepted the "linear" as an attribute of classicism, and the "pictural" as a designation of the baroque. The latter would be outside exact and precise limits, would have a linkage of internal detail, and all objects within the over-all framework would seem to float rather than remain solidly anchored. There would be no sharp delineation of material either in the foreground or background, and all shapes and forms would dissolve into one another. The classical concept of a single central motif would be broken, but without blurring even though the essential character of the baroque might be only "feebly marked." The quality of the baroque in a work of art could be, in fact, simply in the eye of the viewer when he has learned to see differently and thus see different things. All this shift of vocabulary and critical approach from painting to literature can be quite confusing, especially when the literature is that of France. It can become almost meaningless if the baroque in a literary composition is supposed to be a variable depending on the eye and mind of the reader.[8]

The champions of the baroque have made full or partial claim to many French writers of the sixteenth and seventeenth centuries: Rabelais, Ronsard, Montaigne, Du Bartas, Agrippa d'Aubigné, Malherbe, Rotrou, Corneille, Racine, and several other standard figures. Among the irregulars put on the baroque list would be Mathurin Régnier, Théophile de Viau, and Saint Amant; among the rediscoveries and rehabilitations would be poets like Jean de Sponde, J.-B. Chassignet, Jean de Bussières, Jean de La Ceppède, and Martial de Brives. From the group of standard figures, Rousset and Raymond would reclassify Ronsard and make him a baroque poet in his later years; he was after 1574 no longer the "poet of love and roses," but was concerned with images of death, skeletons, and demons. For Imbrie Buffum, Agrippa d'Aubigné's long poem on France's suffering during the religious wars, *Les tragiques*, is an example of the baroque style because it is full of devices like asyndeton, exag-

geration, horror, personification, redness and radiance, oxymoron, metaphoric antithesis, disguise, and metamorphosis.
Raymond Lebègue, Rousset, and Raymond would see qualities of the baroque in Malherbe's early poem, *Les larmes de
Saint Pierre* of 1587; but Raymond would concede that
such writers as Malherbe and Corneille must inevitably be
regarded with a "classical prejudice." For Rousset and Buffum the first plays of Corneille are baroque, and for Buffum Rotrou's excellent *Saint Genest* (which has a play
within a play) is an example of baroque tragedy.

The baroque style, as defined by many of its advocates,
might be seen in Saint Peter's lament from *Les larmes de
Saint Pierre:*

> What is left to me for counsel and for arms,
> But to let my life flow out in a river of tears,
> And driving it from me send it along to the tomb? . . .
>
> My regret is so large, and my fault so great,
> That an eternal sea I demand of my eyes
> In order to weep forever the sin that I have done.

In the same poem, the Saviour speaks of Peter's betrayal:

> All the cruelties of these hands that nail me to the cross,
> The bold disdain that these executioners spit at me,
> The marks, equally full of fury and filth,
> That I endure of their impiety,
> Are not so harsh a thrust into my vitals,
> As the memory of your disloyalty.

Here are to be observed the "baroque" features of water in
movement, tears, antithesis, and violence. Farther along
Peter's remorse becomes so strong that, in hyperbolic metamorphosis, "his sighs turn themselves into winds that batter
the oaks"; and "the conscience of man" becomes "the knife
that brings him death." The first impression derived from
these lines, which have been rendered literally from the original alexandrines, is likely to be one of irritation at the forced

figures and bad taste involved. As far as Malherbe is concerned a generous attitude would be to relegate quietly *Les larmes de Saint Pierre* to his immature and informal period. This poem is a far cry from Malherbe's eighth ode which dates from 1628; in it are both dignity and formality, as shown in the following stanza on the men who fight the King's battles:

> Men in whose blood heat no longer flows
> In vain devote their cares to war:
> Mars is like Love: his labors and his sufferings
> Demand those who are young.

The later poetry of Malherbe has vigor, some warmth and regularity, and classical allusions that are skillfully employed.[9]

The somber and sometimes bitter verses of the Huguenot poet Agrippa d'Aubigné are based on Christian materials and have caused their author to be compared to Dante and Milton. He wrote with a colorful and powerful pen about the upheaval and suffering brought to France by the Wars of Religion. Turbulence, contrast, paradox, metamorphosis, and such things—all "baroque" characteristics—rather naturally permeate his poetry. An example from *Vengeances*, a section of *Les tragiques*, will indicate this matter of shift and change; it has to do with transformations brought to the earth by God's wrath:

> Earth, you that with difficulty carry on your back our woes,
> Change into ashes and bones so many fertile plains,
> Our meadows into mud, our pleasures into horrors,
> Our fields into sulphur, our flowers into carcasses.

D'Aubigné makes use of images of light and color when he describes the salvation of the Protestant martyrs:

> Thus the beautiful sun shows a finer face
> As it blends brightly with the thick cloud,
> And makes itself loved, with regretful desires,
> When its evening rays plunge into the sea.

One might say of the pilgrim (the sun), as it rises from its bed,
That it prefers a white morning and an evening that is red:
You in your birth and childhood had a white morning,
The joys of your setting are reddened in your blood.

The Sun's chariot coursing across the heavens, and the
weather changes involved in the process, was a favorite subject for artists and writers in the sixteenth and seventeenth
centuries. Corneille, whose first plays have been offered as
examples of the baroque, in the 1632 edition of his complicated tragicomedy *Clitandre* has a character ask the sun to
stay in bed a little longer with the sea-goddess, Thetis, so
that the night may be prolonged for further amorous dalli-
ance. It should be said that these lines involving "two more
kisses" for Thetis were removed by the sober Norman when
he revised his plays after 1657. In his first tragedy, *Médée*,
Corneille made use of the famous legend of Phaëthon, and
his efforts to guide the Sun-god's chariot across the sky. The
result was a wild dash of uncontrolled chargers through the
stars and planets, the scorching of the earth, and the death
of Phaëthon (the full story of which is told in the second book
of Ovid's *Metamorphoses*). Corneille employed the legend
when he had Medea, who was the daughter of the Sun, ask
for the privilege of wrecking his chariot on the city of Corinth, from which she had been banished:

Sun, you who see the insult that will be done to your race,
Give me your horses to drive in your place;
Grant this favor to my boiling desire:
I want to fall on Corinth with your burning car; . . .
(verses 261-264)

Corneille borrowed the essence of these lines from Seneca's
*Medea*, verses 32-36: "Grant, oh, grant that I ride through
the air in my father's car; give me the reins, sire, give me the
right to guide the fire-bearing steeds with the flaming reins;
then let Corinth, with her twin shores cause of delay to ships,
be consumed by flames and bring the two seas together."

Here, in best "baroque" fashion, Seneca has filled the heavens and earth with turbulence and climatic change befitting a "baroque" heroine like the sorceress Medea who could fly away in her own chariot drawn by two dragons.[10]

Urbain Chevreau in his *Billets critiques* of 1697 gave a strong argument for the theory that exotic figures of speech, transmutations, stars in peacocks' tails, and such things were the property of all poets in any language and time. He used for illustration the conceit of the Sun-god's voyage across the heavens, which has already been observed in Seneca, Agrippa d'Aubigné, and Corneille. Chevreau quotes first a couplet from a certain M. du Cros—"when these fierce horses that bring on the day announce its return onto the banks of the Ganges"—and says the same thing can be found in the Italian Fulvio Testi. Chevreau then quotes Ovid's version of the similar image (*Metamorphoses*, II, 152-154), wherein the Sun-god's horses are named: "Meanwhile the sun's swift horses, Pyrois, Eoüs, Aethon, and the fourth, Phlegon, fill all the air with their fiery whinnying, and paw impatiently at their bars." This scene is preliminary to Phaëthon's fatal dash across the heavens, when the horses, in Ovid's words, "with swift-flying feet rent the clouds in their path." But back to Chevreau: he goes on with a like picture from Vergil's *Aeneid*, which he gives as "Théophile (de Viau) translated it":

> His horses on coming out of the waves,
> With flame and light all covered,
> Their mouths and nostrils opened,
> Breathe forth the light of the world.

Chevreau emphasizes the point that the "baroque" figure of the fiery steeds of the sun changing the world from night to day has belonged to poets from the time of the ancients down to that of his friend M. du Cros. In his continued analysis of the figured language of poetry, Chevreau states that the transforming of flowers into stars has been done by many French and Italian poets, but that they were not the first to put flowers in the sky and to bring the stars down to earth; in fact, "there are 'flowers of light,' 'flowers of fire,' 'flowers of gold,' in the ordinary language of poets," and it was Plato that called the sky a "meadow filled with stars." As for the question of stars (or eyes) in the peacock's tail, that transmutation in Chevreau's opinion was a standard one for versifiers—and he might have mentioned the story, from the first book of Ovid's *Metamorphoses*, of Juno's transferring the eyes of Argus to the tail of her favorite bird. Sappho, according to Chevreau, made the rose the "eye of the spring-time," and Pindar called all flowers "beams of reddish purple." Latin poets like Catullus, Horace, and Ovid also were fond of vivid colors, and Ovid had a "reddish purple bull." Chevreau piles up several chapters to show that such contrasts and metamorphoses as the above were used freely by Spanish and Italian poets, as well as by the French, but for every figure that he introduces he makes a classical attachment. In other words, the recently discovered baroque style Chevreau would find in full measure among the Greeks and Romans. For him, and he was there at the time, the "baroque movement" in seventeenth-century France would have been nonexistent.[11]

The main current of French critical opinion on poetry, from the sixteenth century on into the eighteenth, rejected the irregularities and contortions of what has since been called the baroque in favor of regularity and formalized restraint. Du Bellay said in 1549 that a poet should even be careful about using exaggerated noms de plume: such names as "the traveler of perilous paths" (assumed by Jean Bouchet), and "the one banished from joy" (taken by François Habert)—as well as all names involving "springtime" and "fountains"—should be avoided. Ronsard echoed the sentiment of conservatism in 1573 when he stated that many

writers are "too inflated"; if their compositions were dis-
membered only "wind" would come out, as from a blown-
up pig's bladder. From another point of view, the pedantic
formalist Barthélemy Aneau attacked Du Bellay and the
Pléiade for their "addiction to periphrases," as well as for
their "syllogistic logic." But these opponents were in agreement as to the necessity for rule and form in the French
language, and would have resisted any unguided "baroque"
exuberance.[12]

In the seventeenth century, Rapin made a strong claim
for both naturalness and clarity: nature is the proper guide
for legitimate metaphors, and all poetic images are false
"when they are not natural." Small poets, in fact, exhaust
themselves in describing "forests, brooks, fountains, and
temples"—all of which Horace called exercises in puerility.
Rapin's contemporay, le Père Bouhours, was also opposed
to the irregular and unrestrained. In Bouhours' opinion,
"our language makes only very sober use of hyperboles,
because they are figures hostile to the truth." As for metaphors, French employs them when they can not be avoided.
Such combinations as "the ship of the soul" being agitated by
"the whirlwinds of fear" are for the French mind "extravagant figures" which should be relegated to the Spaniards and
Italians. It would be acceptable for a Spanish poet to be
fearful lest his "sighs being full of fire ignite the sky, the
earth, and the sea," since such bombast would be "in keeping
with the nature of the Spaniards." The Italians were not
much better, Bouhours thought, in their inclination toward
petty contortion and overembellishment. He resorted to a
bit of metaphor himself in describing the qualities of Spanish, Italian, and French linguistic styles: Spanish is like an
unbridled torrent, Italian is a gurgling brook (which can at
times become swollen with the spring freshets), but French
is a beautiful, well-cadenced river enriching every area
through which it flows—and its waters roll along in meas-

ured and unhurried majesty. There might be room in Bouhours' estimate for a sprinkling of modesty, but he would
leave little space in French letters for the "baroque." He
gives further emphasis to his conservative beliefs in his discussion of *devises* (or "mottoes"): a motto should have in it
"nothing monstruous, nothing irregular"; no wings should
be attached to an animal which, normally and logically,
should have none. As an example of mottoes and antithesis
that he did not like, Bouhours described details from the
*Ballet of the Four Seasons,* which was staged first in 1623.
In the ballet, the *entrée* of Winter symbolized the burning
of love underneath a frozen exterior, with Mount Etna crossing the stage covered with snow and ice and bearing the
motto "There is ice on the outside, but flame on the inside."
Bouhours' formalized and proper soul cringed before such
antics, but he should have taken comfort from the fact that
a ballet, like a machine play, did not pretend to obey any
rules. And, besides, the motto was written in Italian.[13]

Near the middle of the eighteenth century, Charles Batteux continued to voice objection to the irregular, the exaggerated, and the distorted in French art and letters. In the
dedication of his treatise *Les beaux arts* to the Dauphin, mention is made of taste—"taste for the true, for the simple," and
a "taste for nature adorned with its own graces, without the
slightest affectation." Batteux felt, however, that the scope
of poetry was tremendous, broad enough to encompass all
of nature's phenomena: "It [that is, poetry] may rise up into
the heavens to revel there in the march of the stars: it may
bury itself in the depths of the earth to examine there nature's secrets: it may penetrate into the land of the dead
to view the rewards of the just and the punishments of the
wicked: it includes the whole universe." Poetry would
therefore permit "striking metaphors, vivid repetitions, and
singular apostrophes"—like "Aurora, daughter of the morning, who opens the gates of the Orient with her rosy fingers,"

or "the young Zephyrs that frolic over the enameled plains."
Batteux, like Chevreau, would allow all poets of all times the
use of such figured language—but under the guidance of
properly restrictive "laws of imitation." Thus, certain elements of so-called "baroque" effusion would be the property
of the whole world of poetry.[14]

The formalized and classical seventeenth century, in its
listing and its estimate of poets past and present, paid little
attention to the irregulars who have since been adopted by
the *baroquistes*. A slight exception is to be noted in the
lengthy *Bibliothèque française* of Charles Sorel in 1644, which
included everything and everybody. One of the large figures
of the late Renaissance (and one much favored by the protagonists of the baroque), Du Bartas, received a fairly general rejection. It is true, admittedly, that few of the sixteenth-
century poets received any lavish accolades from seventeenth-century critics, as is illustrated by Boileau's cursory
treatment of them in his *Art poetique* of 1674 and his herald-
ing the arrival of Malherbe with his "proper cadences." In
any case, Pierre de Deimier criticized Du Bartas for his
flamboyance and lack of measure. In 1639, La Mesnardière
listed as the "learned troupe" from the Renaissance Ronsard,
Baïf, Du Bellay, and Pelletier. Later in the century, Desmarets de Saint-Sorlin the Modern, in a different judgment,
said that Malherbe rejected the inflation and extravagances
of Ronsard and Du Bartas, and brought French poetry back
from a "precipice." From the earlier part of the seventeenth
century, Saint-Sorlin would praise Desportes, Malherbe,
Louis Guez de Balzac, and Voiture—and reject the ancients
and their admirers. Around 1650, the grammarian Gilles
Ménage listed a group of poets who, according to him, had
brought "majesty" to the use of the alexandrine: they were
Desportes, Du Bartas, cardinal du Perron, and Chapelain.
Chapelain, who was later lampooned by Boileau, was called
by the pedantic Ménage "the Homer and Vergil of France."

Bouhours in 1675, among several men of letters of his century, named Balzac, Voiture, Corneille, Richelieu, the chevalier de Méré, and Boileau—but none of the more recent "baroque" discoveries. At about the same time Rapin mentioned, with some praise and some blame, Ronsard and Du Bartas (both were "barbarous" in their use of antiquity, but both "had all the genius of which their century was capable"); Rabelais ("unworthy of genteel attention in the present century") and Régnier ("lacking in *bienséance*"); Théophile de Viau ("had too much affectation") and Sarrasin (who was good at "small verses"); Malherbe (the first to join "purity with the noble style"); and the salon poet, Voiture ("the most delicate spirit of recent centuries"). Chevreau in 1693 wrote a letter to a certain friend, M. de la F . . . , who played at writing verses, in which M. de la F . . . is praised for having abandoned "his great heroes, Pierre de Ronsard, Jean-Antoine de Baïf, Amadis Jamyn, and Remi Belleau"—all connected with the Pléiade; and for removing from his poetic "idols" Du Bartas and Théophile de Viau. No latter-day "baroque" excavation is included on the list of fallen heroes. Even the irregulars who were known in their day (men like Régnier and Théophile de Viau) did not triumph because under Louis XIII, in the words of Gaxotte, "French society aspired to a reconstruction on a basis of regularity"; and in verse, prose, and novels there was a "universal conspiracy in favor of politeness and *bienséance*."[15]

If the proponents of the baroque in France have been unsuccessful in marking out a "baroque period" in French literature and in clarifying their critical terminology, they have done a service in rediscovering some good poets who got lost in the progressive formalism of the seventeenth century. Jean de Sponde and Jean de La Ceppède, in particular, are worthy of note; and, possibly, the *baroquistes* have made more respectable the free-living and free-thinking Saint Amant, that seventeenth-century combination of Chateaubriand and Edgar Allan Poe. Sponde, the Villon-esque poet of love and death who died in 1595, is worth all the contradictions that have arisen from efforts to implant the baroque on French terrain. His verse is full of shift and contrast, repetition, stars and the wind, ice and fire, and other supposedly baroque characteristics. With it all Sponde mixed the standard Ovidian vocabulary of love—that is, love is a flame, love is a wound, love is a malady, and such things. The first quatrain of the fourth love sonnet blends elements of contrast, repetition, and Ovid's language:

> In vain a thousand beauties may be present before my eyes,
> My eyes to them are open and my heart is closed,
> A single beauty lights the flame in my bones
> And my bones are happy with this fire alone.

In the twenty-fifth love sonnet—Sponde wrote twenty-six sonnets on love and twelve on death—the gold of his love comes out stronger through the test of fire; and in the opening line of the first *Stance* the fire of his passion is doubled by the device of repetition: "Ce feu, ce feu, tout seul peut rallumer mes feux." The fifth love sonnet, in the first line of the first tercet, recalls vividly the Ovidian story of Actaeon's destruction by his own dogs: "Je suis cet Actéon de ces chiens déchiré." Sponde's first sonnet on death is full of the cold north wind, the *aquilon*—later to be favored, it will be recalled, by the Romantic poet Lamartine. The second sonnet on death may well be the best of Sponde; it begins:

> But indeed it is necessary to die, and arrogant life
> In facing death will feel its furies,
> The suns will burn brown these flowers of one day,
> And time will burst this bubble filled with wind.

Sponde, the pre-Romantic, lived a sad and miserable life, and like Villon and Alfred de Musset, died early. He would not have fitted into the seventeenth-century world—as his editor, Marcel Arland, has admitted—of "measure, harmony, and verisimilitude."[16]

J.-B. Chassignet, while still in his teens, wrote odes and sonnets on life and death; they were published in 1594. He also used some sonnets to illustrate in verse an emblem book, which is full of macabre contrasts. The fifth emblem, for example, is described as "a gallows on which is hanging a lute; in the background is a woman carrying a sheaf of grain, next to a cart of manure." In the eleventh emblem, "a death's head, placed on two crossed bones, reposes on a base, beside a ruined wall and a broken column." The last tercet of Chassignet's sonnet for this design runs as follows:

> But do you not see death laughing at your speeches,
> Breaking up your endeavor in the midst of its course,
> And enclosing all your plans under seven feet of earth?

All of which is similar to Victor Hugo's *Hernani* (I, ii), where Hernani tells his beloved Doña Sol that old Gomez is holding onto her with one hand while he is holding death with the other. The fifty-fifth emblem bears the description: "In the midst of a stormy sea, there is a rock on which a kingfisher rests in its nest; in the background, a vessel and a boat shattered by the tempest; the sun is coming through the clouds." In the fifty-seventh emblem, there are two skeletons, one upright and one lying flat—and "at the right is a shattered wall on which is blooming a flower." Most of these visualized contrasts in the emblems are artificial juxtapositions, and Chassignet's illustrative sonnets contain many forced inversions. At times the whole procedure seems a bit naïve. However, there is a striking similarity in this collection of tombs, broken columns, flowers blooming in shattered walls, and so on to the Romantic theory of the poetry of ruins, and to Chateaubriand's predilection for the mossy slabs of an old tomb wherein a bird had built its nest.[17]

Saint Amant, that uninhibited seventeenth-century poet whose formal training was chiefly in drinking, also liked ruins and the eery inhabitants thereof—as may be seen in some verses from his poem *Solitude:*

> How I like to see the crumbling
> Of these old chateaux in ruins,
> Against which the rebellious years
> Have hurled their insolence!
> Sorcerers in them conduct their midnight revels;
> Frolicsome demons inside them take up their abode,
> Demons who with their malicious posturing
> Deceive our senses and bring us martyrdom;
> Inside them are nested in a thousand holes
> Snakes and owls.

Further on in the poem (and in the ruined chateau), an owl "underneath a rafter of accursed wood shakes the horrible skeleton of a poor lover who hanged himself because of a shepherdess that was cold."* Saint Amant exhibits a Poe-like quality in some lines from another poem, *Les visions:*

> A big dog, starved and black, slowly dragging along
> In the company of horror and fright,
> Comes every night to howl at my door
> Redoubling his cries in a frightful way.

In somewhat milder fashion, Jean de Bussières speaks of the sun, fire, snow, ice, the obscure night, marble wounded by the chisel, and the sadness of the rain. Martial de Brives blends together elements of religion, antithesis, and oxymoron as in such lines as "I have the honor to bear these fortunate chains" and "In this powerful and divine weakness my wavering hope finds its surety." Brives' *Paraphrase sur le cantique de la Vierge* begins, in a display of preciosity and bad taste:

> The Virgin who from her vitals
> Sees emerge the God of battles. . .

---

* The rigorous Boileau later in the century said that Saint Amant's images of snakes, snails, and hanged men were "malapropos" and "most frightful" (fourth *Réflexion* on Longinus).

Brives, also, is fond of combining the natural, supernatural, and biblical: at one point, for example, he calls on "dragons, terrible gulfs, and the sphere of fire [the sun]" to join in the praise of God.[18]

All of the pieces of verse excerpted here have been taken from poets from the last years of the sixteenth century through the first half of the seventeenth. Most of the writers involved have been catalogued since by the *baroquistes* as a part of the "baroque movement" of the period. There is no doubt that the attributes of language and style supposed to be indicative of the baroque are to be discerned in full measure in these composers of verse. The same qualities, as has already been suggested, can also be seen in Sappho, the younger Seneca, Ovid, Villon, Chateaubriand, Lamartine, or Baudelaire. Certainly it must be conceded that poets like Sponde and Saint Amant (among others) would have been against the current of formalism developing around the court of Louis XIII. Such irregulars, therefore, would have been the logical leaders of any movement contrary to that of regularity and form. There is one primary objection to this line of reasoning: judging from the evidence of the availability of their works, these poets were simply not known during their own age.

Some indications of their popularity in their own time can be gained by consulting the catalogue of the Bibliothèque Nationale, which was begun officially by Francis I, a far-seeing monarch who demanded that copies of every book published in his realm be sent to the royal library. On the basis of entries, Sponde's religious work was fairly well known: his *Déclaration . . . à s'unir à l'Eglise Catholique* had five editions between 1595 and 1610, and his *Méditations sur les pseaumes* had one in 1588. His more amorous verse appeared in a collection of several poets, which had one edition at Rouen in 1604. Chassignet's poetry of his early youth, *Le Mespris de la vie*, had one edition at Besançon in 1594,

7. Henry IV entering Metz

COMBAT NOCTVRNE, ET AVTRES ARTIFICES DE FEV, EXECVTEZ
DEVANT LEVRS MAIESTEZ, PAR LE SIEVR ABRAHAM FABERT.

8. Fireworks, 1603

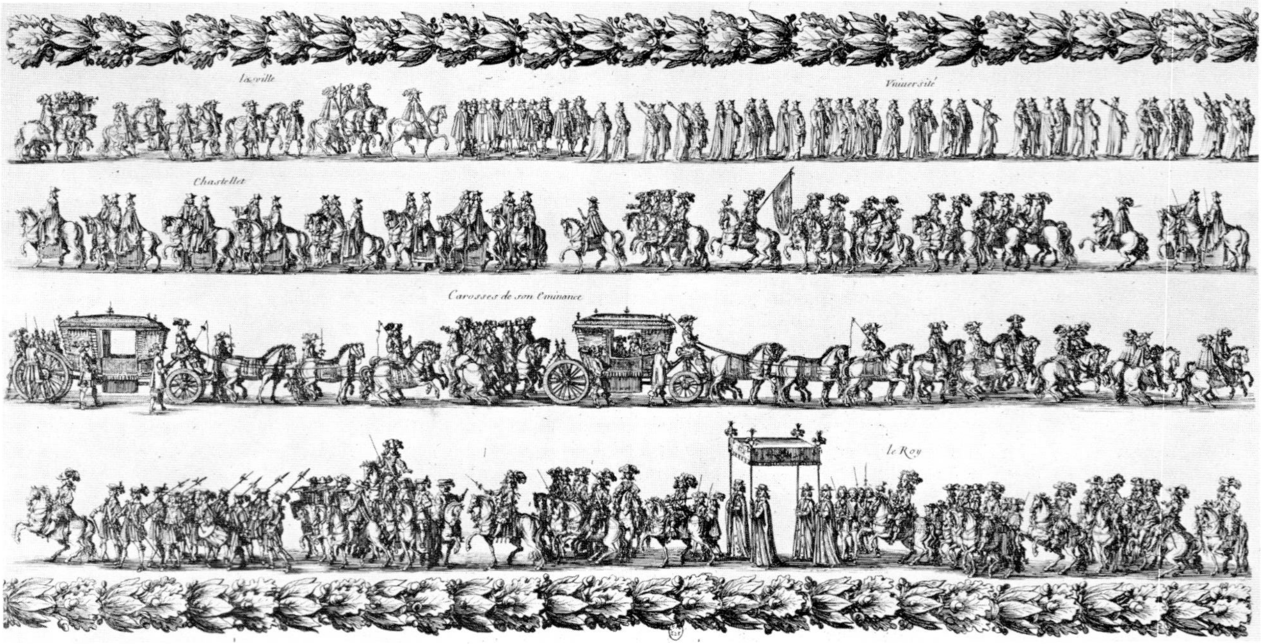
la ville
Vniuersité
Chastellet
Carosses de son Eminance
le Roy

9. Entree of Louis XIV and Marie-Thérèse into Paris

and his *Paraphrases sur les douze petits prophètes du Vieux Testament* had but one edition in 1601. La Ceppède's *Les théorèmes . . . sur le sacré mystère de notre rédemption* has only one listing in the Bibliothèque Nationale catalogue, an edition at Toulouse, 1613-1621. Bussières' *Les Descriptions poétiques* has a single cataloguing, an edition at Lyons in 1649; but his Latin *Flosculi historiarum* was printed in 1649, 1656, 1659, 1661, 1662, 1677, and 1683—and also had three translations into French during the seventeenth century. Martial de Brives faired a trifle better; there were three editions of his works during the seventeenth century but none since.

The "baroque" poets discovered in recent years could have had little influence in their own period. They were engulfed in the rising tide of formalism that marked the reign of Louis XIII. On the other hand, a rather casual sampling of the more ordered and restrained writers of the seventeenth century—some good, some bad, and some indifferent—will show that they were well-known in their own day. In the Bibliothèque Nationale catalogue, that proponent of order and clarity in prose, La Mothe le Vayer, has eleven columns of listings, most of them from the seventeenth century. Le Père Le Moyne, whose epic poem on Saint Louis is scarcely remembered today, has eight columns of entries in the BN catalogue, all but two of which are from the seventeenth century. Benserade, who concerned himself with the court ballet, also has eight columns of listings of his seventeenth-century publications. As for the formalistic critics, Rapin has thirteen columns of his works catalogued, chiefly from the seventeenth and eighteenth centuries; Bonhours has seventeen columns of his writings in the Bibliothèque Nationale records. It seems clear that without the help of the major defenders of classicism and propriety in French seventeenth-century literature—such as Racine, Boileau, and the dignified Bossuet—the outriders of formalism swept aside any "baroque movement" by the mere force of numbers.

# THE FRENCH ACADEMY

O NE OF the primary formalistic influences on life in France, since its establishment in the first part of the seventeenth century, has been the French Academy. It began as a rather unpretentious effort in 1629, on the part of several men of some social and literary position in Paris, to rid themselves of the feminine domination encountered in a salon such as the Hôtel de Rambouillet. All were more or less regular participants in madame de Rambouillet's stylized gatherings, but they felt from time to time the normal masculine urge to get away from the mannered chattering of women. The result was the development of something like a men's luncheon club, which began to assemble about once a week at the home of a wealthy and cultured Parisian, Valentin Conrart. Among those who enjoyed the calm of Conrart's hospitality was the abbé de Boisrobert, minor dramatist, amateur actor, and—most importantly—secretary to Cardinal Richelieu. Boisrobert reported the activities and discussions at Conrart's house to his master, whose intuitive sense of regulation led him to the conclusion that these informal meetings should become a formal organization under his patronage and, inevitably, under his control. The result, though it was not really desired by Conrart and his friends, was the formation of the Académie Française, that august and venerable body which can still today by membership therein bestow the highest of accolades on a French man of letters. To be one of the "Forty Immortals" of the French Academy remains, despite occasional derisory comments from the envious, the loftiest honor that can come to a writer or scholar in France. And it all began in 1635 because the astute and austere Richelieu saw in a men's eating club the possibilities of formalized guidance of the French language and literature.

There had been discussion groups, literary and artistic assemblies, and even academies in sixteenth-century France—in Paris, Lyon, Poitiers, and other provincial areas; but none had the dignity and pretensions to authority of the Académie Française. The most significant and official of these earlier organizations was probably the Académie de Poésie et Musique, which was founded by Jean-Antoine de Baïf, the experimenter in verse forms and member of the Pléiade; and the musician Joachim Thibaut de Courville. The academy was given letters patent in November 1570, by Charles IX, and the promoters were congratulated for having "worked together with great study and assiduous labor for the advancement of the French language." Henry III continued to give support to a literary extension (the Académie du Palais) of the group after he became king in 1574, and welcomed it to the royal palace, a tradition that was to continue later when sessions of the Académie Française were held in the Louvre. The Huguenot poet Agrippa d'Aubigné spoke in 1576 of the reunions of the academy held by the King twice a week "in his Cabinet to listen to the most learned men and even to a few ladies who had done some studying." Among the latter would most likely have been the duchesse de Retz, who wrote good Greek and Latin and who was called the tenth Muse. The Académie du Palais welcomed women into its fold, a policy that was different basically from that of the Académie Française. The male members of this earlier foundation included many of the best-known writers of the second half of the sixteenth century: Pierre de Ronsard, Guy de Pibrac, Philippe Desportes, the cardinal du Perron, Pontus de Tyard, and others. Musical features were sponsored by the Académie de Poésie et Musique on Sunday mornings, and members were admitted to the hall only if they were wearing an identifying medallion—but they were not supposed to interrupt a song by knocking on the door. Both phases of the academy died before 1600, since Henry IV was too busy with the fundamentals of government to take time for cultural niceties. It was, nevertheless, an official instrument of formalism and could have come to Richelieu's mind later when he established the Académie Française. The pedantic mademoiselle de Gournay, who was the goddaughter of Montaigne and who lived until 1645, may have, from her earlier memories of the Académie de Poésie et Musique, helped put the idea into the Cardinal's head.[1]

The rigid and imposing spirit of Richelieu hovered over the Academy long after his death, the spirit of the "grand Armand, the honor of our history." Fénelon, critic and tutor of royal children, said, in his discourse of reception into the Académie Française in March 1693, that Richelieu was "constant in his maxims, inviolable in his promises," and that he "changed the face of Europe in his time." La Bruyère, who wrote a series of character sketches of men of his age, said in his address to the Academy in June 1693 that Richelieu was a "strong and superior genius." The actions of the members of the Academy on the occasion of the death of Richelieu, the "Protector and Instituter of this Body," in 1642 reflect the innate formalism of the organization. It was generally agreed that the anniversary of the Cardinal's demise would be noted with a public celebration of suitable "solemnity" and "pomp." But first there was to be a simple ceremony: one member would do a eulogy of the Cardinal, another would compose an epitaph, and a third would offer a funeral oration. All the other Academicians would, each one, write a piece of prose or verse in praise of His Eminence. It was decided finally that such trifling homage was not sufficiently pompous for an open session, but should be done privately before "the Company." The Académie Française was, indeed, Richelieu's solemn and well-disciplined child.[2]

The early meetings of the informal group of friends at Conrart's house were chronicled in 1652 by Paul Pellisson, the first historian of the Académie Française. Conrart's place was chosen for the reunions because it was "in the heart of the city"—which it was, on the rue des Vieilles-Etuves, not far from the rue Saint-Martin in the fourth arrondissement today. Those present chatted "familiarly, as they might have done on any ordinary visit, and about every sort of thing, business, late news, and belles-lettres." This type of gathering continued for three or four years, "without fanfare and without pomp, and without any other laws than those of friendship." Richelieu's interest injected immediately an element of rigidity and formalism into the sessions, and into the minds of the participants. After they agreed to accept the Cardinal's plans for creating the Academy—they could scarcely have refused—they sent him a letter indicating that one of their official responsibilities would be to "remove from the number of barbaric tongues this language that we speak." The policy was later confirmed in Article 24 of the Academy's statutes, which bore Richelieu's signature, to the effect that the principal function of the institution would be to "give explicit rules to our language and to render it pure, eloquent, and capable of treating the arts and sciences." Louis XIII issued letters patent on January 25, 1635, confirming the title of Académie Française and limiting the number of academicians to forty; the King's "very beloved cousin the Cardinal duc de Richelieu" was allowed to call himself "chief and protector" of the association. In regard to the figure of forty seats, it "was not yet reached" in 1637, as would be confirmed by P. Sevin's contemporary engraving which reveals in formalistic array some thirty seated members, with one imposing chair on a dais left vacant for the Chancellor or the Protector of the assembly (Figure 2). It will be noted that Sevin's engraving—which is itself properly formal with arches, balustrades, fleurs-de-lis, and Italian mottoes—shows certain academicians sitting stiffly upright with their hats still squarely on their heads in keeping with their privileged social status.[3]

As for the "seat" (the *fauteuil*) of an Academician, there was no such reserved place for each member during the seventeenth century, despite the well-spaced chairs in Sevin's engraving. There were reserved seats for the Director (and probably for the Protector, which was Richelieu until his death in 1642), the Chancellor (a variable office), and the Perpetual Secretary (the first was Conrart). In later years, however, it has become customary to speak of a "seat in the French Academy" to designate membership therein. And in 1855 one Arsène Houssaye wrote an imagined history of the "forty-first seat," wherein he installed successively the many great French writers who had never been elected to the Academy. (The most notable name on his list was that of Molière.) It is true that the first forty Academicians—the full complement was not reached until 1639—included more writers of empty formalism or rigid pendantry than of literary genius. Scarcely a third of them would be remembered now; among these would be Jean Chapelain (critic, distributor of the Cardinal's pensions, and would-be writer of epics), Desmarets de Saint-Sorlin (Richelieu's dramatist and later critic of the Ancients), Saint Amant (emancipated inebriate and pretty good poet), Louis Guez de Balzac (the reformer of prose), Vaugelas (important codifier of language), and Voiture (salon poet and writer of letters). Of the original group that gathered at the home of Conrart, even fewer deserve to be listed today, though two members of the earlier club, Antoine Godeau and Claude de Malleville, wrote some pleasant light verses.

Despite mistakes and omissions, the early Academy had important aims and regulatory aspirations. With the support and approval of Richelieu, it was able to set in motion many of its formalistic plans, despite the hostility of the Parlement de Paris, whose type of legal eloquence the Academy ridiculed, and of the University of Paris. By its statutory regulations the Academy was forbidden to take up matters of religion, and given only limited privilege to discuss moral and political problems. But in one of the briefest of its statutes, Article 24, was laid out a program of formalized business that would keep the Academy occupied for centuries: "There will be composed a dictionary, a grammar, a rhetoric, and a poetics under the observations of the Academy." The rhetoric and poetics never got out of the realm of discussion and the project for the grammar was abandoned because Vaugelas, one of the best of the Academicians, was working on his *Remarques sur la langue française,* destined after its appearance in 1647 to become the century's most influential treatise on language, grammar, and usage. It should be mentioned, in passing, that the Academy finally did bring out its own grammar, a thin little volume which did not see the light of day until the 1930's. The question of the dictionary, however, was taken up immediately and received serious consideration.

Both Vaugelas and Chapelain offered ideas on the dictionary, but it was Chapelain's general plan that was put into operation. His hope was that the dictionary (assisted by the proposed rhetoric, poetics, and grammar) would "render the language capable of the ultimate in eloquence." The words included in the work would be subjected to several criteria of judgment. First, it would be necessary to "make a choice of all the dead authors" who have written "purely" in the French language. It would be necessary, next, to effect an analysis of all words, and admit some that have been authorized by "usage" though not found in the compositions of "good authors." A distinction should be made in the listings between words proper to verse and those proper to prose, and the indication should be clear concerning words of a "sublime quality, a middle quality, and of the lowest quality." Accents should be observed carefully and logically, and the open and close quality of vowels should be marked to facilitate their exact pronunciation. Also, the Latin etymologies of words should be given to show the history and logic of their evolution. All in all, it was a lofty and valid project, as Chapelain visualized it. He would have chosen for quotation, as responsible writers of French prose, certain men from the near past; among them were Jacques Amyot (the translator of Plutarch), Montaigne, Saint François de Sales (the most popular religious writer of the first part of the seventeenth century), and the novelist Honoré d'Urfé. Among the poets worthy to be quoted in the dictionary were Marot, Saint Gelais, Ronsard, Du Bellay, Du Bartas, and Malherbe.[4]

Boisrobert was first picked by the Academy to put Chapelain's ideas on the dictionary into operation, but by 1638 Richelieu had not confirmed the appointment of his secretary to the job. Interest in the proposal began to wane, and "eight or ten months passed without any mention being made of the dictionary." Serious work began on it, however, when Vaugelas took over its direction in 1639, encouraged by a generous pension from the Cardinal's coffers. Progress was painfully slow and when Vaugelas died ten years later the compilation had gone no farther than the letter "I." There were rumblings of complaint about the whole affair, though in the beginning there had been much confidence that the dictionary would give order to the language; and it would be an excellent thing for a writer to be supported in his choice of words by "forty of the most intelligent of persons." At the time of Vaugelas' death in 1649 many people thought that the system of having several Academicians sitting in semisomnolent postures around a table, exchanging pompous and pedantic ideas on words, was a rather inefficient way to make a dictionary. Even Boisrobert chided his fellow members in a bit of doggerel for spending six years on the letter "G," and he doubted that destiny would let him live "until H." The project almost died with Vaugelas, since the dictionary was seized by his creditors and returned to the Academy only after much litigation. The zeal of the Academicians had cooled considerably during the long interlude, and was rekindled only by the efforts of Louis XIV's minister, Colbert, in 1683. After the many years of painful labors, the dictionary at last appeared in 1694, and with proper order and solemnity was presented to Louis XIV. Its success in the world of culture and learning was mediocre, due to its omissions, some inexactitudes, and an arrangement of words by roots instead of alphabetical order. This last difficulty was removed in the second edition of 1718 when a more standard system of alphabetizing was substituted for that of roots. Succeeding editions—the eighth was in 1932—have added to the dictionary's dignity and gained for it more general acceptance.[5]

The Academy apparently indulged in some relaxation, aside from verbal interchanges and pontifications, after the publication of the dictionary in 1694. In 1713, the Secretary, M. Dacier, asked the several Academicians to present ideas as to what should occupy the Academy in its future deliberations. Fénelon seems to have been the only member who took the suggestion seriously, and the result was his famous *Lettre à l'Académie*, which the printer had in hand at the time of Fénelon's death in 1715. In it, Fénelon restated in fine critical fashion the tenets of Article 24 of the statutes in regard to the dictionary, grammar, rhetoric, and poetics. He made a strong plea for all four ideas, but his remarks on the dictionary were the only ones to bear any practical fruit. He pointed out very persuasively that a new edition of the dictionary would have great value for future generations by showing them what words and expressions were esteemed to be proper during the last years of Louis XIV. It would be a notable thing, said Fénelon for illustrative parallel, if contemporary dictionaries still existed from the cultivated ages of Greece and Rome—or of the language of the French Middle Ages. The dictionary would be of immediate value, in addition, for even "the most cultivated Frenchmen" who might perchance need to look something up. The solid and proper ideas of Fénelon undoubtedly had some effect in hastening the completion of the Academy's second edition of its dictionary in 1718.[6]

One of the great crises in the French Academy during the seventeenth century was brought about by the assembling and publishing of another dictionary, that of Antoine Furetière. Furetière was the author of a realistic novel in 1666, and a friend of such good classicists as Racine, Boileau, Molière, and La Fontaine. He was also an Academician in good standing until the affair of the two dictionaries caused his dismissal in 1685 from the Academy, an occurrence that has been very rare in the history of the organization. Nevertheless, in keeping with a proper concept of form and regulation, Article 13 of the Academy's statutes provided for the elimination of a member who had done some act "unworthy of a man of honor." Furetière's activities in connection with the dictionary were adjudged to be unworthy, so action was taken by the Academy in January 1685—he had been an Academician since 1662. Furetière's own dictionary came out in 1690, two years after his death and four years before the compilation of the Academy.[7]

As for the Academy's position, it should be pointed out that it was given in 1674 a monopoly on the production of a new dictionary in the French language, and no printer was supposed to bring out any competitive work before twenty years had passed. In some way Furetière obtained for himself a privilege of publishing a "universal dictionary generally containing all the words in French both ancient and modern." The Academy accused him of falsifying this privilege and of plagiarizing its dictionary, all of which Furetière vehemently denied, saying that he had spent twenty years on his work and that it filled fifteen large cases. He was more resentful of the Academy's implications that he was a poor scholar than of its exclusion of him from its register. Boileau was inclined to be on the side of Furetière, though La Fontaine deserted him. The Academy never relented in its condemnation, but Furetière's seat was not filled until after his death. It is of some significance that his dictionary, probably as a result of the Academy's monopoly, was published in 1690 in Holland and not in France. It required three folio volumes, was alphabetized and not assembled by word roots, and has in general been regarded by posterity as a fuller and more usable instrument than the Academy's dictionary of 1694.[8]

Furetière spent the last years of his life blasting the Academy's methods of making a dictionary: the ponderous slowness, the empty pomposity, and the wasted formalistic interchanges. His feeling was that the least capable of the Academicians had been given a lexicographical task too big for them, and that their primary interest was their own "glory." He arranged his attacks in a series of satiric *Factums*, a second satire called *L'apothéose du dictionnaire de l'Académie*, and a third one entitled *L'enterrement (burial) du dictionnaire*. From the second *Factum* comes an imagined session in 1685 of a few Academicians discussing words proposed for the dictionary; the committee functioned as follows: "The one who shouts the loudest is the one who is right; each person gives forth with a long harangue on the slightest trifle. The second man repeats like an echo everything that the first has said, and most frequently three or four of them talk at the same time. In the commission composed of five or six persons, there is one of them who reads, one who offers his opinion, two who chat, one who sleeps, and one who spends his time perusing some dictionary which is on the table. When it is the turn of the second to express his views, the article has to be read to him again because of his distraction during the first reading. That is the way they are writing the dictionary. No two lines are accepted without long digressions, without somebody telling a funny story or a tidbit of news, or without someone else talking about conditions in the country and about reforming the government." With due allowance for Furetière's likely bias, it sounds as though he might have attended such a committee meeting. His satire on the slow procedures of his erstwhile companions in erudition was continued in an epigram that prefaced the *Apothéose* of the Academy's dictionary:

> I am this big Dictionary,
> Which was for half a century in the belly of my mother;
> When I was born I had a beard and some teeth:
> This fact should not be considered very unusual,
> Since I was at the time fifty years old.

Furetière went on with his ridicule of the imagined apotheosis of the Academy's work by saying that the Academicians were so proud of it that they thought it only proper for it to be deified. He then set about the task of picking holes in the Academy's selection of words or the definitions attached to them. Furetière's attack was centered on the first part of the dictionary, which he had undoubtedly seen in an early draft; he was dead by the time the work appeared in 1694.[9]

The policy of the Academy was to reject all words judged to be barbarous, and which would not pass the test of proper usage; usage was, as has been noted in Vaugelas' terms, the manner of speech of "the sanest part of the Court." Such formal limitations and exclusions left many openings for

Furetière's shafts and he was not hesitant in firing away. At times he objected to the Academy's definition of words, and at other times to certain words that the Academy had not included in its book. He was occasionally petty, frequently astute, and sometimes more formalistic than the Academy itself in his criticisms. The Academy had defined *amour* as the "sentiments of one who is in love." Furetière called this a "pitiful definition," and proceeded to describe love as an "interior passion or movement, which inclines the person who feels it toward an object which, appearing agreeable to him, gives him the desire to possess it." Furetière clearly should have left love alone; the Academy at least was wise enough to make a minimal statement on the matter. On the question of the *article*, the Academy had said there were two, one definite and one indefinite. Furetière thought this was not enough "instruction" on articles, so he spent two pages of formal discussion of their varied uses, including an explanation of the partitive construction. In this case he exhibited sound scholarship and gave a piece of grammatical exposition that is still valid. The Academy had put in its compilation *octante* for *huictante* (eighty); Furetière properly called them both outdated linguistic formalisms, since "we say now *quatre-vingts*." According to Furetière, most of the Academy's remarks on language were "taken from Vaugelas," for whom Furetière had respect—but, unfortunately, not enough was borrowed from Vaugelas. Furetière was most regularistic when he criticized the Academy's defining "accusative" as "the fourth case of words which are declined." This was too simple, to his mind, and merely put the accusative on a ladder with the nominative, genitive, and dative, and gave no idea as to its function. With some pedantry (but, it must be admitted, with exactitude), Furetière maintained that "the accusative is the case which designates, which indicates, which accuses the term on which the active verb takes action." In the 1697 edition of Furetière's *L'enter-*

*rement,* from which this discussion of the accusative is drawn, some later formalist has substituted in the margin (in ink now brown and dim) for "takes action," "takes *its* action."[10]

Many of Furetière's objections smacked of pettiness and the splitting of hairs. The Academy's dictionary, in its dedication to the King, contained the statement: "This work is a faithful collection of all the terms and of all the phrases from which Eloquence and Poetry can form words of praise." Furetière gave as his critical estimate of this claim: "This dictionary has been made, then, only for orators and poets who wish to offer words of praise: thus preachers who wish to declaim against vice; and poets who, like Despréaux (Boileau) and Molière, wish to cause vice to be hated, will come in vain to look for words and phrases in this dictionary." The Academy's work had defined *puce* (flea) as an "insect attaching itself principally to the skin of men." Furetière called this exposition inexact: "of men" should be "of man," in the generic singular, since the skin of both men and women was involved. Furetière had authority for his position, because the learned jurist Etienne Pasquier had written a clever poem in the sixteenth century about a flea that nestled in the bosom of a fashionable lady he knew, madame des Roches. Furetière got nearer to the gutter in his notation of the omission from the Academy's dictionary of *compisser;* he admitted that it was a low word, but wondered how an Academician would describe the action of a dog that had wet his *robe de chambre.* Furetière found also many quite proper and correct words that had been omitted from the Academy's collection, apparently by pure oversight or faulty procedures. On this point he exclaimed: "Those who wish to know whether one should say *capitaine* or *capitainesse,* will not be able to be informed by the dictionary, because the word *capitaine* is not in it." In the realm of formalized architecture, said Furetière, a person might want to describe the hall of the Swiss guards at the Louvre, "where you see four caryatids, or statues with women's figures, twelve feet in height, holding up a tribune enriched with ornamentation." A man of scholarly exactitude would get little help from the Academy's dictionary, however, since the word *cariatide* is not in it. Furetière concluded, therefore, on the basis of such evidence that the Academy's work was a "poor and impotent thing, halting and lame."[11]

Saint Evremond, the civilized and sophisticated critic who went into exile in London after the internal difficulties of the Fronde, had several things to say about the Académie Française. He resented the Academy's pretentious authority, which was symbolized by the affixing of its seal of blue wax with a crown of laurel to any document that the Academy considered to be the final truth. A visual manifestation of the Academy's supposed infallible position is to be seen in Gautrel's engraving (Figure 3), with the Forty Immortals listed on the individual leaves of a laurel wreath, surrounded by trumpets, fleurs-de-lis, and the likenesses of the first protectors and sponsors, Richelieu and the chancelier Séguier; and with the Latin motto NOT BELOW MANY above the Sun-god (or the Sun-king) piercing the clouds while the Academy's pompous TO IMMORTALITY rests underneath the orb below. The only concession made to mortality—the engraving belongs to the second half of the seventeenth century—is the collection of fallen laurel leaves bearing the names of earlier Academicians.

It was the Academy's stilted assumption of rectitude that Saint Evremond, who was at home in the relaxed atmosphere of the less rigid salons, did not like. He set out to puncture academic inflation in a rather amusing little comedy, which was called *Les Académiciens*. *Les Académiciens* was published in 1650, though it had circulated in manuscript for the amusement of a select few six or seven years earlier. The printed edition was prefaced by an engraving which had the face of Richelieu in its center with the names of thirty-eight Academicians radiating in a circle of stars around him. It was said that Richelieu saw the engraving before he died and did not care for its rather empty pomposity. *Les Académiciens* has as its cast of characters some seventeen actual Academicians (their names undisguised) who are going about their usual duties of reforming the language. The aged and pedantic mademoiselle de Gournay also drops by their reunion hall to give a little advice. The scene opens with Saint Amant and the minor writer Faret regretting that their fellow members in the Academy have not written material that is of a little better quality. The particular object of their criticism is Chapelain—known as the "Spiderous Chevalier" because of his dirty clothes, moth-eaten wig, and generally unkempt condition—who went around literary gatherings reciting verses from his *Pucelle* (an epic poem on Joan of Arc that received rather general condemnation, specifically from Boileau.) The two decide to leave the hall and retire to some nearby cabaret. At this point Godeau (salon poet, relative of Conrart, and one of the original group that met at the latter's house) comes in and launches into proper alexandrines:

> What! dear nurslings of the Daughters of Memory*
> Who over future ages will gain the victory;
> Handsome darlings of Pallas, preferred favorites of the gods;
> Have you as yet not come to our meeting place?

All of which simply means that he does not see any of his fellow Academicians around; Colletet (one of Richelieu's men and a biographer of poets) soon arrives and obsequiously praises Godeau's verse, which Colletet finds to be "exact and regular, completely well-bred." Godeau preens himself with this homage and says:

* The Muses were the daughters of Memory.

Have I ever in any spot failed to keep the caesura?
Can anyone discover in my writings a single hiatus?
Do I not make everybody speak in proper fashion?
The *decorum* of the Romans, in French *bienséance*,
Is nowhere else so well observed, to my way of thinking.

But then they get into an argument over the merits of each other's poetry, a quarrel that is patched up when Serisay (member of the duc de La Rochefoucauld's household, and occasional writer) appears opportunely. The first act ends with two minor Academicians, Porchères-d'Arbaud and Colomby, on stage; they lament the death of Malherbe, the proscriber of hiatus and supporter of middle-line caesura. Their grief is so strong that they are retiring from the profession of letters.

The second act of *Les Académiciens* opens with Chapelain alone in view, composing some verses (prose is "too low") to a countess. He asks help from Phoebus, the "divine father of the day," and hopes to regain "the warmth of fertility that created the *Pucelle*." With Phoebus' help he gives the lady "twin suns" (for eyes) and an aquiline nose in the manner of the best painters; to leave out an aquiline nose is a "mortal sin." He has completed only twenty verses when he is interrupted by the arrival of other Academicians, but those twenty lines are "magnificent, pompous, correct, and finely wrought." Chapelain abandons his composition and tells his companions that the day has now come when the "whole language of the Court must be regulated." Certain restrictions are suggested, in the midst of which mademoiselle de Gournay enters—"at the age of seventy she is still a *pucelle* (or maiden)," says Boisrobert, in another derogation of Chapelain's epic. She makes a plea for leaving in the language words associated with Montaigne. Serisay states that usage, though it is hard to pin down, must not be forgotten. The third act begins with a fairly full complement of Academicians present, and there is general agreement that

the Muses now "have no other residence except Paris."
Chapelain sees Saint Amant and Faret returning from the cabaret, where "they have drunk extensively."* The two pro-
pose some verses in praise of wine; Serisay says that their
"bacchic stanzas" are excellent and qualify them as being
worthy of the title of "Academic Drinkers." But the rest of
the group have to get down to work, lest they grow decrepit
before they have "reformed the vocabulary." They start
by weeding out *or* (now; it is still in the language) and a
few other words deemed to be out of fashion. There is a considerable discussion of *car* (for). It is finally agreed to "leave
*car* in peace," but Colletet would like to "crack up *néan-
moins*" (nevertheless; it stayed). After these minimal and in-
conclusive decisions Serisay sums up the results: "Thanks be
to God, companions, the divine Assembly has worked so
well that the language is regulated." It is agreed by "the
Troupe" that those who do not recognize the reforms will
be regarded as heretics. The play ends with Saint Sorlin's
departure to put the "Great Seal" on their deliberations.[12]

Along with Saint Evremond's play in its 1650 edition a
pamphlet was published satirizing the rigid seriousness of the
open sessions of the Academy where general complaints
might be brought concerning the use of certain words. One
lady of high position and delicate sensibilities wanted "conception" ruled out because it referred not only to processes
of the mind but also to those of the body. The Academy
promised to look into the matter. And "Margot-pisse-à-terre,
recommanderesse de nourrices" wished to have all her
nurses participate in the Great Days of French Eloquence in
order to insure their linguistic competence in dealing with
the young. The Academy's reply was that, "without approving of the word recommanderesse," it would send deputies to

---

* Saint Amant was a real inebriate; but Faret was not, according to Pellisson: he was unfortunate in that his name rimed with "cabaret," and thus
fitted into bits of doggerel.

check on the nurses' capabilities of "talking to small children." Gomberville's opposition to the word *car* (for which he tried, unsuccessfully, to substitute *pour ce que*) was told straightforwardly by Pellisson in his history of the Academy. Gomberville maintained that he had not used *car* in the whole five volumes of his novel, *Polexandre*—though, in fact, he does not use it three or four times. Gomberville's attack on the word caused many to rise in real or mock defense of it, as has already been seen reflected in *Les Académiciens*. The salon poet Voiture wrote a delightful letter to madame de Rambouillet's daughter Julie asking her to do what she could to protect the poor monosyllable. There was also a question about *muscadin* (fop) or *muscardin*, with a spelling more in keeping with the word's Italian origin. The Academy gave its approval to *muscadin*, though Balzac objected and said in a letter to Chapelain that it was not proper to go around dropping "r's" at random out of the language. Voiture as usual added the light touch in a poem that showed what could be done by inserting "r's"; it contained the line: "But by my faith I am *malarde*."[13]

Despite many jibes at its assumption of formal infallibility, there was genuine respect for the Académie Française during the first century of its existence, just as there is today. As early as 1634 the Academy had in mind, in keeping with French inclinations toward order and regulation, the establishment of a "certain usage of words." It took its stand early against burlesque and popular words used by writers in an effort to win the acclaim of the marketplace, a tendency later attacked by Boileau in his art of poetry of 1674. In Article 45 of its statutes, the Academy stated its privilege of offering judgment on any composition of its own members; in addition, however, it envisaged the possibility "of being obliged by some consideration to examine the works of others." In such a case it promised to give its conclusions without either censure or approbation. Its first and most famous pronouncement of this category was its "sentiments" on Pierre Corneille's play *Le Cid*; the Academy's judgments were made before Corneille became one of its members.* The influence of the Academy even in its first years might be measured from Corneille's letter to Balzac on November 15, 1637 in which the dramatist said that he was awaiting with impatience the Academy's decision; until then, he wrote, "I do not dare use any word with a feeling of surety." The Academy assumed in the beginning of its career, with complete confidence, that it was the proper body to decide concerning the regularity or irregularity of a piece of writing. The composer of an irregular work would be advised to correct it, but not forced to do so if the Academy was "satisfied with the general order of composition, with the correctness of the divisions, and with the purity of the language." The organization even took a hard look at the poetry of one of its puritanical ancestors, François de Malherbe, and came up with that most dastardly of criticisms: some of Malherbe's verses simply were "not French." The Academy spent about three months in examining Malherbe's stanzas but did not finish inspecting them "because it had other thoughts in mind and because the vacations of that year (1638) came up soon afterward." The august deliberations of the almost-forty immortals could not compete with the regular August departures from the city of Paris. A century later, in 1738, the marquis d'Argenson poked a little fun the time spent by the Academy in its sober linguistic discussions: "The Académie Française has been occupied this whole year in deliberating on this great question: whether one should say the *patton* of a shoe,** or the *pâton*—that is, with a short or a long "a"; and finally the matter appeared so

* For a fuller examination of *Le Cid* and the quarrel around it, see Chapter V.

** The 1740 edition of the Academy dictionary had *pâton*, a piece of leather reinforcing a shoe.

important and complicated that the meetings were closed without any possibility of a decision."[14]

In the midst of amused or serious criticism directed toward it, the Academy never veered from its sober position of rectitude and authority, a position that has had general recognition throughout the years. Vaugelas in 1647 dedicated his famous *Remarques* to monseigneur Séguier,* chancelier de France and the "protector of this illustrious company which is making our language as flourishing as is our empire." Vaugelas' statement is understandable, since he might be expected to be prejudiced in favor of an assembly of which he was such an important member. But the precise and contentious grammarian, Scipion Dupleix, said in 1651 that the climax of influences purifying his own style was that "in the Academy." It was Dupleix, too, who in a moment of grudging admiration called Vaugelas "that pivot of the Academy." Ménage in 1672 remarked to the chevalier de Méré that, "since the establishment of the Académie Française," our language has not only become "the most beautiful and richest of all living languages, but indeed the most circumspect and most modest." The fine critic Bouhours had respect for the Academy and frequently called on it for support; he spoke of it as an "oracle." In an argument with Ménage in 1675 over the admission of *urbanité* into the language, Bouhours said he would believe "this word to be completely French as soon as the Academy will have made a declaration on it." Fénelon spoke in 1713 of the Academy's power to foist a new word upon "the public," but he felt that such power should be employed with careful judgment in view of the nature of the French, who are a people living "under a temperate sky." They would not enjoy, therefore, "the harsh and bold metaphors" appropriate to inhabitants of "hot countries"—and here climate would be

---

* Le Moyne called the chancelier Séguier, "a minister embellished and cultivated by the Muses," as well as a distinguished magistrate. Séguier's house in Paris was designated by Le Moyne as the temple of the Muses.

seen to become a basis for formalized restraint. Recognition of the Academy's importance continued on into the eighteenth century. The critic and dramatist La Harpe claimed in 1772 that the Académie Française in its accolades to writers had found the "sole means of honoring great men in the name of the nation."[15]

One of the most delightful and unintended pieces of homage paid to the Academy in the early eighteenth century was done by madame Dacier, wife of the permanent secretary of the organization. Madame Dacier was a fine Greek scholar and had translated the *Iliad* in 1711, completely and in three volumes of prose. La Motte-Houdart, a Modern and with little knowledge of Greek, made a verse adaptation and condensation of the *Iliad* in 1713. In a letter to Fénelon on December 14, 1713, La Motte said that he had read five or six books of his version to the Académie Française and "those [members] who know the original poem best congratulated me." Madame Dacier may have known of this reading session; at any rate, she saw La Motte's translation and excoriated him for maltreating, truncating, and abusing Homer. As for the Academy's attitude toward Homer, she blasted it with a full salvo of verbal artillery: it is quite a "fatality" that "from the Académie Française, from this so celebrated body which should be the rampart of the language, of letters, of good taste, have been issuing for fifty years all the heinous attacks that have been made on Homer." Only Boileau and her husband, she said, have risen up against these "deviations from reason." The Academy, "this famous company," has remained silent, though it could do so much to stop the maltreatment of divine Homer.[16]

The discourses of reception made by new members as they were received into the Académie Française became important in the seventeenth century and on into the eighteenth. It all began, according to Pellisson, with the admission of Olivier Patru, an excellent legal orator, in 1640. He made such a gracious speech of appreciation that it was decided to formalize the procedure and have all new members deliver an oration. In 1672 these occasions were opened to the public. In theory, the newcomer gave a eulogy of his predecessor combined with some lofty words of praise for the founders and protectors of the body. There were deviations from time to time from this custom, especially when a new member was disinclined to pile encomiums, for one reason or another, on the man whom he succeeded. In 1671, for example, the pompous and formal Bossuet said not a word in his opening discourse about the man who had preceded him in the Academy. He did, however, indulge in some proper and dignified oratory concerning the Académie Française as an institution. He began by saying that Richelieu, who had wished in every way to carry to the highest possible degree "the glory of France," had added to it by assembling in Paris, the capital of the realm, "the élite of the most illustrious writers of the nation to make out of them your corps." French should have an immortality of its own, Bossuet stated, and not be dependent on the languages of Rome and Athens; the Academy was born to lift French to the height of perfection of the two classic tongues. And for eloquence that will "inflame men to virtue," the Academy should continue to "employ so majestic a language on subjects worthy of it." Bossuet's discourse of reception concluded with a paean of praise for Louis XIV, "great in peace and in war . . . and, in public and in private, admired, feared, and loved"—all, in reality, because of the "discipline in his armies" and the "order in his household." It was, indeed, a resonantly formal oration. La Bruyère's discourse of 1693, when he came into the Academy, praised its founders and contemporary Academicians and gave brief mention to the man he succeeded. In a later preface accompanying his discourse La Bruyère defended the public sessions of the Academy as being one of the few places in Paris where one could still hear "eloquence of a proper cadence." Fénelon in his opening discourse, also in 1693, praised Richelieu and the great Academicians of the past. Voltaire, upon being admitted in 1746, spoke of the influence of poetry on the essence of languages, while Buffon on his entrance in 1753 gave a very formalistic speech, his notable *Discours sur le style*.[17]

Membership in the Academy, with its implications of rectitude and power, came to be much sought after as the seventeenth century progressed along its way. Election, dependent upon a majority vote of the members, had first been done by an open counting but was changed in the second part of the century to a secret ballot. A good deal of intrigue entered into the selections and a man who had submitted his candidacy might find a strong cabal allied against him. Pithy epigrams against a given candidate might be placed on the tables of Academicians in an effort to influence their decisions. Women entered into the picture since the men of the Academy were visitors from time to time in the salons and would let fall there morsels of Academic gossip. It was said of the marquise de Lambert, whose intellectual salon was at its height in the early eighteenth century, that it was necessary to go through her house to reach the French Academy. The marquis d'Argenson regretted her death in 1733 (at the age of eighty-six) because he was losing a good friend; also, she had wanted to present him to the Academy, an almost certain guarantee of acceptance, since she had "created half of the Academicians." In 1749, according to the story of the duc de Luynes, one monsieur de Belle-Isle was taken into the Academy despite the early objections of some of the Academicians to the methods used by the maréchal de Richelieu (a descendant of the great Cardinal) in foisting Belle-Isle on them. Finally, everything was smoothed out, and "there was not a single black ball, every one of them was white."[18]

Men of military and political stature began to get into the French Academy fairly early. The tough old maréchal de

Villars, in speaking of the honors that had come to him in 1715, remarked: "I was also accepted as a member of the Académie Française, and I made a discourse which seemed to me to have been rather well received." In 1722, Villars was the chancelier of the Academy, a position he minimized when he compared it to his military distinctions. Soldiers and statesmen have continued to be elected to the French Academy on down to modern times. Clemenceau and marshal Joffre, of First World War fame, come immediately to mind. Marshal Pétain, the hero of Verdun and accused of collaborating with the Germans in the Vichy government, remains one of the very few Academicians ever to have been dismissed from the corps.[19]

The Académie Française had no fixed place of meeting until 1643, when it began assembling regularly at the Paris house of the chancelier Séguier and continued to do so until his death in 1672. Louis XIV then installed the Academy in the Louvre where it remained till it was suppressed by the Terror in 1793. The convention in 1795 created the Institut de France, made up of the Académie Française and other academies of later formation. The Institut was given a home in the handsome and domed Collège des Quatre Nations, completed in 1688 from a bequest left by Mazarin. Today this same building (now the Palais de l'Institut), bright and shining from recent cleaning, lifts its burnished dome toward the sky. And the Académie Française, the matron of the French academies, carries on its ordered and ritualistic work, *sous la Coupole*.

On September 27, 1965 an Associated Press dispatch from Paris appeared in the American press. It read in part: "The French Academy, in its endless review of the French dictionary, has reached the letter 'G'. . . . The Academy, established in 1635, guards the integrity of the French language against unseemly modernism and alien corruption."

# ⋅ V ⋅

# RIGORS OF THE THEATRE

THE FRENCH theatre came out of the Middle Ages in a rather formless condition. There had been a variety of types of plays, but few rules and regulations concerning them. The most pretentious medieval concept of drama, the fifteenth-century mystery play, ended up by being a hodgepodge of the serious and farcical that was finally forbidden by the Parlement of Paris in 1548. Dramatic entertainment before 1500 might be a one-act skit with two fools beating each other over the head and indulging in comic acrobatics, or an interminable Biblical history of over sixty thousand lines. The place of presentation could be a street corner, an unoccupied stall in the central market, a public square, a hall in the palace of justice, or a partially covered tennis court not being used for the moment by players of the "game of the palm." Actors were clerics and clowns, charlatans selling their doubtful wares, and law clerks with time on their hands; brickmasons, solid bourgeois and carpenters who liked to put up scaffold stages. They were bound together in several loosely knit organizations, the most important of which was the Brotherhood of the Passion, the belated builder in 1548 of the Hôtel de Bourgogne, the first public theatre to be constructed in Paris. It was ironic that the passion plays were prohibited during this same year by parliamentary edict. Understandably, the farce was the only medieval type of play to pass on through the sixteenth century into the seventeenth. It had no rules for construction, but it had a lustiness and verve that gave it popular appeal. Its language was rough and its pantomime often gross, as when the shyster lawyer Pathelin describes his stomach malady in the fifteenth-century farce of the same name. It took two centuries of dramatic propriety and formalized regularity to clean up the farce. The cleansing processes led to the comedy of Molière.

The sixteenth century saw plays being submitted to rules and form, in keeping with principles that had come down from the Greeks and Romans. Dramatists began to try to follow the laws of Aristotle and Horace, with a large admixture of the bombastic tragedies of the younger Seneca. The unregulated forms of medieval drama were cast aside, and the admonitions of the ancients began to be listened to and obeyed in strictest fashion. Horace had said, for example, that a tragedy should have exactly five acts. Until well beyond the middle of the eighteenth century, French tragedy and much French comedy* were fitted into this mold. By the middle of the sixteenth century the *Poetics* of Aristotle, first brought out in Greek text by the Aldine press in Venice, was becoming known in France and the so-called Aristotelian unities commenced their more than two centuries of regulation of French tragedy. To the unities of action and time— the latter only suggested by Aristotle—was added the unity of place by the Italian critic Castelvetro. When the French after 1570 heard about this third unity, they gladly added it to the list of rules to be obeyed in tragic composition. The French, out of the depths of their logical hearts, showed here their propensity for making rigid precepts out of somewhat flexible suggestions. Over Renaissance tragedy and over later seventeenth-century tragedy in France the Aristotelian unities exercised a congealing rigor of dominion.

---

* But comedy, born out of the old farces, was never as formalistic as tragedy.

Part of the reason for the absolutism of Aristotle, Horace, and Seneca in sixteenth-century drama was the influence of the scholars and professors. There was no public theatre in France at this time and no popular audience to be catered to. The scholars by 1550 were initiating the translation of Euripides, Sophocles, Plautus, and Terence into French, but these adaptations were intended primarily for an educated reading public. The professors wrote Latin plays for their pupils and encouraged them to try their hands at compositions in both Latin and French. The results of such endeavors would normally be presented before an audience of pedagogues, admiring parents, and some interested nobles. It should be mentioned that the Jesuits a bit later in the century began their use of plays as a part of their program of instruction; these creations were likely to be more interesting than the other schoolboy productions, but the Jesuit rules in a different way were also quite strict: their plays had to be written in Latin on a theme of impeccable morality and without any feminine roles. Plays, also, were for a time presented at the Court by young ladies and gentlemen before an elegant audience—as, for illustration, Melin de Saint Gelais' *Sophonisbe* (translated from an Italian tragedy of the same name) at Blois. The royal and noble spectators must have shed proper tears over the sad love affair between the Carthaginian lady, Sophonisbe, and the Roman general, Massinisse. However, after the death of Henry II the widowed queen, Catherine de' Medici, forbade the presentation of any more tragedies at Court for fear of their being symbols of bad luck for ruling dynasties. The schools and scholars laid down the correct framework for tragedy during the French Renaissance.

The first tragedy of the Renaissance in France to be composed in accordance with the rules from antiquity was Etienne Jodelle's *Cléopâtre* which appeared in 1552. Jodelle was a young man in his early twenties, with little of the Greeks' knowledge of human problems, so *Cléopâtre* is not much of a play. Nevertheless, it showed Jodelle's training in the classics under proper professors, and set the essential form of tragedy for over two centuries in France: it was in five acts, it was partially in alexandrine riming couplets, and it terminated each act with a choral ode after the fashion of Seneca. The play was performed in the courtyard of one of the Parisian *collèges,** and Henry II liked it sufficiently to grant its author five hundred crowns reward. The members of the Pléiade were so pleased with the accomplishment of their fellow-versifier that they entertained him with a big party in the little town of Arcueil outside Paris, where Jodelle in best Greek tradition was given a goat as prize. Ronsard in a poem describing the celebration said that the goat was sacrificed in Dionysic pomp, but later denied this complete pagan ceremonial. Jodelle's next dramatic effort was *Didon,* a series of lamentations on the part of Dido because of Aeneas' departure; it was no masterpiece but it further fixed the form of tragedy: the whole play is in alexandrine couplets except the lyrical choral odes. It remained only for the seventeenth century to eliminate the choral ode and thus set the tragic mold as it was used by Corneille, Racine, and Voltaire.[1]

Tragedy continued to be correct but pallid throughout the sixteenth century, because it was never submitted to the vigorous criticism and demands of a public theatre. Its progress was also deterred by the Wars of Religion and the lack of interest in the genre on the part of the informal warrior-king, Henry IV. Comedy during the period came in its turn under the regularizing influence of the Romans. The five-act form of Plautus and Terence was copied, as well as the prologue and the stylized Roman setting of a small square (or street intersection) with the houses of the protagonists fac-

* A *collège* would be roughly the equivalent of an American preparatory school; only the Collège de France would have university status.

ing on it. Unfortunately, these formally designed plays were, like their tragic counterparts, lacking in appeal. They were not publicly performed nor did they depict French mores; but many later techniques—such as asides and servants' roles —were taken from them and used in the seventeenth century. Around 1600 the coarse and unregulated farce was favored in Paris, as professional dramatic companies and a public stage came into existence. Farceurs with names like Gros Guillaume, Gautier Garguille, and Turlupin drew a noncritical following, and their position was solidified by the lack of formality around Henry IV's court. Tragedy, which was introduced publicly at this time, consisted of the blood-and-thunder spectacles of the prolific Alexandre Hardy, who obeyed no rule though his plays had zest. Such uninhibited compositions and unrestrained spectacles were contrary to the essence of the French spirit, and so they lasted for no more than two decades. Rigor returned to the theatre with Cardinal Richelieu's patronage of it, and the demands of the cultivated ladies at the Hôtel de Rambouillet. The unities, which had been ignored by Hardy (except the unity of action), reared their three-pronged head again and assumed a vicelike control of tragedy.

The critics—and France has long been a nation of literary critics—never forgot the unities once they had been heard about in the sixteenth century. A remarkable phenomenon is the fact that the scholars and critics were able to impose the rigors of the rules upon tragedy after it became public entertainment. Some explanation might be found in the formal and upper-stratum audience that went to see and hear tragedy; but this is an incomplete answer since the *parterre* (or pit) in French theatres until near the end of the eighteenth century was filled with several hundred noisy, untutored, and standing customers. They, too, patronized tragedy as well as comedy, and listened—not always quietly—to a regulated type of drama that would never have had popular

support in England or Spain. In any case, the unities remained relatively intact until the French Revolution; and the
seventeenth century, when obedience to dramatic rule was
at its height in France, has been designated as the century of
the three unities, sometimes with derogatory implications,
especially on the part of German writers like Lessing.

The Italian analysts of Aristotle helped to plant the unities
on French soil, and the Latin poetics in 1561 of Julius Caesar
Scaliger played its part. Scaliger gave a definition of tragedy
modeled very much on that of Aristotle, and advocated a
unity of time much more strict than that suggested by him:
for Scaliger a tragedy should be concerned with incidents
that would consume no more than five or six hours of
elapsed time. The minor dramatist Antoine de Riveaudeau
sponsored in 1566 the ultimate rigor of the unity of time.
For him no more events should be considered in tragedy
than could happen during the acting time of the play. No
one took this overly zealous restriction too seriously, but
the very good dramatist and critic Jean de la Taille did look
into the whole problem of the unities in his *L'art de la
tragédie* of 1572. For the first time in France, La Taille
stated the unity of place along with those of time and action. He would allow more reasonably the incidents in a full
day for the playwright to use in carrying out his maneuvers
on stage. La Taille's treatise was the best of the formalistic
guides of the period and did much to destroy the stage mechanics of the mystery play which had had no regard for any
sort of rule or limitation. Even Ronsard had some remarks
on the unities in the 1587 edition of his works, in his preface
to the reader in the third tome of his *Franciade*. Tragedy
and comedy, he said, are like mirrors to human life, but they
must teach a lot of things in very few words, "since they are
limited and compressed in a small space, that is to say one
whole day." Ronsard then offered what he deemed a clever
ruse for writers who wished to ease the restrictions of the

unity of time: "The most excellent masters of this profession extend them [that is, plays] from one midnight to the next, and not from daybreak to the setting of the sun, in order to have a greater extent and length of time." There is little evidence that composers of tragedy made any application of this suggested plan, though some later melodramas did begin in the middle of the night. Vauquelin de la Fresnaye in his art of poetry of 1605 (written some years earlier) laid out specific unities of time for both tragedy and the epic—tragedy was to be based on an "argument" of a whole day, while an epic could deal with happenings that might take place in one year:

Now the epic writer like the ancients following his narrow path
Must fit his work into the course of one single year;
The writer of tragedy or comedy into one day
Compresses what the other does in the course of his year:
The stage never should be filled
With an argument longer than of a completed day:
And an Iliad should, in its lofty endeavor,
Be completed in the circuit of a year, or not much more.

Vauquelin, in formal alexandrines and with the Frenchman's normal inclination toward the setting down of a rule, has put a definite time limitation on the epic not to be found in Aristotle's poetic laws.[2]

An opposing voice was raised by Pierre de Laudun in his *Art poétique* (1597). Laudun gave a long discussion of tragedy and comedy, and devoted the final chapter of his work to "those who say that tragedy must be about things that are done within one day." He was thoroughly opposed to the unity of time and stated that, if the play is to consist of five acts, "it is completely impossible for all that to take place in one day." Laudun, who was somewhat emancipated from the earlier doctrines of the Pléiade, was one of the first critics to come out categorically against an Aristotelian unity. There is little chance that he had seen this early a performance of

Amphiteatre de la place Dauphine

Iean Marot fecit

*10.* Amphitheater at the Place Dauphine

11. A 1623 funeral procession

any tragedy by one of the first traveling troupes of profes-
sionals, though before 1600 such a group was in Bordeaux.
He does forecast a period of disregard for the unities. As has
already been noted the dramatic interests of Paris during the
first years of the seventeenth century was focused on the
farce-players. Nor were the insipid pastorals that were given
private and some public representation during the early
1600's submitted to the demands of the rules.[3]

Chapelain, the critical voice of Richelieu and the dispenser
of the Cardinal's pensions, sought to put drama back on a
straight course in 1630 with his *Lettre sur la règle des vingt-
quatre heures*. Chapelain based his whole argument in favor
of the rule on the idea of *vraisemblance*, or verisimilitude,
and maintained that nothing could be "less in keeping with
verisimilitude than the poet's representation of the events of
ten years in two or three hours." Hardy had done exactly
this sort of thing in his *La force du sang*, wherein a child is
born and reaches the age of seven in one act. Chapelain argued further that the ignoring of the rules from antiquity
brought confusion and no satisfaction with a play, "for there
is nothing so certain as the fact that the production of pleasure, as with everything else, is done through order and verisimilitude." The street entertainers and farceurs would appeal
only to "idiots" and the "dregs of the people." Despite a few
dissenting murmurs, the proponents of a regulated theatre
won out, and their victory was signaled by the success of
Jean de Mairet's tragedy *Sophonisbe* in 1634. Mairet had
himself spoken out for the rules a bit earlier, and *Sophonisbe*
showed his belief in the unity of time by being filled with
expressions like "before the sun goes down" and "before the
end of the day."[4]

The greatest dramatic poet of the first half of the seventeenth century, Pierre Corneille, fitted himself into the rigors
of the rules, although he did not like the restrictions of the
unity of time. The unity of place, an attribute of the unity of

time, was accepted by Corneille and other dramatists without much complaint, since a public square, a room in a palace, or some such fixed spot was a logical location for the action of a play. Corneille admitted that it made little sense for a drama to be set in both Rouen and Paris, even though one could go conceivably from one city to the other within twenty-four hours.* The rather wooden critic, the abbé d'Aubignac—who wrote in 1647 a detailed manual for dramatists, *La pratique du théâtre*—maintained that a play could not be set in two areas of Paris that were not contiguous to one another without violating the unity of place. The same décor, for example, would be unable to include both the Louvre and the cathedral of Notre Dame, since such juxtaposing was contrary to reality. As for the unity of time, Corneille would have liked to extend it to thirty hours for extraordinary material, but rigorous critical opinion never allowed it.[5]

There was much discussion over the "natural day" and the "artificial day"—that is, over whether a play should be allowed for its action a full twenty-four hours or the approximate twelve hours of daylight. D'Aubignac favored the artificial day since, "in keeping with verisimilitude," people sleep at night. Something of the ultimate in pedantic rigor was reached in an interchange between D'Aubignac and Ménage as to whether a play should be given possibly fifteen hours if it were in the summertime when the period of light was longer. A more confident critic, like Boileau, in the second half of the seventeenth century phrased the rules with more directness. Boileau stated simply, in his *Art poétique* of 1674, the three unities for tragedy as "one place, one day, one single action completed," although "beyond the Pyrenees" a versifier might put years into just one day. One year later

* Corneille said in his *Discours des trois unités* that this journey could be done in twenty-four hours "en poste"; but the fastest coaches from Paris to Rouen in the seventeenth century required two full days.

in 1675, the Reverend Père Le Bossu made some interesting comparisons between epic and tragedy in his lengthy *Traité du poème épique*. He felt that the unities of time and place were proper to the theatre, since a spectator would think it unnatural to sit in his seat and spend "days and nights without sleeping, without drinking, and without eating." Aristotle had put no time limit on the epic and it really was not necessary to do so, said Le Bossu, because a reader could stop anytime for repose, good red wine, and some solid nourishment. However, Le Bossu could not avoid laying down a rigorous and strict rule for epic action, evolving out of the theatrical unities: "it is necessary to say in regard to its duration that the period of a year is for epic narration what the period of a day is for tragedy; and that the winter is as little appropriate for the great work as the night is for the theatre." He would thus limit the epic to a single "campaign" just as the action of tragedy would be compressed into an artificial day. The *Aeneid* was not specifically marked as to time, according to Le Bossu, but Vergil packed its action into "a single campaign, making it begin in summer and terminate before the end of autumn in the same year."[6]

Le Bossu would find in the form of tragedy the mold in miniature for the epic; the longer narrative action of the epic would thus be an extension of the episode of tragedy. In an elaboration of this theory he made a rather amusingly precise analysis of the *Iliad*, which for him had an over-all duration of forty-seven days. Nine days might be omitted since they were concerned with the pestilence that struck the Greeks before Achilles' quarrel with Agamemnon, and eleven days of truce were then given to Priam and the Trojans; twenty-seven days remained, eleven of which were needed for the convalescence of the Greeks, and eleven more were consigned to Achilles for the burial of Patroclus. The combats around Troy, therefore, began and ended within five days—and Achilles, "the first hero of the poem, fought only one day." The primary action of the *Iliad* was reduced, in essence, by Le Bossu to tragedy's twenty-four-hour rule, though he readily conceded that there were other ways of "counting time" in an epic. Madame Dacier, who as has been noted did a translation of the *Iliad* in 1711, took a slightly different approach to the unity of time in tragedy and its connection with the epic; she contended that, in keeping with Aristotle's advice, an epic should be of such length that "it can be read completely in a single day."[7]

The eighteenth century continued to struggle with the unities. La Motte-Houdart, the Modern, objected to their limitations and would have added a fourth one, a unity of interest. He also believed that the primary aim of the theatre was to please the public, and that any play that did so obeyed a unity not yet discovered. But the best writer of tragedy in the eighteenth century, Voltaire, could never forget his classical training with the Jesuits. He sought to add novel and exotic features to tragedy, but was unable to get away from his basic allegiance to measure and form. Nevertheless, after 1750 tragedy and the unities underwent some powerful attacks, including the thrusts of the proponent of a bourgeois drama in prose, Denis Diderot. La Harpe in 1772 spoke of the "barbarous declaimers" in the theatre who had "taken nothing from the Greeks except the rule of the three unities," though he would not put Corneille and Racine in the category of the emptily regular. L.-S. Mercier, a supporter of Diderot's prose drama, in 1773 blasted the legacy from antiquity and maintained that "methods, rules, poetics have spoiled and are spoiling" the most inventive minds, and that the best way for a young dramatist to start his career was by "first throwing all arts of poetry into the fire." Corneille, according to Mercier's way of thinking, would have been freed from the rigors of the rules and had more appreciation if he had lived in London. In a "scrupulous subservience to the unities of time and place," Corneille showed only one side of the dramatic picture instead of "blending his colors" as did Calderón, Shakespeare, Lope de Vega, and Goldoni. Mercier thought that a writer could ignore the unity of time, "which has been fixed at twenty-four hours," without making any great mistake; and the same thing could be done for the unity of place, which was even "more irritating, more inconvenient, and much less respectable." The only unity that Mercier supported was the indeterminate one of interest. The other "minutiae of regulations" he blamed on the, to his mind, cold and rigid Boileau. Despite the attacks of such critics as Mercier, the unities died slowly and received their final blow only from the Romantics.[8]

Tragedy was not only rigidly encased by the unities in France, but also by other limitations that the French regarded as necessary to the genre. Among these would be the avoidance of deeds of violence on stage, the exclusion of any scenes of low comedy (there had been comic relief in the mystery plays), and of any language that was not properly elevated and dignified. The last restriction would eliminate a word like *mouchoir* (handkerchief) and substitute for it the more refined *tissu* (tissue). The whole process led in the seventeenth century to a severely limited classical vocabulary that was Ciceronian, Senecan, and Ovidian (for matters of love). When Corneille used words like "magnanimous," "generous," and "honest," they were employed with a distinctly Roman connotation. As for the subject of tragedy and the characters therein, Jean de la Taille had said in 1572 that it should be created around the "extraordinary adventures of historically important people." This naturally involved the representation on stage of kings and high nobles, a practice which led to Diderot's calling in the eighteenth century the personages of tragedy nothing but stilted crown-bearers. However, many of the French have all along the way defended their formalized version of tragedy. Voltaire, despite an early admiration for Shakespeare, called his plays "monstrous farces" and could find little justification for the grave-diggers' scene in *Hamlet*. The French have discovered, as a near equivalent of Shakespeare in their own literature, Alexandre Hardy—who had a nature of "extreme liberty" and whose art was "far from being subjected to precise rules." One of France's present-day Academicians, with limited modesty, has made the following claim: "There are in the history of literatures only two tragedies, Greek and French."[9]

In defining tragedy the French were rigidly Aristotelian, although for some decades into the seventeenth century they thought the ending should be unhappy, a prescription that Aristotle did not make but which was made by Scaliger in 1561. In following Scaliger's lead, therefore, Corneille's *Le Cid* in 1636 (or early 1637) was first designated as a tragi-comedy because of its happy ending; it has since been called a tragedy. And French critics of the Renaissance tried to justify the pompous and oratorical choruses inherited from Senecan tragedy. Jacques Peletier du Mans said in 1555 that the chorus should "speak sententiously, fear the gods, correct vices, menace the wicked, and show the way to virtue." Vauquelin de la Fresnaye stated near the end of the sixteenth century that the "tragic subject would show only virtuous deeds, magnificent and grand, sumptuous and royal." La Mesnardière later in 1639 had a great deal to say about tragedy, which he considered "pompous and sublime, grave and filled with majesty." It was too pretentious to have any appeal for the people, but it should be terrifying to princes when they saw what disgraces might happen to "their kind." Despite its disturbing qualities, in La Mesnardière's opinion tragedy was "the poem suitable for kings" in their nocturnal reading. As for the portrayal of queens in this sober type of drama, they should be depicted as being "chaste, modest, grave, magnificent, tranquil, and noble." La

Mesnardière said, in his definition of the genre, that it was "the serious and magnificent representation of some somber action, complete, of great importance, and of reasonable grandeur." He was not writing merely as a theorist, but with added knowledge from having seen tragedy performed at two public theatres in Paris, the Hôtel de Bourgogne and the Théâtre du Marais.[10]

By the time of Louis XIV and the great era that began in the 1660's it was generally supposed that tragedy needed little more in the way of rigorous definition, since the cultured elite were acquainted with its aims and its rules. Both Boileau and Racine said that the primary purpose of tragedy was "to please and to move." This was a deceptively simple explanation for a formal and sophisticated audience that knew the regulations and had already heard of Aristotelian catharsis. Rapin thought, however, in 1674 that he should mention certain foreigners that had veered away from Aristotle, "who is the only one that should be followed." Rapin offered a rather original idea on the purification of the emotions when he argued that tragedy corrects by "moderating fear and pity, which are obstacles to virtue." The freethinking Saint Evremond at about the same time issued a complaint against restrictions: never, he asserted, have there been so many rules "for making beautiful tragedies" and so few beautiful tragedies. A possible flaw in Saint Evremond's statement is the fact that it was made in 1672 when Racine, the superb conformist to the laws of tragedy, was near the peak of his distinguished career. Saint Evremond found a more legitimate example of mediocrity when he quoted a supposed remark of monsieur le Prince: "I am pleased with monsieur d'Aubignac for having followed so well the rules of Aristotle, but I do not pardon the rules of Aristotle for having assisted monsieur d'Aubignac in the creation of so terrible a tragedy."* Saint Evremond summed up his attitude

---

* "Monsieur le Prince" was probably the Great Condé; the tragedy re-

toward the rigors of Aristotle's legacy as follows: "One must admit that the *Poetics* of Aristotle is an excellent work; however, there is nothing sufficiently perfect to regulate all nations and all centuries." Aristotle introduced catharsis or purgation, according to Saint Evremond, in order to make the gods more palatable to the Athenians—this "purgation which nobody up to now has understood, and which Aristotle did not understand very well himself in my opinion." But Saint Evremond was talking to a very small audience, since a well-disciplined tragedy fitted quite snugly into the formalism of Louis XIV's court.[11]

A tragic hero was expected to be pompous, in the Roman sense of the word, that is, splendid and magnificently ordered. Corneille's great figures in this sense were pompous, magnanimous, and honorable men; Roman and Plutarchian, and devoted to duty. Horace in the play of the same name carried the rigors of duty and patriotism so far that he killed his own sister who upbraided him for slaying her fiancé, a deed demanded by Rome. Not many persons today would have great sympathy with the rigidity of Horace's character; nevertheless, to stiffen the souls of the French, *Horace* ran continuously at the Comédie Française during the first battle of the Marne in World War I. Corneille's portrayal of Augustus (in *Cinna*) was probably the ultimate in royal pomp, in dignified and correct imperialism. Racine's personages, notably his heroines, also possessed a proper grandeur along with psychological subtleties lacking in Corneille—the decorous Andromaque, the ill-starred Phèdre, and the majestically ruthless Athalie. But a well-balanced critic like Fénelon thought both Corneille and Racine were too precisely formal in the verses they put into the mouths of some of their characters. Fénelon would call Rodrigue's complaint at the end of the first act of Corneille's *Le Cid* (the famous

ferred to could be either D'Aubignac's *Sainte Cathérine* (1642) or his *Zénobie* (1647). Neither was a masterpiece.

"pierced to the depth of my heart by a shaft unforeseen as well as mortal") too bombastic: "Never did serious grief speak a language so pompous and so affected." For Fénelon the story of the death of Hippolytus in Racine's *Phèdre* should not have consumed almost two pages of alexandrines; his tutor and companion should have reported simply: "Hippolytus is dead; a monster sent by the god's anger from the depths of the sea destroyed him; I saw it." It was unnecessary to include "the most pompous and flowery description of the face of the dragon." Fénelon in reality knew the answer to his own question: the French have always liked long and formal speeches in their plays, and have applauded them from Jodelle to Giraudoux.[12]

But tragedy was subjected to more and more criticism after 1750. Mercier said that in it "all the heroes walked with big strides, lifted high their heads ornamented with floating plumes, held themselves stiff and rigid; they spoke, or rather they bellowed, through the speaking tube of the poet." The speaking tube of the poet was the rhymed couplet, which Mercier considered a dull formality: "Our alexandrine meter is heavy and labored, and the eternal monotony that it produces makes itself felt even in Racine and Voltaire." Mercier, like many others of the eighteenth century, would have preferred plays in prose. The "useless yoke" of rhyme, he said, had already been shaken off in England and Italy, but "we cherish our chains." Mercier was right about the cherishing of chains; the rigors of rhyme in the French theatre continued to be accepted, with some modifications, well into the nineteenth century in the drama of the Romantics. And Victor Hugo was not averse to piling up two or three pages of alexandrines in a single speech.[13]

A conservative and strict code of acting came into the French theatre in the early 1630's with the appearance of such performers as Bellerose and Mondory: Bellerose at the

Hôtel de Bourgogne and Mondory at the Théâtre du Marais. They brought dignity to a stage that had known chiefly the rough antics and gross language of the farce-players. A more polished audience began to demand more proper plays and more decorous performances, which these two chiefs of their respective troupes sought to supply. Bellerose was famous for his impressive portrayals of kings, while Mondory's technique was so noted that it was imitated in private theatricals by Boisrobert, the secretary of Richelieu. The Cardinal was very much the sponsor of Mondory's troupe and frequently had it tread the boards in his own theatre, before a proper and, at times, royal audience. Acting must have been resonant and stentorian, full of well-marked cadences and demands on the vocal cords. Mondory, who was famous (according to D'Aubignac) for his depiction of a "demi-passion," had to retire in 1637 because of a paralysis of the throat and tongue which struck him while he was playing the role of Herod in a tragedy of Tristan l'Hermite. Montfleury, who was a trifle overweight and who was satirized in Rostand's *Cyrano de Bergerac*, was quoted as saying on his deathbed that he was not dying of pleurisy but of "pushing" the part of Orestes in Racine's *Andromaque*. Such pompous and oratorical interpretations were ridiculed by Molière in his farce *Les précieuses ridicules* when he said the Hôtel de Bourgogne was where they "rolled out the words." Molière might have been somewhat jealous of the actors at the Bourgogne, since he himself lacked tragic presence on stage. The tradition of Bellerose and Mondory was carried on in the second half of the seventeenth century by the great tragedian Floridor. And the formation of the Comédie Française in 1680 guaranteed the continuation in France of a stylized and rigorously formal type of acting, though there have been some innovations in recent years. However, those who may have heard in the 1920's the resounding and set periods of Albert Lambert fils at the Comédie Française can well imagine what it was like at the Bourgogne in the seventeenth century when the actors were rolling out the words.[14]

Richelieu's interest in the actors and plays and his demands for dignity and correctness in them were to set a fashion in lofty and royal circles for almost a century. After the death of Louis XIII in 1643, the widowed Anne of Austria still liked to "go to the comedy"* and she often took little Louis XIV with her. Mazarin would at times entertain the dowager Queen with his intricate machine plays, where gods would sit pompously in a mass of clouds or a dragon lift its arrogant head out of the sea. Even Corneille, whose "beautiful pieces" could serve as a "lesson to correct the unbridling of human passions," wrote two plays with machines, *Andromède* and *La toison d'or*. In an engraving that was made of the former, Andromeda is chained to a very symmetrical rock while Perseus flies through the air on a confident horse to release her. Louis XIV's love of the theatre and ballets is well known. For his court and his favored ladies, he would frequently have musical and theatrical composers like Lully, Corneille, Molière, and Quinault collaborate on precisely groomed mixtures of plays and ballets. The setting might be Versailles, Fontainebleau, Chambord, or some other chateau. One of the most notable of these comedy-ballets was Molière's *Bourgeois gentilhomme*, which had its première before a royal audience in the great hall of Chambord in 1670. Louis always enjoyed the play; later, when he was older and sadder and had married the serious madame de Maintenon, he liked to see the comedy performed "in his room." But, in the famous scene where the would-be gentleman, Jourdain, is initiated into the imaginary Turkish order of *mamamouchi*, the King (in a gesture of formalized piety) would not allow the Bible to be used for the Koran in the ceremony.[15]

A most formal and grandiose presentation before the King

* In the seventeenth century, *aller a la comédie* meant simply "to go to the theatre."

was that of Racine's tragedy *Iphigénie* at Versailles in 1674. The historian Félibien gave a full description of the setting. As a preliminary to the dramatic features of the evening, in best French fashion, "Their Majesties had a collation to the sound of violins and oboes." Then the King got into his caleche and, followed by all the Court, went to the end of the *allée* that led to the Orangerie, "where a stage had been set up." The décor was made by statues, vases, marble basins, orange and pomegranate trees, with a tent in the background that "covered the orchestra." It must all have been very proper, since "between each tree there were great candelabra and azure and gold tables which supported girandoles of crystal lit with several candles." It was on this stage that "the troupe of the King's Comedians* represented the tragedy of *Iphigénie*, the latest work of sieur Racine, which received from all the Court the esteem that his pieces have always had." It must have been a correct and difficult evening, though probably not as stiffly formal as the production of Racine's *Esther* by the girls of madame de Maintenon's school at Saint Cyr in 1689; on this occasion Louis had as his guest the exiled King of England, James II. During his last years Louis XIV "went no more to the comedy," but when any report of improper plays reached his ear the comedians faced punishment or banishment. The Italian company was forced to leave Paris by royal edict in 1697 when they advertised a spectacle supposedly based on the private life of madame de Maintenon.[16]

The marquise de Sévigné, whose letters gave such a colorful picture of the formalized ritual of Louis XIV's court, found therein one episode which possessed for her all the rigors of tragedy: the broken romance between the comte de Lauzun and the Grande Mademoiselle (the King's first cou-

* The *troupe des Comédiens du Roi* would at this time have been the troupes of the Hôtel de Bourgogne, the Théâtre du Marais, and Molière's; they would be officially designated as the Comédie Française in 1680.

sin); their proposed marriage was disallowed by Louis himself. Madame de Sévigné wrote about it to monsieur de Coulanges, courtier and writer of light verse: "You know now the touching story of Mademoiselle and of monsieur de Lauzun. It is the exact subject for a tragedy according to all the rules of the theatre. We were drawing up the acts and the scenes for it the other day; we gave it four days instead of twenty-four hours, and it made a perfect play. . . . Monsieur de Lauzun has played his role to perfection; he has borne this misfortune with firmness, courage, and at the same time a grief mixed with profound respect which has made him admired by everybody. . . . Mademoiselle has conducted herself very well also; she has indeed wept; today she has taken up again her royal duties. . . . Now it is all over." Madame de Sévigné thought, in regard to the actual situation, that Mademoiselle should have ignored regal formalities and married monsieur de Lauzun in greater haste; nevertheless, she thought the affair was the essence of Cornelian tragedy (she preferred Corneille to Racine), in which Lauzun was comparable to Corneille's martyred hero, Polyeucte.[17]

The theatre, both public and private, was less rigorously proper under the Regent and Louis XV than it had been in the previous century. The duke of Orleans as Regent allowed the return of the Italians who had been dismissed by Louis XIV—a move that was symptomatic of the general relaxation of the Regency. Louis XV preferred hunting, and his mistresses, to any kind of a theatre. According to the maréchal de Villars, in 1723 "comedies began at the Court," though the King was not very much interested in them; therefore a large loge was set up for him so he could come and go without disturbing the spectacle. In this way the ritual of the royal theatre functioned, and a "diversion very necessary for the Court was reestablished." If Louis XV was not greatly inclined toward the theatre, the same could not be said for his favorite, madame de Pompadour; she loved the mannered preening that the stage allowed. She not only patronized drama, opera, and ballets, but also liked to act in them. Though this elevated bourgeoise seemed to have been cordially disliked by the proper nobility around the Court, everyone was amazed at the energy that was in her "ravaged chest" and fragile body. The marquis d'Argenson said that she maintained a constant round of ballets and parties, and nobody knew how she did it. She gave her protection to the blood-and-thunder tragedian, Crébillon, many of whose plays, despite her support, received only a modest popular acclaim. In early December 1749, at Versailles, she performed in Destouches' comedy Le philosophe marié and "played superbly." Early in 1750 several plays were produced at Versailles "in the cabinets." These included Destouches' Le préjugé à la mode, in which madame de Pompadour carried the role of Constance, the faithful wife; and Voltaire's tragedy, Alzire, in which madame de Pompadour played a native Peruvian princess and for it received "great praise." During this period operas and ballets were given three times a week at the Court, in the marquise de Pompadour's effort to "amuse the King to such a degree that he has no time to think." The rigors of the theatre by 1750, along with the other elements of formalism, had begun to relax. Comment was made at the time concerning the gaudy decoration and spectacles of the Opera, all monuments "to the reign of bad taste and to the disappearance of the beautiful, the noble, the simple, and the magnificent."[18]

The eighteenth century did make two gestures toward the mechanics of formalism in the theatre that were worthy: the spectators were removed from the stage in 1759; and the parterre, the noisy rabble that had stood on the main floor of French theatres since the earliest years at the Hôtel de Bourgogne, was seated in a new hall constructed for the Comédie Française in 1782. It is remarkable that the great tragedies of Corneille and Racine could have been produced in the presence of such a milling mob as the parterre. La Harpe blamed it, with some inaccuracy, for having "made fall" Racine's masterpiece, *Phèdre*, and for Racine's having been "lost to France and the theatre for eighteen years." La Harpe's analysis of the parterre is intriguing: "Dramatic representations will not have any decency and dignity, and public judgments about them will not be clear and marked, until all the spectators are seated. . . . It is evident that cabals and cliques are hidden easily in a crowd that is standing and in tumult, and they would be discovered quickly in a peaceful assembly of seated men. . . . Then the parterre would no longer be a field of battle where each side is divided into squadrons, and it would no longer be asked of everyone who arrives (as monsieur de Voltaire expressed it recently), 'Are you coming to applaud?—get over there; are you coming to hiss?—get over here.' . . . They are talking about building a new hall for the Comédie Française. Without doubt in it one will be rid of this remnant of barbarism which brings dishonor to the theatre and the nation." The new theatre was built and given the formalistic Greek name of Odéon which it retained until after World War II.[19]

From the sixteenth century into the eighteenth, criticism of plays and their authors, particularly of tragedy and the writers thereof, was as rigorous as the rules affecting the genres. The critics inevitably had their effect upon the authors, and Corneille admitted that he had known nothing of the unities until he heard and read about them in Paris; he therefore claimed in his more mature years that some of his early and irregular plays had been written in fun. Molière and Racine both lashed back at their critics, especially when the criticism was personal rather than literary, and Boileau often lent a helping hand to his two friends when he thought they were being abused. In the early eighteenth century the rather wooden dramatist Destouches made the standard objection of the creator to the critic—"art is difficult but criti-

cism is easy." In most cases the critical estimates from their
own contemporaries were an added rigor for dramatists. Etienne Jodelle in the sixteenth century, however, probably received better treatment than he deserved. Peletier du Mans
said in 1555 that Jodelle's *Cléopâtre* would bring "honor to
the French language." Nearly fifty years later Vauquelin
mentioned that he had seen *Cléopâtre*, though he considered Robert Garnier (and rightly so) the more likely master
of the tragic form.[20]

The greatest critical furore of the seventeenth century was
over Corneille's *Le Cid*. The story of it was told in full by
Pellisson in his history of the Academy, and has been repeated many times since. The pamphlets and documents involved would fill a sizable volume. The general nature of
the criticism—from the writers, Georges de Scudéry, Jean
de Mairet, and others—was rigorously pedantic: Corneille
had violated the principal rules of dramatic construction, he
had borrowed from the Spaniards (who were automatically
suspect and unregulated), he had written many bad verses,
and he had ignored decorum and verisimilitude. None of
these accusations had any effect upon the popular success of
the play, and the final one, the *Sentiments de l'Académie
Française sur la tragi-comédie du Cid*—done at the behest of
Richelieu—came out long after *Le Cid* was firmly embedded
in the minds of the public. Chapelain edited this lengthy report, which was both legalistic and ambiguous; its first form,
which appeared toward the end of 1637, ended with the admission that Corneille had "elevation and delicacy in several
of his thoughts," and that the play had an "inexplicable at-
tractiveness mixed in with all its faults." Later in 1667 Boileau had a neat couplet on the Quarrel of the *Cid* and Richelieu's supposed opposition to the play:

>    In vain against the *Cid* a minister forms a league,
>    All Paris for Chimène* has the eyes of Rodrigue.

* The heroine of *Le Cid* and Rodrigue's beloved.

And in 1687 La Bruyère said that Le Cid was one of the "most beautiful works that could be constructed," and that it was stronger than the "authority and politics" that tried to destroy it. Despite later encomiums, Corneille learned a great deal from the criticism of Le Cid. His next play, Horace, in 1640, was based on a solid Roman subject, it fitted easily into the unities of time and place, and it was dedicated modestly and obsequiously to Richelieu.[21]

Molière and comedy in general were subjected to the rigors of the rules. Vauquelin de la Fresnaye stated as early as 1605 that comedy had been cleaned up by ignoring Aristophanes and imitating the Romans and Italians; and in 1670 Desmarets de Saint-Sorlin complimented French comedy on its fine language, and said that he did not know in all Aristophanes a single spot which "would make a gentleman laugh." Boileau thought that Old Comedy in Greece was unrefined, and that for correct comedy one should "study the Court and know the culture of the city." The dirty puns of the farces were worthy only of the attention of lackeys; in fact, in Molière's farce Les fourberies de Scapin Boileau did not "see the author of the Misanthrope." Rapin praised Molière in spite of the "defective ordering" of his plays, and regarded the character of Alceste, the misanthrope, the "most finished" on the French stage. Fénelon looked upon Molière as a great comic poet, though at times he gave a "gracious turn" to vice. Molière was attacked on many sides for making Tartuffe in the play of the same name a successful religious hypocrite, so he changed the ending in the final version; also, his L'école des femmes was criticized for being indecorous, especially in one verse which spoke of babies being born "through the ears." And the rigid and unyielding Bossuet, bishop of Meaux, gave Molière's comedies a general condemnation for their "impieties" and "infamies."[22]

But the formal and correct dramatists of the seventeenth and eighteenth centuries—Corneille, Racine, Molière (in most respects), and Voltaire—received the accolades of the formal and correct critics. Boileau, who said tragedy should speak a "pompous verse," consoled Racine for the cabal of *Phèdre* in 1677 by saying that the play appealed to Louis XIV, the Great Condé, Colbert, and La Rochefoucauld—all formal and proper gentlemen; the rabble could spend their untutored admiration on the "skill of Pradon,"* or possibly on the clever Quinault, whose verses lacked any "great force." Bossuet, who really did not like the theatre, admitted that Corneille had "force" and "vehemence," and that Racine possessed "justice" and "regularity." La Bruyère compared Corneille to Sophocles and Racine to Euripides, and Racine's plays were "just, regular, founded on good sense and human nature." The abbé Raynal around the middle of the eighteenth century said that Corneille manifested a "pompous majesty" and Racine an "enchanting charm," though a disintegrating public taste preferred operas and ballets. And La Harpe in 1772, when the rigorous frame of tragedy was being broken, found in Racine a symbol of good taste and decorum, the tradition of which was being carried on by Voltaire. Shakespeare for La Harpe was "too often the poet of the people," while Racine's *Phèdre* and Voltaire's *Mérope* were the "delights of cultivated men." Therefore statues should be erected to both Racine and Voltaire on which would be carved four words: "the beautiful" and "the true."[23]

The rigors of the rules in the French theatre gave way before an age of less restriction and more relaxation. But there is still one house in Paris, facing on a shady square off the rue de Richelieu and marked by two matching fountains, where the dignified Roman heroes of Corneille still stride the boards and where Racinian heroines still couch their emotions in proper alexandrines: the Comédie Française.

---

* Pradon's play *Phèdre et Hippolyte* competed with Racine's *Phèdre* and, because of Racine's enemies, the Pradon tragedy was momentarily successful.

# ⁏ VI ⁏

# MANNERS AND SOCIAL RITUAL

THE FRENCH have long been conscious of the formalized mechanics of manners, and have at times been accused of substituting correct social ritual for morality. The
plays of Meilhac and Halévy in the nineteenth century, for
example, have been described as reflecting a milieu that was
"perfectly urbane and completely depraved." One of the
primary complaints of Molière's misanthropist, Alceste, in *Le
misanthrope* was that in Louis XIV's Paris, amid the bowings
and scrapings and mannered social effusions, it was difficult
to know who was a friend and who was an enemy. The
French language has played its part in offering stylized and
almost automatic formulas of politeness to fit any occasion.
With the proper application of these linguistic devices the
wheelworks of society have been able to turn, despite Alceste's
objection, without open and informal outbursts of hostility.
The French by their very nature, in preparation for most of
life's encounters, prefer a morning coat to a sport shirt; and
many and repeated shakings of the hand to a casually waved
farewell. It would be useless even today to invite a Frenchman
for a cup of tea or an apéritif on an hour's notice. He would
prefer to know about such a ceremonial occasion several days
in advance; or possibly a week.

Formalism in French manners took its lead from life at

the Court, and a royal court began in the sixteenth century with Francis I. Until his time, as has been noted, a "court" had referred to a legal assemblage; but with the first of the Valois-Angoulême monarchs courtly procedures became more regularized—and the plan of action included a liberal sprinkling of attractive ladies.* The externals of manners became more refined than they had been in medieval France, and many of these, such as handkerchiefs and forks, came from Italy. Francis was himself, as a result of his military expeditions into Italy (unsuccessful as they were), intoxicated with the culture and style of the land. To the native formalistic instincts of the French, Francis added a touch of the Italian niceties, taken from the princely courts of Florence, Mantua, Ferrara, and Urbino. He was not only a man of the Renaissance, but of two Renaissances, the Italian and the French. All of this was symbolized by his chatting with courtiers, poets, and scholars in the gardens of Fontainebleau after his midday meal; by his interest in and patronage of the arts as a distinguished amateur; and by his visits to such a chateau as Chambord (which he built) where his well-mannered ladies and gentlemen could watch the hunting of the stag from the roof while making plans for the evening's entertainment. The Gothic and austere living in fortified chateaux like Loches and Chinon, made obsolete by gunpowder and artillery, was abandoned for a more civilized and conversational existence in such examples of Renaissance architecture as Chambord, Azay-le-Rideau, and Chenonceaux. For over two centuries the royal and upper-stratum families of France, in their dislike for the smells and bourgeois noises of Paris, spent a large portion of their lives in chateaux: Henry II liked Anet, which included Diane de Poitiers; Louis XIII was often at Saint-Germain-en-Laye, on

---

* The genteel quality of living in sixteenth-century France has been treated with some degree of fullness in an earlier book of mine, *The Gentleman of Renaissance France* (Cambridge, Massachusetts: Harvard University Press, 1954).

a hill overlooking Paris; Louis XIV loved his own Versailles, but also went to Chambord, Vaux-le-Vicomte, and Chantilly; Louis XV enjoyed Fontainebleau, Chantilly, and Marly, among others. An invitation from the King to a lady or gentleman to accompany the royal retinue for a visit to some chateau put considerable demands not only on wardrobes but also on knowledge of the social proprieties.

It must have been a major problem for the King's Household when Francis I decided to visit one of the chateaux of the Loire, because he wanted to take everybody along, in a train of horses that stretched out for miles. The Royal Household at this time consisted of six major divisions: pantry, wine, cuisine, fruits, stables, and kennels, with proper functionaries in charge of each. There were also the grand chamberlain, the grand squire (who carried the King's sword on ceremonial occasions), and the grand falcon-master, all with necessary subordinates. The King's Household (as well as the Queen's) became more extensive by the seventeenth century, but the royal guest list for a weekend at a chateau became more limited under Louis XIV, though he did have thousands of nobles living at Versailles to lend luster to its décor. And the parties given by the King at Versailles itself were nothing short of stupendous in setting and execution. Madame de Sévigné in a letter to madame de Grignan (her daughter who spent most of her time producing children), dated July 29, 1676, described what must have been a relatively simple affair at Versailles, after Their Majesties had finished dinner at noon: "At three o'clock the King, the Queen, Monsieur, Madame, Mademoiselle, all the princes and princesses, madame de Montespan and her suite, all the courtiers, all the ladies, finally what may be called the Court of France, is assembled in that beautiful apartment of the King that you know. Everything is furnished divinely; everything is magnificent. You would not be conscious of feeling warm in it; you can go from one spot to another without being crowded in any way. A game of *reversi** is the order of the day, and draws full attention. The players are the King, madame de Montespan (who is dealing the cards), Monsieur, the Queen and madame de Soubise, Dangeau and company, Langlée and company. A thousand louis are spread out on the table—there are no other chips." The game lasted from three o'clock until six (Dangeau won all the money), at which time everybody got into caleches and rode around the grounds of Versailles. Many of the ladies were ornately "embellished with curls and diamond pendants of infinite beauty." Somewhat later in the evening, according to madame de Sévigné, "we take a ride on the canal in gondolas, we have music along the way, we return at ten o'clock and see a comedy; midnight sounds and we have a little repast: that is the way Saturday was spent."[1]

The noble chateau of Chantilly (Figure 4), the home of the Great Condé in the time of Louis XIV, was much admired in the seventeenth and eighteenth centuries. Madame de Lafayette—a great lady of the seventeenth century and author of the first French psychological novel—said of Chantilly in 1673: "of all the places that the sun shines on, there is none that can compare with that one." Madame de Lafayette volunteered this opinion in spite of the fact that the weather had been bad on her recent visit to Chantilly; however, she had been able to follow the hunt most satisfactorily in a glass-enclosed carriage, the latter a formalized adjunct to the chase brought into France from Italy by the fashionable maréchal de Bassompierre. There were certainly some properly grandiose celebrations at Chantilly to do homage to Louis XIV. In late April of 1671, when the springtime was returning to the valley of the Seine, the King and his court traveled forty-one kilometers northeast of Paris to visit "monsieur le Prince" (Condé) at Chantilly. It was estimated that this royal inva-

---

* The game of *reversi* is a card game in which the player with the fewest tricks and smallest number of points wins.

sion would cost "monsieur le Prince" some forty thousand crowns a day for suitable entertainment, which would include among other things four correct repasts, for which would be needed "twenty-five tables with five services." One small item would be one thousand daily crowns to be expended for "jonquils." The King apparently enjoyed the whole affair, and hunted the stag by the light of the moon. One incident occurred that dampened the festivities: the "great Vatel"—Condé's maître d'hôtel and former maître d'hôtel of Nicolas Fouquet, the King's erstwhile superintendent of finances—learned at eight o'clock one morning that the fish had not arrived for the royal dinner later in the day. In deep mortification and feeling that he faced disgrace because the fish course would be missing from the ritualized meal, he committed suicide. Thus was sacrificed to form a man "whose fine head was capable of handling the affairs of a nation." The day ended and the night came on; but the fireworks were a failure, though "they cost sixteen thousand francs."[2]

The handsome chateau of Vaux-le-Vicomte (Figures 5, 6), some forty kilometers southeast of Paris, was the creation of Fouquet. Such artists and designers as Le Brun and Le Nôtre decorated it, and Fouquet welcomed to it both nobles and writers. His entertainments were properly lavish, with banks of violins on the terraces and costumes with mythological motifs. Madeleine de Scudéry thinly disguised the chateau under the name of Valterre in her novel *Clélie*, and praised the life therein. In August 1661, Fouquet staged for Louis XIV an incredibly ornate and formal series of events at Vaux-le-Vicomte. Among other features of the festival was Molière's first comedy-ballet, *Les fâcheux*. The King thought all the stylized spendor was misplaced, and suspected Fouquet of the misappropriation of royal funds to underwrite it—an opinion that was supported by Fouquet's successor, Colbert. Fouquet was arrested one month later, and after a lengthy trial was sentenced in 1664 to exile despite the lamentations of many persons in high position, including madame de Sévigné who wrote more than a dozen letters concerning the superintendent's downfall. The rigidly correct gardens of Le Nôtre at Vaux-le-Vicomte remain intact today for a more informal age to see and admire. As for Fouquet's loss of favor, it was borne with philosophic calm by Condé, since as a result of it the great master of gastronomic functions, Vatel, went to Chantilly where he died because the fish did not arrive on time.[3]

Louis XIV, with a group of select companions, continued to frequent the chateaux even as he was growing older. A visit to Marly (a little more than twenty kilometers from Paris) was planned toward the end of August 1684, but complications arose and the voyage was canceled: "The fete which was supposed to take place at Marly on the following Sunday was called off, because the King had planned on there being no more than 50 women on the trip; so many of them showed up at Versailles that the King counted up to 108." The King did not want to "make the choice" and so, rather wisely, abandoned the whole project. There was an interesting party at Marly in January 1686. At five o'clock in the afternoon the chateau was "brilliantly lighted" and in the salon were set up *boutiques* for each season of the year: "Monseigneur and madame de Montespan presided over the autumn boutique, monsieur le duc de Maine and madame de Maintenon over the winter one, monsieur le duc de Bourbon and madame de Thianges over the summer one, madame la duchesse de Bourbon and madame la duchesse de Chevreuse over the spring one; there were in the little shops magnificent fabrics, silverware, and everything else suitable for each season; and the ladies and gentlemen of the Court gambled for the contents of the shops and took away all that they won." Later the King gave away everything that was left in the boutiques after the game of chance had been completed. It is little wonder that all the ladies liked to go to Marly. Louis XIV, for his part, continued to enjoy Marly—which he made more and more ornate—until the end of his days. The maréchal de Villars, one of France's finer soldiers, said the King invited him to Marly in 1704, and had the kindness "to make the waters play just for me."[4]

The proper persons carried on into the eighteenth century their mannered existence in the royal and noble chateaux, but the mores became less rigorously controlled. After the excesses of the Regency, Louis XV while in his teens started his rounds of the chateaux in keeping with established ritual. The young King was at this time more interested in hunting than in the society of ladies, so in 1724 he spent a month at Chantilly where there was an abundance of stags (there were few in the environs of Versailles). For this sojourn, however, at Chantilly—"Chantilly, the most beautiful place in the world"—he needed to have with him seventeen ladies and about forty gentlemen. The magnificences at Chantilly did not cease to be "sumptuous, prodigious, and excessive"; even for a simple hunting party, there had to be maintained at the ready "five or six tables with eighteen covers, all very delicate." In 1727 the King pursued the stag at Rambouillet until eleven o'clock in the evening, which some of his noble entourage thought to be too extensive an interest in venery. Within a few years Louis XV began to combine his riding to the hounds with a developing inclination toward women. Chantilly remained a formalized clearing house for both endeavors, and was often crowded with the King's collection of grand seigneurs; but the frank marquis d'Argenson, who was a strong proponent of the position of the nobility, said in 1732 that "this house of Condé is a hotbed of factions and avarice." In November 1737, there was a big assembly at Fontainebleau because it had been rumored that madame de Mailly was to be proclaimed the mistress of Louis XV. Therefore, in a tinsel gesture of formalism, "the loftiest princes of the blood took possession of madame de Mailly during the hunt, and gave her the best places in their caleches." The royal group was rather relaxed in its inspection of several chateaux near Paris during April 1739: "In the trip to La Muette that the King made the party was gay and independent. The ladies, who usually come along and to whom everybody is accustomed, had been invited. Dinner was at [the chateau] Madrid; supper took place at La Muette; the afternoon was given over to Bagatelle with the maréchale d'Estrées; the time was passed most pleasantly, with a bit of lovemaking if such were desired; everything was in perfect order." At about this same time efforts were made to remedy the "misery of the provinces" but to no avail.[5]

Versailles and Fontainebleau were, naturally, the centers from which evolved these distinguished operations. A very fine ball was held at Versailles in 1739, "worthy of the Court of France"; the gallery was superbly decorated and illuminated, the masks and refreshments were elaborate and correct. The whole affair was arranged with "order" and "politeness," except that monsieur de la Trémoïlle, who was in charge of placing the people, created some "disorder" in ranking the guests. Fontainebleau, along with Versailles the official residence of the King outside Paris, was visited by the royal family in October 1749. There was some confusion in the ritual of reception: "Traditional usage held that the governor of Fontainebleau should come to receive the King and Queen at the entrance of the forest, and that at the foot of the mountain on this side the provost and chapel wardens should come to present to Their Majesties some fruits, which ceremony was preceded by a little harangue"—and then very properly would be handed over to the King the keys to the palace. On this occasion, however, the royal procession was delayed in its arrival at Fontainebleau, much to the frustration of the functionaries in charge: the presentation of the fruits and the harangue had to be postponed until the following day, although some dramatic spectacles and music in the chapel were provided for the King and his court according to plan.[6]

The manners and social ritual of the French Court were essential to its functioning; and the stylized ceremonials of the Court were based on the fact that French Kings, especially Francis I and Louis XIV, enjoyed being in properly chosen crowds, and living their private lives publicly. Louis XIV, in particular, relished an existence in a gilded goldfish bowl, and his getting up in the morning as well as his retiring at night became ritualized procedures and special opportunities for showing favor. Under such conditions the correct manners of a courtier became of primary importance, and as early as 1630 one Nicolas Faret wrote a very popular manual on the art of being pleasant at Court. The great nobles (like the duc de la Rochefoucauld), who had been progressively shorn of their political powers since the time of Richelieu, resented their position of empty formalism and social decoration under Louis XIV. But for the majority of France's upper classes, proper conduct in the King's aura became the primary aim in life. La Bruyère spoke perceptively of Louis XIV's entourage: "The Court is like an edifice built of marble; I mean that it is composed of men who are hard but who are highly polished." A "man of the Court," according to La Bruyère, should use the best of his family names, and bring frequently into the conversation both his paternal and maternal forebears; he should "have his halls decorated with genealogical trees, with escutcheons quartered sixteen times, and with pictures of his ancestors and friends of his ancestors." He should look around superciliously at various courtiers in an assembly and say that this one is not a "man of quality" and that that one really is not a "gentleman"; if such a man talks loudly and often, "he will be heard." On the royal levees and retirings, La Bruyère said that "a thousand scarcely known persons made up the crowd" who jammed their way into them; the King obviously could not see everybody and thus made many people "unhappy." La Bruyère went on with a rather embittered picture of the Court as a "region where the old men are gallant, polished, and civil," and the women declining in beauty because of overindulgence in cosmetics. In summation, he said: "Whoever has seen the Court has seen the most beautiful, the most specious, and the most ornate spectacle in the world; whoever disdains the Court, after having seen it, disdains the world." La Bruyère, the tutor of the grandson of the Great Condé, had been close enough to make a report on life around the Sun-King.[7]

The French Court earlier in the seventeenth century saw its concepts of manners and dress suffer a defeat at the hands of the dashing duke of Buckingham, English emissary in Louis XIII's domain and possible beguiler of the Queen, Anne of Austria. In 1625 there was a "grand ball at the Louvre," and the Queen had invited to it "all that there was of greatest charm and gallantry among the ladies." The gentlemen who had been asked were, in their turn, all properly groomed and had neglected nothing that might be "most advantageous" to their appearance. It was "the most beautiful and brilliant assembly that could be imagined." Into the midst of it came the "duc de Bokingant," arrayed in the most inconceivably outlandish clothes. He had on a costume "of a Persian fashioning," with a velvet hat covered with plumes and glittering precious stones; and, of all things, *chausses* (pants) pulled up so high that his knees were visible —this was in an era when French courtiers wore baggy plusfours with the bit of lace dangling from the bottom. All the correctly dressed Frenchmen curled a disdainful mustache at the ridiculous Buckingham on his entry, and greeted him with a sneering smile; the ladies added their touch of mocking laughter. Before the evening was over, however, the dynamic Englishman had become the main attraction of the party, and had "effaced French concepts of fashion, as well as the greatest gallants of the Court." Buckingham continued to cut quite a swath in France. The discreet madame de Motteville, who was devoted to Anne of Austria and after 1643 chronicled her every breath, said of him: "He was magnificent, generous, and the favorite of a great king [Charles I], all of whose treasures he was free to spend; and all the jewels of the crown of England were available for his adornment." Madame de Motteville was certain that Anne of Austria's virtue had remained intact despite Buckingham's onslaughts: the Queen had indulged only in "what is called ordinarily genteel flirtation in which no specific commitment is made." In the middle 1620's, George Villiers, the first duke of Buckingham, unquestionably left his imprint on the manners and courtly ritual of France.[8]

The logical French—whether courtier, churchman, or bourgeois with pen in hand—never ceased to speak out about the life at Court. The well-mannered chevalier de Méré (whose *Conversations* began to appear in 1668) said, "the Court has made progress in spirit and gallantry," and will go farther "under this great Prince [Louis XIV] whom everybody admires." At about the same time the Jesuit Le Moyne was writing to the charming duchesse de Schomberg to the effect that few, like her, could live at the Court "without being stained by its vices." In 1717 the marquis d'Argenson commented on the changes in form and ritual that occur in a royal Court: "a modern Court takes pride in ridiculing and in treating with ill-placed superiority all the functions, manners, and objects of respect of the preceding Court." One formalistic feature that remained rather standard from the sixteenth into the eighteenth century was the matter of men's hats: no gentleman kept his hat on in the presence of the King and the King doffed his hat to nobody. The King wore a headdress whenever and wherever he pleased, indoors or outdoors. At this time a gentleman did not normally remove his hat in a social gathering unless it were done to show deference or respect. Even a king could make such a gesture occasionally, as Louis XIV did at a dinner in 1686 when he stood up and, bareheaded, drank to the Pope; then he sat down and put his hat back on. On a promenade through the gardens of Versailles in November 1700 the King had his courtiers "cover themselves," to the surprise of some Spanish visitors who were along. Louis explained that it was normal ritual for his men to be uncovered in his presence, but that he had abolished form on this wintry day because he did not want the whole Court to come down with colds.[9]

Hats could be political as well as formalistic symbols. After the death of Louis XIV in 1715, the duc d'Orléans hoped to become regent during the minority of Louis XV. The duke had promised the peers of France, however, that he would use his influence in persuading the first president of the Parlement de Paris* to doff his hat when he addressed the peers, as was done for "the legitimate princes while calling them by name and for the other princes without naming them but in making to them a bow." The legitimate princes were opposed to the whole idea, since such a ceremony would indicate that their rank was too near that of the peers. Louis XIV in his last days had been consulted on the issue, but had decided that the Parlement de Paris should make its own decision—Louis in his time had had plenty of trouble with the Parlement. When the Parlement de Paris sat in full session to decide on its preference for a regent, the duc d'Orléans became wary: he had heard that the stubborn Parlement was opposed to having its first president doff his hat to the peers of France, so the matter was not brought up

---

* The Parlement de Paris was the governing body for control of the internal affairs of the city of Paris; it was very jealous of its prerogatives and could at times oppose the wishes of the King.

at the opening meeting. Nor was it brought up later, despite the fuming and frothing of some of the peers. In any event, the profligate Philippe duc d'Orléans became Regent, though the peers of France were not given the formalistic accolade of having the first president of the Parlement de Paris doff his hat in their homage.[10]

Many of the great nobles, particularly men of the sword, disliked the regime of the Regent and the later one of Louis XV, and said they were glad to leave the Court where there was nothing but a continual round of pleasures. Most of the triviality was blamed on madame de Pompadour, who was such a "low-grade mistress." In spite of the criticisms the ritual of form continued, and madame de Pompadour was properly installed at Versailles in the apartment formerly occupied by madame de Montespan, "just underneath the King's." On another tangent, it was hopefully suggested in 1739 that Louis XV might have a "penchant for order" because he kept a card-index system on five or six "packs of hounds," an inclination that might in time be transferred to more important affairs of state. In 1740 some worry was expressed over the libertinage around the Court and about the King's possible loss of religion; but there was no need for concern, according to the marquis d'Argenson, because the King was going his "usual way with his mistress" and mumbling his "paternosters and prayers with accustomed decency." An intimately formal detail was given by the maréchal de Villars in 1725 concerning a visit made by him, "monsieur le Duc,"* and the grandmaster of the wardrobe to the bedroom of Louis XV and his new Queen: "We entered the next morning into their room while the Queen was still in bed. Modest compliments were exchanged; they both exhibited the real satisfaction of the newly wed." Some years later in 1749, when the King's tastes in feminity were

---

* This would be the grandson of the Great Condé, the duc de Bourbon, who was known by this title.

more varied, the correct duc de Luynes said, in connection
with madame de Pompadour's occupying royal quarters, that
she was "acquainted with the King." In further assurance of
the correctness of procedures at the Court, Luynes asserted
solemnly in 1750 that the Queen's ladies in waiting were
very busy seeking culture—"without missing the hours of
the King's levees and unbootings, or the visits they made to
madame la Dauphine, or the Queen's gambling parties."
Aside from these interruptions, "Mesdames" were turning
seriously to reading and study under the direction of monsieur Hardion, "of the French Academy and a very learned
man." He made for them extracts of history and "the parts
of philosophy"; he even gave them "a smattering of Greek"
to set their manners and conversation on a classical foundation.[11]

The manners and social ritual away from the Court were
during the age of formalism an echo in many respects of the
royal scene. The great gentlemen and ladies of France liked
to base their actions on an age of chivalry, one earlier even
than that of the "chivalric King," Francis I. Madame de
Sévigné wished for the "preservation of all chivalry," and
boasted to her cousin, the comte de Bussy Rabutin, that
their family reflected "three hundred fifty years of chivalry."
When the maréchal de Bassompierre died in 1646 he was
lamented as a representative of an age (no longer in existence
because of Mazarin) when "civility and respect for women
were in vogue." But this was a prejudiced lamentation and
ignored such well-mannered gentlemen as the chevalier de
Méré and many like him. And the great private houses that
were built in Paris during the seventeenth century were the
settings for social and cultured activities in most precise form.
There was a very good and correct dinner party in 1671 at
the home of monsieur de Chaulnes: "Service was arranged
for two tables in the same room, with fourteen covers at

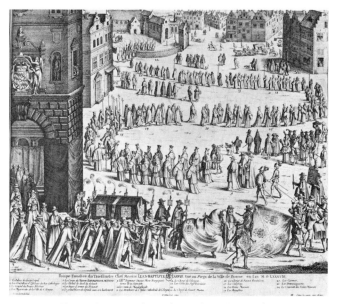

*12.* Funeral procession of Baptiste de Tassis, 1588

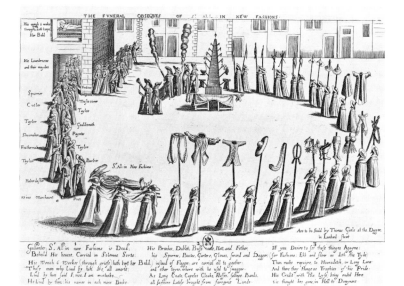

*13.* The Funeral of All-in-New-Fashions

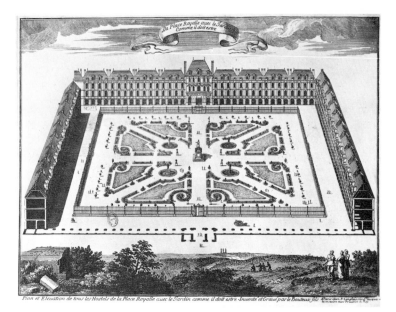

*14.* The Place Royale

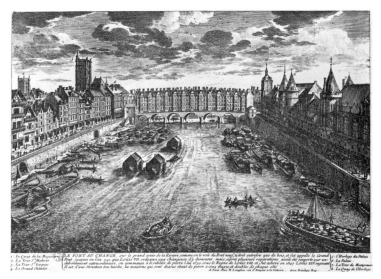

*15.* The Pont au Change

each table; monsieur de Chaulnes presided at one of them and madame at the other. It was quite a sizable feast, even excessively lavish; platters of roasts were taken back which appeared not to have been touched; in order to bring in the pyramids of fruits, it was necessary to take off the doors." One pyramid "with twenty porcelains" was smashed at the entrance and the noise "drowned out the violins, the oboes, and the trumpets." Dancers appeared later and did "gypsy steps and those of lower Britanny." During the spring of 1672 "monsieur le Duc"* staged a hunting party one Saturday at the chateau of Saint Maur, followed by an early supper featuring "the most beautiful fishes of the sea." Then the genteel guests were escorted back to Paris where there was served at the Hôtel** de Condé a midnight repast consisting of "the most exquisite viands," to the accompaniment of oboes, musettes, and violins. It must have been a wearying day, with little opportunity to relax in a pair of old pantofles. Well-mannered society could not always find peace and quiet even after the party was over. In 1671 the house of the comte de Guitaut, on the rue de Thorigny in Paris, burned down at three o'clock in the morning. All the best representatives of the *haut monde* came out for the occasion, although they had little time to change from their informal nightcaps and nightshirts. Nevertheless, the Venetian ambassador showed up in a stylish *"robe de chambre* and in a wig and preserved very well the gravity of his most serene highness."[12]

Dress was an important part of social ritual and took its lead, whether for men or women, from the Court. The fertile madame de Grignan was advised by her mother to cut off her hair and pile it up on top of her head in curls in order to be fashionable: this was the mode of the 1670's estab-

---

\* This would be the son of the Great Condé, Henri Jules, who was at the time some twenty-nine years of age.

\*\* *Hôtel* in the seventeenth century did not mean a hostelry, but a private town house of large dimensions.

lished by the Queen, madame de Montespan, and madame de Nevers. As for rouge there was much objection to it by many men—Molière and La Bruyère among them—on the theory that it injured feminine skin and that it was an unsuccessful effort at hiding old age. But the correct and proper ladies wore rouge, "this rouge that is the law of the prophets, and it is on this rouge that turns the whole of Christendom." On the other hand, when a lady became devout she ceased to wear rouge and hid her bosom, as did madame de Thianges in 1674. A lady could bedeck herself in clothes too fancy for proper good taste; this is what happened to madame la Coetquen and it was not ignored by her feminine friends: "She had made a black velvet skirt with heavy embroidery of silver and gold, and a fabric cloak the color of fire, silver, and gold; and although she was indeed resplendent, everybody thought she looked like a comedienne and laughed at her so much that she did not dare wear the dress again."[13]

Women during the formalistic period, despite their manners and courtesies, were at times less than kind to one another. The same thing to be sure could be said of the proper gentlemen, but their difficulties were more likely to be settled with a sword than with a velvet-wrapped stiletto. The hostility between madame de Montespan and madame de Maintenon, who were in competition for the favors of the same King, is understandable and has been well chronicled. Madame de Sévigné was, in general, rather fair to her own sex, though she did not care much for the women of Holland. She related a rather amusing incident concerning a visit of Condé's son to the Low Countries: "Monsieur le Duc is very much bored in Utrecht; the women there are horrible." Evidently a partial reason for monsieur le Duc's boredom in Utrecht was the fact that one of the ladies of the city rejected his advances with a well-formalized rebuke: "In the name of God, monseigneur, your highness is having the kindness to be too insolent." Something of a crisis between ladies of high position arose at an exhibition of fireworks in Paris during 1722, an affair that was graced by the presence of the King. In getting to the seats, there was the "matter of a quarrel involving mesdames de S. . and de P. . , both of them as distinguished by their birth and that of their husbands as by their beauty, their gallantries, and their intrepidity in every adventure. The duchesses de Brissac and d'Olonne, whose birth did not match that of their husbands, put themselves above the first two ladies without any excuse or compliment; the latter abstained from beating them with their hands only because of the presence of the King. They did excoriate the two duchesses, their husbands, and the maréchal de Villeroy, a relative of the first." Young Louis XV was so upset by this breakdown in mannered ritual that he left the display of varied fireworks before it was finished.[14]

On into the later eighteenth century, the manners and fashions of women were important to the social structure. It was generally agreed that, in following madame de Pompadour's lead, feminine coiffures had become so high that they blocked the view of the stage in the theatre. In the city of Paris, as a further example of the French propensity for regularization, there was evolved a formalized hierachy of prostitutes: in an ascending order of importance, they were *filles publiques, courtisanes, filles entretenues*,* and *matrones*. As for madame's toilette, it was well portrayed by Boucher and other artists of the eighteenth century. The critic L.-S. Mercier, who had much to say about etiquette and manners, stated that milady really made two toilettes. The first was secret and had to do with basic cleansing processes and foundation garments. The second was a "game invented by the coquettishness of woman" and was acted out

---

* *Entretenue*, "entertained," or "entertained intimately" (thus "kept"); a confusion over the meaning of this word brought on the most famous duel of the sixteenth century.

to show off a well-turned limb, in the pleasant aura of powder and perfume; and accompanied by "ribbons touched with
a thousand colors, rouge, *billets doux*, epigrams of the day,
and a whole army of pins." The second toilette was a carefully timed and formal ceremonial destined for the sight of
man. It could, however, be ineffective and lacking in impres-
sion. The well-bred and bored young Charles de Sévigné
said, with youthful oversimplification, that woman was nothing but "breasts, thighs, and an excess of kisses."[15]

Women were at their best in the salons over which they
exercised direction and in which they set the code of manners
and politeness. The salons were a social and literary phenomenon that developed outside the regime of the Court;
the most famous salon of the seventeenth century—the
Hôtel de Rambouillet under the direction of the cultured and
proper marquise de Rambouillet—was organized to counter-
act the crude atmosphere around Henry IV. The salons
demonstrated, too, that woman had won the centuries-old
*Querelle de la Femme* and that she was no longer man's
chattel in society's marketplace. Courtier and savant alike,
therefore, visited the salons and knelt in ritualistic obeisance
at the feet of woman. Not that much approval was given to
"learned" women: Molière ridiculed them in *Les femmes
savantes*, wherein a servant is dismissed for not "speaking
Vaugelas" and affairs in the kitchen are neglected because
the mistress of the house is fascinated by poetry and astron-
omy. La Bruyère spoke his mind on the subject: "A learned
woman is to be put in the same category as a finely wrought
instrument of arms: she (like it) is artistically chiseled, ad-
mirably polished, but of no practical use." Nevertheless, the
cultured and polished madame de Rambouillet had a host of
followers; and La Bruyère himself respected the most learned
woman of his day, madame Dacier.[16]

Back in the sixteenth century there were learned and civilized ladies who had their coteries. Marguerite de Navarre,
the sister of Francis I and the erudite patroness of poets, has

been in more recent years called a *précieuse* before the time of preciosity. The mesdames des Roches received properly and culturally at their home in Poitiers, and the charming Platonist Louise Labé at her gatherings in Lyon was supposed to have embraced philosophers for the love of Greek. However, it was in the seventeenth century, after Henry IV's rough and slashing Gascons had been cleared away and in the midst of Louis XIII's rather boring reign, that women and the salons came into their own. It was at the Hôtel de Rambouillet that refinement was learned, along with a "proper deference to ladies and the regulation of the sexes." The fine town house of madame de Rambouillet was on the rue Saint Thomas du Louvre (now no longer in existence), adjacent to the palace of the Louvre but far removed from official or royal oversight. It was in this hotel, designed by the mistress thereof, that madame de Rambouillet (with the assistance of her daughter, Julie) received courtiers, poets, Academicians, and society in general if it were civilized. Poetry was read, theatrical pieces were performed, collations were provided (at which madame de Rambouillet preferred that a well-bred guest say "I esteem the melon" rather than "I like the melon"). Maxims were composed and there was discussion of the philosophy of Descartes; but, above all things, there was conversation—polite, well-ordered, and tinged with artificiality. The Hôtel de Rambouillet became the center of the correctly mannered social structure of its age. Because of the incorruptible but not prim morality of its mistress, the salon of the marquise de Rambouillet managed to steer a proper course between dissipation and prudery, which latter quality was later to receive a lambasting from Molière.[17]

For conversational purposes the Hôtel de Rambouillet popularized the architectural device of the *alcôve*, a small room within a room cut off from the main expanse of floor by a balustrade and containing a bed and a few chairs.

Very private (but correct) discussions were carried on by madame de Rambouillet herself in such a milieu, and by 1651 the Queen was receiving "while on her bed in her alcove." The privileged group that participated in the restricted conversations with madame de Rambouillet came to be known as *alcôvistes*, and were the favorites of her salon. To them can be credited the development of the superstylized language of preciosity, catalogued by Somaise in his *Dictionnaire des précieuses* and satirized by Molière in his farce, *Les précieuses ridicules*. It is doubtful that the habitués of the Hôtel de Rambouillet, as Moliére would suggest, described a chair as a "convenience for conversation" or a mirror as the "counselor of the graces," except in mock seriousness. There was, indeed, room for polite reform of the rough language of soldiers and the farce-players in the theatre; and madame de Rambouillet did not want the linguistic manners of her group to be confused with those of the grubbing bourgeois or meat-dealers in Les Halles. Most of the précieux locutions listed by Somaise have disappeared from present-day French; no longer would one say for "lackey, put out the candle," "useless one, remove the superfluity of this ardency," or for "it is raining," "the third element is descending," or for "the feet," "the dear suffering ones"; but "to let the conversation die" is still perfectly good in either French or English. The mannered phrases of preciosity were most fashionable around 1650; later in the century they were considered insipid along with the romances of mademoiselle de Scudéry, herself a prime précieuse. In 1687 it was said that a fop who wanted to appear witty in society did not talk simply, but in "pompous gibberish, involved phrases, and big words that signified nothing." In spite of later criticism, the woman's world of the Hôtel de Rambouillet made a contribution to both manners and vocabulary; in frowning on uncouthness and ruralism it taught, as a contemporary Academician has said, men to "talk like gentlemen."[18]

Madeleine de Scudéry continued a feminine influence on manners after the turbulence of the Fronde (around 1652), which had seen many of France's great families for a time in opposition to the Crown. Though a bourgeoise, mademoiselle de Scudéry attracted many nobles to her salon in Paris on the rue de Beauce. Her stylized novels, *Artamène ou le grand Cyrus* and *Clélie*, despite their loss of favor with the later classicists of the 1660's, were in their day veritable "manuals of gallant civility." In them everyone observed the proper social amenities, and gentlemen had good manners along with a courage refined by love. Mademoiselle de Scudéry died in 1701 after having influenced the structure of polite society for some sixty years. The duchesse du Maine carried the salon tradition on into the eighteenth century at her chateau of Sceaux just outside Paris; her entertainments, the famous "nights of Sceaux," were spectacles done in the park, with torches and a splendid collection of ladies and gentlemen. The marquise de Lambert took into the eighteenth century a real concern for refinement in language and the cult of manners. Her salon was an intellectual center in the midst of the Regent's debauchery. And there were many other ladies who had their effect upon men and manners in France before 1750. Saint Evremond, the liberal-minded gentleman who knew such varied ladies as the uninhibited Ninon de l'Enclos and the duchesse de Mazarin, said that he enjoyed the society of women; he relished their conversation and felt that it was distinctly worth while to try to please them.[19]

One of the most natural of the formalistic instincts of the French has been their mannered approach for centuries to food and drink. The first Gaul in the caves of the Dordogne must have served his raw dinosaur and salad as separate courses, even though the *carte du jour* that he probably carved on the walls has not yet been discovered. By the sixteenth century more proper instruments and receptacles had come into fashion, and it was no longer correct for a gentleman to cut a portion of meat from the communal chunk in the middle of the table and then consume it with his knife and fingers off a moist slice of bread. A complete *couvert* of knife, fork, and spoon was available, frequently with ornate handles in chiseled vermeil. Cups could be in crystal and enameled, under the influence of the great Renaissance *émailleur*, Bernard Palissy. And the fine sixteenth-century architect and engraver Androuet du Cerceau etched on the inside of a silver cup a series of mythological stories on the life of Diana. Basins, used for washing the hands before and after meals during the sixteenth and seventeenth centuries, were often highly wrought; this fashion disappeared with Louis XIV who did not like water—he wiped his hands on a damp napkin. Plates made out of Limoges enamel appeared in the sixteenth century; as for liquids, by the seventeenth century an affluent society preferred to drink them out of gold cups since silver ones were not considered to be very clean. In the eighteenth century Louis XV had a fancy basket—fitted out with knife, fork, salt, and pepper—for the consumption of soft-boiled eggs. During the period of formalism in France paleolithic instruments of gastronomy were definitely not in vogue.[20]

Although there had been specialty cooks in France as early as the thirteenth century—bakers, poultry cooks, meat-roasters, and cake-makers—Francis I brought in from Italy rather unnecessarily what he thought to be more proper culinary artists. Rabelais in his *Five Books* reflected the early Renaissance's great concern over food, sometimes from the gourmand's rather than the gourmet's point of view; but in the visit he has his wandering giants make to the land of the Gastrolastres, or food worshipers, Rabelais gives an encyclopedic array of the meats, fishes, crustaceans, and wines that were available to the upper-class gastronome in sixteenth-century France. Montaigne, along with others, spoke of the "science of the gullet," and felt, after his travels in other countries of Europe, that the most civilized alimentation was to be found in his own land, a conclusion which would still be acceptable to most Frenchmen. The sixteenth century made progress in adding variety to things that were eaten, and in correct techniques of consuming them. Catherine de' Medici, Henry II's Queen, was greatly interested in exotic edibles; she loved artichokes, and the combs and kidneys of capons, all to the point of gluttony and resultant obesity. It was only the loftier social classes that had the privilege of ritualized courses and imported delicacies from the Far East and the New World; the peasants had an unstylized diet of bread, some milk products, peas, leeks, onions, and cabbages. But cabbages should not be downgraded, since the genteel philosopher Montaigne said he hoped to die among his.[21]

A formal dinner in the seventeenth century had both order and quantity. If around thirty persons of "high distinction" were to be served, a vacant chair might be left between each *couvert* so that all the guests would have plenty of room for their movements. Such a meal would consist of about eight courses in the following gastronomic progression: (1) soups, hashes, and the like; (2) ragouts, fricassees, tongue, hams, sausages, venison, pâté, and melon; (3) roast lamb, turkey, rabbits, pheasants, chicken; (4) larks, thrushes, and other small birds; (5) trout, brochet, whole salmon, shrimp,* and fricasseed tortoise; (6) celery, eggs, congealed meat juices; (7) fruit and nuts; (8) jams, sweetmeats—and toothpicks. If the dessert needed a little added pretentiousness, it might represent a chateau (or the Louvre or Versailles) in confected cake and sugar. For the great receptions at Versailles the Hall of Mirrors might be filled with small trees in silver boxes or porcelain *cache-pots*, with comfits hanging from the branches to intrigue the guests; and the guests, certainly,

---

* A reversal of the present-day order of the fish course.

on their way to dinner could sip a few hot drinks, wines, brandy with fruits, or liqueurs. Madame de Sévigné had a sumptuous and well-ordered feast at her town house in Paris on Christmas of 1678; a feature of the décor was "two bushes of shrimp surrounded by four tortoises." Louis XIV himself was evidently not lacking in appetite. The Princesse Palatine said she had seen him consume "four full platters of different soups, a partridge, a whole pheasant, two large slices of ham, a large bowl of salad, lamb in its juices and with garlic, hard-boiled eggs, pastries and fruits." Louis XV was also a robust performer at the table, though the culinary arts did not make much progress during his reign. Some of the hostesses in the eighteenth century simplified the order and number of their courses at their suppers. It was said that madame de Geoffrin might offer her guests only an omelette, spinach, and a *poulet*, but it was all mixed with interesting philosophical conversation. And at times a great political issue could be decided "between the pear and the cheese."[22]

The marquis de Coulanges, a cousin of madame de Sévigné and man about town until he died in 1719, had a few remarks to make about the manners of children in his time. As for their actions at table, they should be quiet, consume their food "politely, with both a fork and spoon," and make proper use of a napkin. He gave some good advice to fathers of families:

> In order to bring your children up well,
> Make good use of both nurse and tutor:
> And until they are fully grown
> Do not let them talk in company,
> For nothing is so utterly boring
> As listening to another person's child.

In the best French tradition Coulanges liked to linger over a meal, in relaxed freedom of conversation: "How delightful it is to be a long time at table! . . . My friends, why do you hurry me along?" Even a poor dinner should have its proper processes; but Coulanges' example of a "poor" dinner sounds rather attractive:

> Figs, melons, cabbages, and no *potage*,
> For a single entree a little salty beef,
> For the roast only some well-aged partridges,
> A ham, some walnuts, and some cheese,
> Some cool wine, and no one in a rush.

Boileau in his third satire gave an amusing picture of a pseudo-formal dinner at which the host followed a precise ritual of service that had one major flaw: the food was not fit to eat. After the soup, a rooster appeared "in pompous regalia" masquerading as a capon. A bit later a complicated dish was brought in consisting of a hare flanked by six "emaciated chickens" and three rabbits still "smelling of the cabbages on which they had been nourished"; around this mass, larks were piled up on the edge of the platter along with the "burned skeletons" of six pigeons. Everything reeked of rancid butter, the wine was sweet and insipid, and the salad floated in oil. Some of the "countrymen" present tried their hand at literary criticism, which brought on an argument and the end of the party with some plate-throwing across the table where the guests were crowded too close together for proper ceremony. In the eighteenth century, according to Mercier, manners in the dining room had become simpler and only with the lower bourgeoisie would be practiced the "fastidious ceremonials so familiar to our ancestors." Formerly, demoiselles sat up rigidly straight at the table, silent and motionless, and eating nothing; and "at the dessert they were supposed to sing." Today demoiselles "eat, and sing no more."[23]

For a long time the proper adjunct to civilized eating in France has been wine, and the French have never been negligent in their homage to Bacchus. The French, it must be admitted, did not invent wine but they have probably been

more ritualistic in its use than any nation that ever cultivated grapes. Homer's nectar of the gods contained wine
(along with odoriferous flowers and honey), and the
Greeks created drama out of their festivals to Dionysus; the
Romans, even though Roman ladies of quality were not supposed to drink until the age of thirty, consumed their share
of the warm vintages from the south. It was the French,
however, with a soil that produced infinite varieties of wine,
who put it on the level of high ritual and made of it a symbol
of both great and small occasions. By the sixteenth century
there were wines of reputation in France, and Rabelais named
many of them in his book. Some would not be known today,
but the red of Burgundy was supreme even then. The formal French, in their natural inclination toward wine, recognized early its well-mannered preeminence among potable
liquids. Beer and cider, therefore, for the Frenchman have
lacked tone. Around 1600 in Amiens a couplet was sung
that expressed the feeling:

> Gaudeamus, and may we be of good cheer,
> Let us drink our wine, and ignore beer.

During the seventeenth century coffee and chocolate began to be served in French town houses, but the reception at
the time was rather tepid. Madame de Sévigné is supposed to
have said the vogue for coffee was a momentary fancy and
would pass even as the vogue for Racine.* Coulanges
thought the new importation should not be drunk just to be
fashionable but for the sake of health; with this purpose in
mind, you should "wrap yourself in a thick veil and swallow
it in small sips." Coffee did gain in popularity and it was
shown on stage in a popular comedy of Boursault. Montesquieu spoke of it in his *Persian Letters* and said some
people thought it added wit to conversation. As for choco-

---

* I have never been able to find this much-quoted remark in the letters
of madame de Sévigné.

late, madame de Sévigné was of the opinion that it brought on "vapors and palpitation" and worse: "It flatters you for a time, and then suddenly causes a steady fever, which brings on death." Chocolate had other dangers: "The marquise de Coëtlogon imbibed so much chocolate last year while she was pregnant that she gave birth to a little boy as black as the devil; he died." Coffee and chocolate, obviously, have both now been fitted smoothly into the French social plan; but it was the good wines of France that kept the formalized eight-course banquets from becoming ponderous and dull.[24]

A somewhat surprising feature of formalism in France, from the late sixteenth on into the eighteenth century, was the high-level pattern of gambling. It was no back-room poker game carried on by men in shirt-sleeves and cigar smoke, nor a rolling of dice on a dirty floor. It entered rather into the best of salons, and was carried on in its many forms by well-mannered ladies and gentlemen. Henry IV loved gambling, though he did not think of it as a social ritual. He preferred to win the money of the lusty maréchal de Bassompierre with three dice on a small table in the royal bedroom; or to wager on his own prowess with a racquet in a vigorous match of *jeu de paume*. Since the King was an excellent player of court tennis he frequently brought home a quantity of *écus* that never got into the hands of his collectors of revenue. As the seventeenth century went along its way games of chance became more and more a part of polite society. It was said of the popular salon poet Voiture that he was successful both in love-making and in gambling—but that he preferred gambling. Royalty gave its accolade to gambling as a proper diversion, and the halls of Versailles, the Louvre, and Fontainebleau were the scenes of some spirited engagements at cards, tricktrack, and dice. Madame de Motteville said of the dowager Queen, Anne of Austria: "She is presently fond of gambling, and spends several hours

of the day at it. Those who have the honor of participating
in it with her say she gambles like a queen, without passion
and without insistence on winning." Not all of those who
played in the King's ambiance were so detached about winning or losing. The story was told in 1671 about the master
of the King's wardrobe, monsieur de Cessac, who was dismissed from the Court for obtaining 500,000 *écus* (an incredible sum) by the use of "adjusted cards." There were
some large games that went on in the provinces, too, especially in an area where sessions of the States-General were
in progress. Madame de Grignan, who lived in the south of
France, was continually admonished by her mother to cut
down on her gambling losses. Le Moyne wrote a poem on
gambling to a friend of his, madame d'Oradou; in civilized
Jesuit fashion, he preaches moderation:

> Of all the rules to be learned about gambling,
> The first, Doralis, is to gamble very little.
> Every excess is burdening, in the conduct of things;
> One can be stifled under a pile of roses.
> Gambling, like studying, undermines the health,
> If it is done assiduously, unto excess.

Gambling at the Court increased even as Louis XIV advanced in years. In 1698 in the King's party on a trip out
from Paris there was a "prodigious game" in progress all the
time. And in May 1700: "Madame la Duchesse lost ten or
twelve thousand pistoles* gambling; and not being able to
pay she wrote to madame de Maintenon about her embar-
rassment. Madame de Maintenon showed her letter to the
King, who had all her debts settled"—but with the admonition that "madame la Duchesse" not incur any more. The
marquis d'Argenson claimed that he was not much of a
gambler although in 1719 he won two hundred louis at

* Dangeau, from whose *Journal* this story comes, does not identify her
further; the pistole was worth around eleven francs.

*biribi,** a very popular game during the reign of Louis XV. Gambling became so prevalent as a well-mannered vice that in 1722 the maréchal de Villars, who bore at that time the formal title of "dean of the tribunal of the marshals of France," issued an order against games of chance in the "royal houses" of Paris because of recent heavy losses and resulting disturbances. But Louis XV set the fashion of high stakes though "it was scarcely proper for a king" to do so: "The game was a very big one at Marly [in 1726], and the King and Queen lost 200,000 francs in two months time." Many of the more conservative nobles thought that this was improper, and that Their Majesties should have been satisfied with a modest session of *piquet.* But the heavy gambling continued, and in 1731 at the home of "madame la Duchesse" a young man had been losing so consistently that all his money was gone. He necessarily left the table, visited the buffet, and very courteously brought a young lady an orange; she with equal courtesy lent him an *écu* with which he won several thousand.[25]

In 1739 it was said that there were more than three hundred gambling houses in Paris where biribi and *pharaon*** were played, and in which "all the young gentlemen were being ruined." Several were well-established town houses, like the Hôtel de Soissons and the Hôtel de Gesvres, which had evolved from proper families and had official protection; their décor was elegant, food and drink were formally served, and a man could lose his money in a correct environment. Many government officials did just that, a large portion of

---

* *Biribi* was a game of numbers played with 64 participants sitting around a table, betting on numbers from 1 to 64. However, the numbers in a box went up to 70, so the banker had a 13 percent advantage over the players. The game was outlawed in 1787.

** *Pharaon* was a card game involving a banker and any number of players, who bet to the "right" or "left" of the banker in a circle around a table. A card on the winning side was paid double, while the banker got the wagers on the losing side. He also won if his card and the betting card were of equal value.

their losses being in public funds. Outcries were raised against the gambling establishments, but it was difficult to close them down in view of the mode of living set by the royal house. In October 1749 a piece of construction was completed at the end of the "new garden" at Fontainebleau; it contained an assembly room with three windows, which was "simply decorated but with taste" and "sufficiently large for six gaming tables to be put in it." This was felt to be a needed addition to royal installations, since it had become a mannered routine to "gamble with the Queen" at Fontainebleau on Sundays and Fridays.[26]

During the age of formalism in France Paris was the clearing house of proper functions, including well-planned visits to chosen chateaux in the environs. Paris was where the sophisticated tragedies of Racine were being performed, or where one could listen with La Rochefoucauld to a reading of Boileau's *Art poétique* before its publication, or where madame de la Fayette's garden could be admired when it was at the height of its bloom. Paris was the compensation for spending a few days in a "little dog of a village six leagues from Lyon," even though the streets of the capital might be filled with petty bourgeois and the intimacy of one's own bedroom disturbed by "bitches of bedbugs." And as for going to a terrain like Canada, it was "a sad thing to live in a new land, and to abandon one that is known and loved, to go to share a climate with people that one would not bother to see in the society that one is leaving." Certainly not in Canada of the seventeenth century would one find a cook who would be able with "correct taste" to construct a ragout of beef and cucumbers; nor a bathtub made of marble and trimmed in velvet, even though the contraption was too cold to sit down in; nor a *chaise percée* covered with red or blue damask, or possibly, red morocco; nor a *gantière* studded with pearls on which "persons of quality" put their gloves. It was rather in the correct and formalistic world of France, symbolized by Paris, that one could slip into Mignard's studio and peek through a hole in the door while the great artist was doing a portrait. And it was in Paris that "the air, the tone, the gesture, the accent are subservient to usages that must be respected, and these accepted formalities enrich the pleasures of relationships instead of destroying them."[27]

# ENTREES AND CEREMONIALS

PROBABLY NO nation through the centuries has given more attention to the formalities of uniforms, ceremonials, and parades than the French, unless it might be the Italians. Not that a monopoly could be claimed for the French and Italians on external manifestations of formalistic display; nor could it be said that the pomp and circumstance of marching horses and men was a ceremonial limited to the centuries of formalism. Both Hitler and Mussolini discovered in our own time that resplendent costuming and a rigid goose step could be effective in a quick building of power. Mussolini at the peak of his career constantly filled the cities of Italy with strutting soldiers and military bands, to such a degree that a café-sitter in Rome in the 1930's might see three different units pass by his table within an hour. Nevertheless, the entrees and ceremonials of sixteenth-, seventeenth-, or even eighteenth-century France had a correct dignity lacking in the manifestations of more recent dictators, though the purposes of both were the same: a visualization for the people of a governing authority. When Henry II or Louis XIV rode into Paris with full processional accompaniment it was to give the populace the privilege of seeing and admiring the majesty of the King. The continuation of this sort of proper ceremonial would be evidenced today by a royal coronation—accompanied, to be sure, by popular admiration but only symbolic obeisance—in England, a land regarded by Frenchmen of the age of Louis XIV as being a trifle uncouth.

Royal entrees in France had had importance in the Middle Ages, but they came into full flowering in the Renaissance when cities were larger and more capable of providing majestic receptions. The techniques of entering and receiving were borrowed to a considerable degree from the ducal courts of Italy, which had begun before 1500 their influence on invading Frenchmen in regard to the proprieties of manners and dress. Mythological motifs, taken over from the Italian Renaissance, gradually replaced after 1500 medieval themes in the statues, chariots, and decorations along the route as the royal party wended its way into Lyons, Rouen, or Paris. When Charles VIII made an entry into Paris in 1484 and into Rouen in 1485, the decorative scheme of things was medieval, with allegorical personages out of the *Roman de la Rose* in view; but in 1514 when Louis XII married Mary of England he was in an atmosphere that was becoming formalistically pagan: as he proceeded to the square of the Châtelet, where a throne had been erected, he was surrounded by such proper antique deities as Minerva, Diana, and Apollo, with "Bon Accord" pushed into the background. There could also be exchanges of formalistic splendor, as was the case when Francis I went to see Pope Leo X at Bologna in December 1515. The Pope was in full pontifical array while Francis I shone in habiliments of black and silver, accompanied by six thousand archers every one of whom had a gold salamander (Francis' emblem) embroidered on his tunic. Arches of triumph were erected at several street crossings, and they bore inscriptions honoring the French King. To do homage to Francis I before his departure at the end of 1515, Milan gave him three weeks of "uninterrupted fetes," with such a combination of lavish décor and dark-eyed femininity that Queen Claude (who was left at home) was pleased when he got out of Italy. It was difficult to realize that he had gone down there to wage war. When he arrived in Marseille in January 1516 his entree into the city was ostentatiously correct: Neptune welcomed him, and a galley came into port bringing him as a gift a rhinoceros from Africa. The fetes lasted four days—a relatively brief interlude, since the reception given the King upon his arrival at Lyon in February 1516 was so properly colossal that he stayed three months. Francis thoroughly enjoyed going with full retinue into the various cities of his realm. He spent most of 1517 and 1518 in such formalized procedures; it was during this time that Rouen gave him a most brilliant entree, wherein Pallas asked Jupiter to lift the King from this petty sphere and put him among the brightest of the constellations. Francis I and Henry VIII of England indulged in pompous interchanges at the Field of the Cloth of Gold in 1520, where there were golden apples hanging over the tents, and when these baubles were "stretched out in the sun it was a marvelous sight to see." Another mark of brilliance was the entrance to Henry VIII's tent, where there were two pillars, one representing Cupid and the other Bacchus, from which flowed jets of wine into "large silver cups for whoever might wish to drink."[1]

Henry II continued the tradition of paying regal visits to the urban areas of France. In September 1548 there was, according to the contemporary report of the proceedings written in Italian, "the magnificent and triumphant entree of the most Christian King of France Henry II . . . into the noble and antique city of Lyon." Several arches were erected to honor the King and a "comedy" was staged for him and his Queen, Catherine de' Medici, by the "Florentine nation." Engravings were made of the ceremonials, some of which were included in the Italian account—in particular, two detailed ones of a "white, black, and red galley" and a "white and green galley" which fought an "antique" sea battle on the Saône River in homage to Their Majesties. The second galley, for an added touch of ornamentation, had shining at the top of its mainmast a "very fine crescent moon." One of the most splendid of the royal entrees— and one that has been amply described by the chroniclers —was that of Henry II into Paris in June 1549. It involved the erection of triumphal arches, pyramids, and obelisks, and an abundance of gold and azure hangings. Poets like Jean Daurat and Ronsard wrote commemorative verses for this entree; Ronsard composed a pompous poem, *Avant-entrée du Roi*, in anticipation of the King's arrival, and in which the fine soldier and athlete, Henry II, is visualized as being victorious in a tourney amid the noise of lances, the gleam of armor, the sound of trumpets, and the murmured applause of ladies. The Wars of Religion, which burst out in earnest in the 1560's, interfered with the ceremonial grandeur of the royal entrees, although Paris managed an excellent one for Charles IX and his new wife, Elisabeth d'Autriche, in 1571; and the poets, artists, and artisans contributed their talents to it. One poet, however—Jean Passerat—in a sonnet took a rather jaundiced view of the whole formalistic outlay and thought the capital was not big enough to afford it; the first quatrain runs:

> The apparatus is superb, and so is the magnificence
> That so many workmen and so many clever minds are building;
> Yet I fear, o citizens, that you are to be reproved
> For having made in this entree a useless expenditure.

This was bold language but Passerat was capable of such: he wrote an epitaph for Catherine de' Medici in which he accused her of being the "ruin of France," but hoped that she would rest in peace, "the one thing that she hated." As for Charles IX's 1571 entree, the city of Paris was able to contribute to the King sumptuous pieces of gold ware in spite of the expense involved. And Catherine de' Medici was not economy-minded in her pompous *Ballet comique de la reine* of 1581, which demanded all sorts of ornate costumes and complicated mechanisms, including a chariot for Minerva and a magic fountain.[2]

The weak and effeminate Henry III did not care for formalized entrees, though he did maintain externals of piety and was fond of nocturnal religious processions. It was he who founded in 1578 a new order of chivalry, the Order of the Holy Spirit, which required five days of ritualized ceremonial to create twenty-six new chevaliers who wore at one service of ordination cloaks of black velvet touched with fleurs-de-lis of gold. The first of the Bourbons, the vigorous Henry IV, liked to get about over the country and see the cities of his newly-won kingdom. In the winter of 1603 he traveled with his Queen, Marie de' Medici, to the eastern frontier of France and made an entree into the city of Metz. The whole affair was described in detail in a contemporary report of some seventy-two pages, with several accompanying engravings. Despite the cold weather two arches had been erected as well as a grotto "begun but not finished." There were many laudatory Latin mottoes scattered about, and batteries of "young soldiers who marched under their own flags." The King went into the city through an arch "sous le daiz" (Figure 7), on a prancing horse and accompanied by outriders. At night there was staged for Their Majesties a colorful "nocturnal combat and other artifices of fireworks" which look quite spectacular in the engraving (Figure 8) and even a trifle dangerous. Henry IV probably enjoyed every bit of it.[3]

The most elaborate entree of the seventeenth century was, as might be expected, that of Louis XIV when he brought his new Queen, Marie-Thérèse, into Paris on September 26, 1660. The record of this spectacular and formal event was inscribed by poets, chroniclers, artists, and engravers; it was undoubtedly the most pretentious of official visitations made by any French sovereign into the

capital of his realm. Cardinal Mazarin, who was no mean
discoverer of art in all its forms, had in his collection at
least two engravings concerned with the entree: a large one
by G. Ladame showing a triumphal arch through which
Louis XIV and Marie-Thérèse passed, and another depict-
ing the formal façade of the Hôtel de Beauvais on the rue
Saint-Antoine as it was arrayed for the royal passage. Also,
the correct and dignified Charles Le Brun did an oil painting of the chancelier Séguier as he rode in the procession
on a white horse, surrounded by pages, umbrellas, and a
big hat to protect him from the sun. Five full-folio engravings, a set of which is now in the Cabinet des Estampes of
the Bibliothèque Nationale, were required to show the complete line of march. In the last of these appears an informal
detail that must have caused some of the proper participants
in the parade to relax in a smile: three dogs are being chased
by men on foot (apparently with little success) to get them
out of the column.

The full story of the formalistic affair was told in a
document which bore the imposing title of "the triumphal
entree of Their Majesties Louis XIV King of France and
of Navarre and Marie-Thérèse of Austria his spouse, into
the city of Paris the capital of their kingdoms, on the return
from the signing of a general peace through their happy
marriage, enriched by several plates, harangues, and various
details of considerable importance for history." The
anonymous author of this report, which was published in
1662, evidently sought to describe everything that was connected with the entree, including the visual picture shown
in the five folio engravings. For example, in proper order,
"the march of the cavalcade of the Court was opened by
the train of monsieur le Cardinal Mazarin, in front of whom
were two of his Swiss guards on horseback preceded by
two trumpeters dressed in his colors, and followed by
seventy-two mules head to tail divided into three bands by

two officers on horseback, and indeed most distinguished by their harness and other accouterments." The chancelier Séguier was on a "white palfrey" and "dressed in a cassock and council robe of gold cloth, with a hat of black velvet bordered with gold braid and with a cord of the same material."[4]

The following units* in the lengthy procession are marked on the engravings: Corps de ville, Corps of merchants, Royal stables, Chancellerie, Archers de ville, Chastellet (the city constabulary), the University, the City, the Carriages of His Eminence (Mazarin), the Train of His Eminence, Royal Houses, Marche du Roi (with trumpeters), the King, Cour des monnaies, Cour des aides, the Parishes, the Four Beggars, Chambre des comptes, Parlement, Dais carried before the Queen, the Queen's Carriage. Some idea of the appearance of the long line may be gained from the third engraving, which represents it as progressing in snakelike windings (Figure 9). The representatives of the University are moving along on foot; though the doctors of the Sorbonne were a powerful group they probably would have been ill at ease on horseback. The careful chronicler of the occasion described minutely the costuming of and the numbers in the various units; for illustration, "the march of the Cour des aides [a tax court] was led by two companies of archers . . . preceded by two trumpets; they had shoulder straps of blue velvet, sewn with fleurs-de-lis and markings in gold embroidery, and their plumes and trimmings were blue and incarnadine." Madame de Motteville, the great admirer of the dowager Queen Anne of Austria, gave a very interesting description of this entree from a feminine point of view:

"Near the beginning of September [1660] there was

---

* The units are not listed in absolutely exact order, since the five folio engravings were intended as one, stretched out approximately ten feet in width and showing the full procession winding in a continuous line. It would be impossible to match everything exactly without tearing the plates out of the volumes.

made into Paris the entree of the King and Queen, who, while awaiting this notable day, had continued to stay at Vincennes.* I shall speak little about it, leaving the details to those who want to instruct the public. It was really a beautiful affair, and delightful to see. The Queen was in a triumphant chariot more handsome than the one that is wrongly given to the Sun; and her horses would have won the prize of beauty over those of this god of the fable. This princess was gowned in a black dress with gold and silver embroidery, with a quantity of precious stones of inestimable value. The color of her shining hair, and the white and pink of her complexion which set off the blue of her eyes, gave her an infinite brilliance, and her beauty was extraordinary. The populace was delighted to see her, and transported by its joy and love, gave her thousands and thousands of blessings. The King was such as the poets paint for us these men that have been made divine. His clothing was of gold and silver embroidery, as beautiful as it should be in view of the dignity of the one who was wearing it. He was riding a horse fitting to show him off to his subjects, and followed by a great number of princes, and the greatest noblemen of his realm . . . The Queen Mother saw the King and Queen pass by from a balcony on the rue Saint-Antoine." This rather glowing description, especially of Marie-Thérèse, was somewhat different from an earlier comment made by madame de Motteville on the new Queen: "Her bosom appeared to us well formed and sufficiently plump, but her dress was horrible."[5]

As the entree of Their Majesties moved through the streets of Paris, the monarchs were greeted by the music of trumpets, violins, oboes, and other instruments, while these "beautiful words of the abbé de Boisrobert" were sung at the Queen:

* This would be the chateau of Vincennes, built in the sixteenth century at the southeast gate of Paris and in the present Bois de Vincennes.

Come, oh triumphant Queen!
And receive our good wishes, and give us laws.
    Come and reign over the hearts of the French
And lose without regret the fine title of Infanta,
    In the arms of the handsomest of Kings.


    See in his pompous brilliance
This husband so famous through so many great deeds,
    Who comes to limit his glory as you may choose.

It would have been a good idea to find for the occasion a
better poet than Boisrobert; his insipid verses have lost
little in translation. Many strange and impressive edifices
were constructed along the route of the procession. At the
entrance to the rue de la Tissanderie was erected a mountain "forty feet high"—this was "Parnassus." The peak was
covered with laurel trees (symbolic of Apollo) and "its
slope enriched by two fountains as beautiful as could have
been those of Castalia and Hippocrene."* At one side was
a grotto with little Cupids playing around in it, and over
the whole of Parnassus ruled Apollo, whose "long blond
hair" was bedecked with laurel and hyacinths and who was
wearing "that fine scarlet cloak which Ovid in the second
of his *Metamorphoses* put on his shoulders." All nine of
the Muses were present and paid graceful obeisance to
their patron god. It is obvious that someone not unacquain-
ted with classical mythology was in charge of the décor of
this properly antique Parnassus, with its implied similarities
between Apollo and Louis XIV.[6]
On the Place Dauphine, at the western end of the Ile de
la Cité, an amphitheater was built for Their Majesties, along
with a decorative arch through which could be seen the
statue of Henry IV across the Pont Neuf. It was sufficiently
ornate for Jean Marot to make an engraving of it (Figure
10), in which can be observed several correctly garbed and

* These two ancient fountains sacred to the Muses have already been encountered in the poetry of the sixteenth and seventeenth centuries.

beplumed gentlemen and ladies. The area earlier in the century had been a favorite spot for outdoor entertainers and charlatans like the unguent-salesman Tabarin, but he had never carried on his operations before such an elegant audience. As the day went on there were fireworks—no royal visit even to a provincial city would be complete without fireworks. For the 1660 entree of Louis XIV and his Queen, the display was so extraordinary that four pages of text were needed to describe it. The pyrotechnics concluded with "Louis et Marie Thérèse" being formed in capital letters by "two hundred fifty stars." The end of the celebration came with the chanting of a *Te Deum* in Notre Dame, and an absolute finale of more fireworks. Paris had done its proper best by the nation's King and Queen. By the time of the eighteenth century formalized entrees into French cities were much less in vogue for the ruling monarchs. The coronation of Louis XV at Rheims in 1722, however, required lengthy advance preparations and a correct ritual; and, it was said by the marquis de Villars, there was so much "magnificence" that it was a bad lesson for a young king.[7]

Formalized ceremonials for the important living, during the sixteenth and seventeenth centuries in France, were possibly less ornately proper than equivalent ceremonials for the dead. The French have long been conscious of the pompous rites owed to the deceased, as is suggested in the still current term for funeral arrangements, *pompes funèbres*. The ultimate in dignified and somberly formal procedure would be, most naturally, the burial of a king or high nobleman of important governmental position; and for such personages the record of the last sad homage accorded them was likely to be kept with infinite detail. Such was the case in regard to Francis I, after the death of the knightly King at the chateau of Rambouillet on March 31, 1547.

The full story of Francis I's death and final rites was told by Pierre du Chastel, bishop of Mâcon, who delivered two sermons during the proceedings of interment. Du Chastel's account of almost one hundred pages (which included the sermons) was published by the royal printer, the distinguished Robert Estienne, and bore the title: "The death, obsequies, and interment of the very noble, very powerful, very magnanimous, very Christian Francis by the grace of God King of France, first of this name, clement prince, father of the arts and sciences. The two funeral orations pronounced at the said obsequies, one at Notre Dame de Paris, the other at Saint Denis in France." According to Du Chastel, Francis died between one and two o'clock in the afternoon in a terminating "flux du ventre." The remains then lay in bed for one day while a death mask was made; after a process of embalming, three caskets of lead were required: one for the heart, one for the entrails, and a larger one for the body.* The three caskets were carried in procession to the nearby priory of Haultebrière before being transported to Saint Cloud, "into the house of the bishop of Paris." Three persons had been designated to take charge of the funeral arrangements: Claude d'Annebaut, marshal and admiral of France; François cardinal de Tournon; and Pierre du Chastel. Church bells sounded for two full days, two altars were erected in the priory, two high masses were said each day and continuous low masses. The coffins were resting on a bed covered with cloth of gold during this part of the services. On April 6, the caskets containing the heart and entrails were taken into the church of Haultebière and placed in the vault; on April 11 the body of Francis I was carried to Saint Cloud.[8]

In the chateau of Saint Cloud the body of the King was

---

* Three lead caskets were required at this time because of inadequate techniques of embalming. A lead casket, sufficiently thick to conceal the putrefaction of the whole royal body, would have been too heavy to lift.

placed on a "bed of crimson satin canopied with rich embroidery, in a richly tapestried room of the said hôtel, and continually accompanied by chosen servitors and officers, and forty-eight monks of the four orders." The friars carried out their religious duties at Saint Cloud for approximately seven weeks; but during this time there were strange and macabre features in the ceremonials honoring the dead King. On April 24 the focus of the ritual was shifted to a lifelike effigy of Francis I, a creation that had been fashioned by the fine artist François Clouet and his assistants; it had very realistic features and hands, and was handsomely dressed. Du Chastel gave a full description of its appearance as it lay in a room next to that containing the body: "The effigy of the said king, as natural as if he were alive, was put on a parade-bed nine feet square, blanketed with a covering of crinkly cloth of gold bordered in ermine. . . . The said effigy had its hands joined, and was clothed with a camisole of crimson satin, a tunic of blue satin sewn with fleurs-de-lis of rich embroidery; and over this a great royal cloak of crimson-violet velvet flecked with blue, and sewn also with fleurs-de-lis of rich embroidery, and furred in ermine, the tail of the said cloak being more than fifteen feet long." The effigy wore a crown and also the insignia of the Order of Saint Michel; two pillows on each side held the royal scepter and the hand of justice. One practical detail was given on this formalistic setting: the "sky of tapestry" over the bed cost "fifty crowns" an *aune*, which was a measure of a little more than a yard.[9]

For eleven days, in a ritual that was regally formal but not religious, dinner and supper were served to the effigy as though it were sitting at a table. According to Du Chastel, the "gentleman usher, the maître d'hôtel, the master of the pantry, the pages of the royal chamber, the overseer of the kitchen, and the inspector of the royal service" did their normal duties. The "most worthy personage" gave a napkin to "the seigneur," while a cardinal blessed the table and all the viands and courses were presented "to the chair of the said seigneur" in a normal routine of services including wine. A cup was offered to the effigy in accordance with the standard habits of Francis I, who "had been accustomed to drinking twice with each one of his meals." At the end of eleven days of this nonfunereal routine, the emphasis was shifted from the colorful ceremonial around the ornately accoutered effigy back to the body of the dead king. The mood became more solemn and religious, and the décor was changed to black. The effigy was put into the background and the coffin was brought into prominent display, covered by a black canopy relieved only by the arms of France in cloth of gold. All the motifs around the royal corpse, as well as the costumes of those in attendance, were in black. It was at this period, on May 18, that the new King, Henry II, came to Saint Cloud to asperse the body of his father—and this was his first official appearance. Since he represented the living power of the French throne he was not dressed in black. Also, in recognition of the regal proprieties, he made no visit to Saint Cloud while the effigy was the object of such lavish attention; if he had there would have been for the moment two kings of France.[10]

On May 21 the next phase of the funeral ceremony of Francis I began: at one o'clock in the afternoon the convoy of his casket left Saint Cloud for the church of Notre Dame des Champs on the rue Saint Jacques in Paris. The procession was preceded by housing officials who went ahead to prepare "lodgings" and "suppers" for important personages in the somber line of march. The order of the convoy was given in detail by Du Chastel: (1) the five hundred poor in mourning, each one carrying a torch of four pounds of yellow wax and a black baton; (2) riders of the stables in mourning, on horseback; (3) provosts of the household in mourning, on horseback; (4) gentlemen servants of the cardinals and princes, in mourning and on horseback; (5) five hundred Swiss guards in mourning, on foot; (6) two hundred gentlemen of the household on horseback, ensigns in the scabbard; (7) petty officers of the household, on horseback; (8) the master of the gratuities chamber, controller, and clerks, on horseback; (9) valets of the wardrobe, surgeons, valets de chambre, and doctors, on horseback; (10) serving gentlemen, pantry-masters, cupbearers, and carving valets, on horseback; (11) maîtres d'hôtel with black batons, on horseback—with the premier maître d'hôtel in the rear; (12) the first overseer of carving with a pennon "sewn with fleurs-de-lis"; (13) twelve pages all in black, on chargers; (14) stable masters on horseback; (15) forty archbishops, bishops, and prelates; (16) masters of arms; (17) twenty-four archers; (18) a squire on horse-back, carrying the King's spurs "covered with black crepe;" (19) a squire on horseback with the King's shield; (20) a squire with the King's coat of arms; (21) a squire with the King's helmet and gauntlets; (22) the *cheval d'honneur*, entirely covered with "violet velvet azured and sewn with fleurs-de-lis"; (23) the grand equerry on a large horse covered with black velvet marked with a white satin cross; (24) the *chariot d'armures* in which was the body of "the said seigneur," covered with a black velvet mortuary cloth, relieved by cloth of gold and fleurs-de-lis, and drawn by six great chargers hung with black—and surrounded by four equerries, four valets, and twenty-four friars, each carrying a candle of "ten pounds of white wax"; (25) admiral d'Annebaut (in charge of the convoy), with several cardinals and princes "in deep mourning"; (26) chevaliers of the Order of Saint Michel, and other notables; (27) gentlemen of the royal chamber; (28) four hundred archers of the guard. Twenty-four criers of the city of Paris met the procession at the rue de Vaugirard and were placed at the head of the five hundred poor; also two "presidents of the Court" came out to offer the homage of the Parlement de Paris. They were asked to return the next day to accompany the cortege to the cathedral of Notre Dame. The coffins of the King's two sons—the Dauphin François who had died in 1536 and the duke d'Orléans who had died in 1545—were brought (along with their effigies) to Notre Dame des Champs where a "burning chapel" of candles was made for the three royal bodies.[11]

On May 22 (it was a Sunday) the funeral procession of Francis I made its way from Notre Dame des Champs to the cathedral of Notre Dame, after having been joined by various officials of the city of Paris among whom was the cardinal du Bellay, bishop of Paris. The coffins of the two princes were taken back to their places in the royal tombs of Saint Denis, but the three effigies of the King and his sons were in the impressive march to Notre Dame—and their realistic splendor must have caught all eyes. The cortege was increased by the addition of nine "colleges," various "ambassadors," and "oboes and trumpets," all added to Du Chastel's first list and making the complete line about a mile long. Criers preceded the procession, which was seen by Henry II secretly from a house on the rue Saint Jacques, and asked for prayers for "the very noble . . . King of France." Upon entering Notre Dame the effigy was placed on top of the King's coffin inside a brilliantly lit "burning chapel." The effigy was a pompous symbol (and almost a pagan one) of undying imperial glory, and was in some ways in conflict with the religious phases of Francis' interment; the dual features of the ritual have already been noticed in the brilliant setting for the effigy at Saint Cloud in contrast with the somber décor around the King's actual body. The seating of the cortege inside the cathedral of Notre Dame was done with scrupulous exactitude and in proper order: the princes in mourning were

*16*. The Louvre

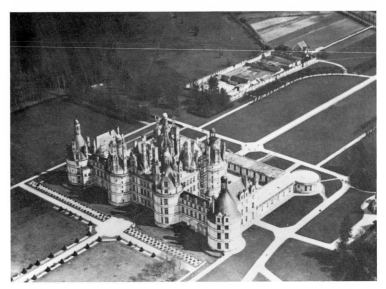

*17.* Chambord

*18.* Val-de-Grâce

placed in the choir, the bishop of Paris was in front of the high altar, and other participants were arranged according to their rank. The two days of movement from Saint Cloud to Notre Dame de Paris had been fatiguing, so the formal service on the evening of May 22 was quite short.[12]

On the morning of May 23 all those concerned with the final rites of Francis I reassembled in the cathedral of Notre Dame and Du Chastel delivered the first of his sermons; this one lasted about an hour. It began with quotations in Latin from the Bible (like *humiliata est in pulvere nostra anima*, "our soul is humbled in the dust"), and continued with a listing of Francis I's bodily and spiritual virtues, his patronage of all the arts, and his interest, even while "eating and drinking" in sacred and profane letters. This solemn encomium concluded with: "O Christian and Catholic kingdom of France, destitute of the glorious and fruitful life but adorned and embellished by the memorable death of this great King; people, nobility, and judiciary of France whom he continued to love and remember until the moment of his death; ministers of the Catholic Church whom he upheld and defended in the authority and hierarchal order of the church militant: should you not keep him perpetually in your memory and forever in your prayers?" After Du Chastel's oration the assembly inside Notre Dame disbanded for dinner; at two o'clock in the afternoon it regrouped in processional form and departed for Saint Denis, some six miles north of Paris. For this final march in homage to Francis I many of the nobles and dignitaries who had been on foot chose to mount their horses.[13]

As the long line came into Saint Denis the religious aspects of the royal funeral were taken over by the abbot of Saint Denis, the cardinal de Bourbon. The same processes of the burning chapel were repeated upon entering the basilica of Saint Denis, then vespers were said, and the weary participants retired for the night. The next morning, May 24, another sermon was delivered by Du Chastel; it, too, was filled with pompous Latin although he said it was essentially a message of comfort for those grieving for the dead king. It ended with praise for Henry II and asked the people of France to "render thanks to God who has shown this kindness to this very Christian realm, in giving us from a very splendid father a very splendid son who is seated and reigning on the throne of his royal house." One leavening incident was reported in connection with Du Chastel's statement that the soul of the King had gone "straight to Paradise": the chief steward said that Francis wanted to see everything, and so there was little doubt that he stopped off in purgatory "for just one drink." In any case, after the sermon the body of Francis I was with appropriate ritual ensepulchered, with the symbols of power placed beside him in the tomb. The royal banner of France was dipped by the admiral d'Annebaut as he entoned "the King is dead," which was repeated three times by the herald at attention; the admiral d'Annebaut lifted the banner of France with the cry "long live King Henry the second of that name." There followed the final homage to Francis I: the funeral dinner at which time the chief steward "broke the baton" to symbolize the dissolution of Francis' Household and the new regime of Henry II.[14]

This full pomposity of funeral rites for French kings was continued through the sixteenth century. The last complete ceremonial done after the fashion of Francis I's, with effigy and other stylized accouterments, was that of Henry IV in 1610. By the time of Louis XIII processes of embalming had improved and evisceration was no longer necessary; nor were the strongest porters of Paris, the salt carriers, needed to hoist the lighter (because less lead was used) coffins. In regard to Louis XIII, there was one story that would indicate that his death was treated rather casually: "The day after the death of Louis XIII [in May 1643],

King Louis XIV, the Queen [Anne of Austria], the duc d'Anjou, the duc d'Orléans, and the prince de Condé left Saint-Germain [the chateau of Saint-Germain-en-Laye where Louis XIII died] to return to Paris; and the body of the late king remained alone at Saint-Germain without any other group around it except that of the people, who came to see it out of curiosity rather than through any tenderness. . . . Of all the courtiers who had paid their respects to him the day before, none stayed to show respect for his memory: they all followed the Regent." Formalized pomp and extended ritual in the burial of the kings of France was progressively reduced in the seventeenth and eighteenth centuries. The ultimate in simplicity was reached in 1793 with the guillotining in the Place de la Révolution of Louis XVI, whose body was thrown within an hour's time into the handiest graveyard.[15]

A royal or ducal funeral could have formalistic elaboration in other cities of Europe besides Paris. One of those for which a most complete pictorial record was kept was that of the archduke Albert VII in Brussels in 1623. A large set of folio engravings of the ceremonial appeared in 1624, and they give detailed information on such things as death's heads and skeletons, the burning chapel, and important personages who participated in the event. The procession was led by the "chariot of Memory," drawn by six be-plumed horses with riders named *Benignitas, Nobilitas, Prudentia, Amor Virtutis, Ratio, Providentia*. Memory sat in the embellished car with an eagle on her head. Many of the French provinces were there, with the names of their representatives listed on an engraving (Figure 11). Some idea of the pageantry can be gained from the delegations of Bourgogne and Artois shown on the plate, where the banners of the rampant lion of Bourgogne and the fleurs-de-lis of Artois are lifted high on staves marked with coroneted *B*'s and *A*'s. The two powerful chargers shown repeat in their turn the emblems of Bourgogne and Artois, while their heads and cruppers are bedecked with ornate plumage, and their incredible tails wave in the breeze.

A somewhat simpler *pompe funèbre* was that of one Jean-Baptiste de Tassis, who was slain in battle in 1588 (Figure 12). From this less lengthy procession can be derived a more exact idea of the nature of such formations and the methods of their progress. The first feature to strike the eye is that the line of march is not straight, but moves in curved and snakelike windings through the square, the same procedure observed in the entree of Louis XIV and Marie-Thérèse into Paris. Many of the essentially formal elements of the royal corteges, but less ornate and extensive, are visible in that of Tassis. The coffin as it leaves the church is apparently near the middle of the procession; it is being carried on the shoulders of several men—a less pompous technique than the chariot of arms which would bear the body of a king. The coffin is, however, accompanied by torches to which are attached the coat of arms of the dead man. His riderless charger, on the covering of which is embroidered the same coat of arms, in next in order. To the right of the horse is a single trumpeter, a considerable reduction in numbers from the musical corps in attendance at a regal funeral. Then comes the banner of the deceased, carried by two men and marked with the same coat of arms with bars. Immediately in front are the pages of the dead warrior holding batons and his grand blazon. Several dignitaries of the clergy and members of Low Country nobility are next in line; the front of the procession is headed by the minor friars, the Dominicans, the Carmelites, and the Augustinians. Many onlookers are standing around in the square staring at the solemn ritual, as well as the inevitable dogs—in this case to the number of seven—two of which are on a leash. In the background, detached from the official proceedings, is a very handsome carriage drawn by four horses; out of it is peering a lady who might be the wife of the dead man, if the engraver had put her in mourning rather than a low-cut dress. Despite this detail of feminine costuming, the funeral procession of Jean-Baptiste de Tassis (who, though a Frenchman, was apparently buried in Cologne) was properly formal and dignified.

A rather amusing satire on French and Continental burial ceremonials is to be noted in a seventeenth-century English engraving entitled "The Funeral Obseques* of Sr. All-in-New-Fashions" (Figure 13). At first glance the last rites of this gentleman would seem to be progressing properly with marchers and mourners in the usual curving line, and the coffin of the deceased approximately in the middle of it. The first unexpected discovery is that the dead man is not in a coffin but that his stiffened body is being carried along uncovered, with a hat pulled down over the eyes and his beard projecting comically into the breeze. Almost half of the pseudo-solemn cortege turn out to be the dead gentleman's creditors, and are labeled "spurrier, cutler, taylor, shoomaker, feathermaker, haberdasher, wine merchant, poet (a surprising listing), barber, paynter, gouldsmith, musissioner, fendsor"; four "taylors" are indicated on the engraving, so Sir All-in-New-Fashions must have had an extensive wardrobe. The end of the visible procession as it comes out of the church is made up of other unpaid servitors of the corpse, "his launderesses and their maydes." Over the church door is an open window through which can be observed a somewhat unexpected sight marked: "his wench 6 weekes through griefe doth keepe her bedd"; and the sorrow-stricken lady is stretched out at almost her full length. A large portion of the procession is centered around the gentleman's wearing apparel, each portion of which is suspended from a long staff and held

* The English spellings on the engraving have not been changed.

up for everyone to see; the various objects are enumerated in some verses underneath the engraving, which were possibly written by the unpaid "poet" mentioned above:

> His breeches, dublet, buffe coat, hatt, and fether,
> his spurres, bootes, garters, gloves, sword and dagger;
> instead of flagges are carried all to geather:
> and other toyes wherewith he used to swagger.

The writer of these lines thought that such sartorial display was the result of "fashions lately brought from foreyne lands." The opening stanza of the poem gives a very good picture of the gentleman's financial condition:

> Gallantes: S$^r$. All-in-New-Fashions is dead;
> Behold his hearse, carried in solemn sorte:
> His wench 6 weekes (through griefe) hathe kept her bedd
> Those men who livd by him are all amorte;
> Livd by him said I; noe, I am mistooke.
> He livd by them: his names in each mans booke.

In addition to the objects of clothing lifted high on poles in the procession, a sort of pyramid in the center of the square displays hats, spurs, and other bits of the deceased's personal gear. All of it, according to the legend in one corner of the engraving, is "to be sold by Thomas Geele at the (sign of) the Daggere in Lumbard Street." The whole emphasis in the ceremonial of Sir All-in-New-Fashions' funeral is on satirizing his desires for formal and ornate clothes he could not afford. But it does show the influence of pompous ritual that could come in from "foreign lands."

In regard to pomp and ceremonial, the funeral of Cardinal Mazarin was somewhere in between Francis I's and that of Sir-All-in-New-Fashions. When Mazarin died in 1661 a large portion of the French nation was delighted; many thought that it was only after his death that Louis XIV "began to be King." The last rites of the dead cardinal were enacted at the church of Vincennes on March 11, 1661—without, it was said, a great deal of ceremony. Some cynics maintained that a stone had been found in his heart, an infallible symbol of the harshness of the man. The many epigrams attacking Mazarin during his lifetime continued as scathing epitaphs after his death; one of them ran:

Here lies His Eminence number two:*
God save us from number three.

Nevertheless, in 1665 the death of Mazarin was the subject of an "epic poem" entitled *La pompe funèbre ou éloges de Iule Mazarini, cardinal, duc, et premier ministre*, by one V. du Val. The poem is seventy-seven pages long, and it would be hard to find a more pompous or emptily formalistic collection of verses. Mazarin in it is imagined to have left this sphere to make his ceremonial approach to the "glorious temple of ministers of state," which is so marked in gold letters over its entrance. All of the famous ministers are there, headed by the "incomparable Armand," duc de Richelieu, who thought that Mazarin was his worthy successor in the earthly land of France and deserving of joining him in the gold-embossed temple of ministerial immortality. In confirmation of Richelieu's good opinion the *Génie* of the temple recites in pedantically dull alexandrines the list of Mazarin's exploits; the citation concludes with the following verses:

At the height of their glory we have seen ministers
Whose careers have ended in sinister reverses:
Proud colossi, who fall underneath the scythe
And leave at their death their designs incomplete,
Pompous images, whose fragile bases
Carry heads of gold on feet of clay:
But this divine spirit for whom we weep,
Having in full good fortune accomplished his projects,
Can see forever his virtues confirmed,
Before the tribunal in which lives Renown.

The "august Richelieu" is pleased with this eulogy, and

* His Eminence number one would have been Richelieu.

Mazarin, whose funereal pomp became more pompous in verse than it had been on earth, is ready to spend eternity with the other dead ministers.[16]

The French propensity for entrees, parades, and ceremonials could inspire Du Val's morose couplets on the funeral of Mazarin; such an attitude could also produce the delightful marching and countermarching in Furetière's amusing allegory in 1658 on the "troubles in the kingdom of Eloquence." It all started when Princess Rhetoric, wearied with the undisciplined actions of Allusions and Equivoques, decides to send them to the land of Pedantry. They revolt and enlist in their support battalions of Antitheses, Hyperboles, Allegories, Epiphonemes, and a few other formalistic warriors, all led by Galimatias. But Princess Rhetoric has a very solid leader of her forces, her prime minister Good Sense who calls in the aid of the "feudatory barons" of Academy: Chapelain, Voiture, Saint Amant, Colletet, Conrart, and others, who march into the conflict with legions of comparisons, descriptions, glosses, idylls, epigrams, madrigals, and similar well-disciplined troops. The proper organization of the war can be confirmed from the following tactical alignment: "The advance guard was composed of prior Analytics, the rear guard of posterior Analytics; and the battle corps of Topics, in eight battalions under the command of General Aristotle. In this corps were enrolled Dilemmas, Sorites, Enthymemes, Inductions, and several others. But their principal force consisted of Syllogisms." The primary clash is between Tropes and Figures, and Usage and Good Taste, with the latter pair scoring a resounding victory. The columns of Galimatias are put in disarray and sent back to reside in the land of Pedantry.[17]

The French in the age of formalism liked their festivals and ceremonials in prose, poetry, engravings, or in a properly groomed square of Paris. Or the correct pageantry might be in evidence on the waterways of France as when madame de Montespan took a trip to Vichy on a painted and gilded boat. Or in 1686 Louis XIV might receive the ambassadors of Siam very officially "on his throne"; then the Siamese showed all sorts of respect for the King by retiring at the termination of the audience, to the very end of a long gallery, "backwards, not wishing to turn their faces from the King." All the rigors of form could be demanding: in the process of a long ceremonial at Versailles in 1714 on a winter's night, a page carrying a torch correctly in a cold gallery ended up with a frozen arm. The King took measures, however, and ordered all pages to be issued heavy sleeves so that for the future "such accidents might be avoided." On the other hand, it must have been a problem of heat rather than cold when Louis XIV went out into the field, with the proper retinue of "all the ladies and gentlemen of the Court" to review his troops and "fourteen millions [of francs] were burned in powder." In the eighteenth century further resentment was expressed at the money being lavished on fetes and ceremonials: for a royal wedding in 1739 the city of Paris made an outlay of 800,-000 livres and twelve workmen were killed in falling from scaffolding while preparing the displays. The marquis d'Argenson took a very bitter view of the whole affair and thought that the money could have been better spent on "supplies of wheat." The same thing could be said for the ornate trip made by Louis XV to the Channel in 1749, to show madame de Pompadour the sea and "to eat some fish." The city of Rouen had to provide proper accommodations and suitable entertainment along the way, a needless expenditure just to produce "royal indigestions."[18]

Although the pompous ceremonials and processions around the Court produced some mutterings in the eighteenth century, many of the established rituals continued in a fully ornate routine until past 1750. In the "ceremony of the Order" (the Order of the Holy Spirit) eight new chevaliers were properly dubbed in 1728, much to the disgust of some noblemen who had been passed over; and there was a large ceremonial of the Order in 1750, in which some thirty-seven chevaliers participated. As for religious parades and festivals, Mercier said that Corpus Christi was "the most pompous fete of Catholicism." He had once seen two noblemen at Saint Sulpice carrying the long red robes of two cardinals even as lackeys might hoist the train of a duchess. But Mercier thought the formalism of religious processions was impressive: "the most solemn pomp accompanies these corteges; the flowers, the incense, the music, the heads bowed down, all would create the belief that Catholicism does not have a single adversary."[19]

# BUILDINGS AND GARDENS

THE CITY of Paris today, though rimmed in its suburbs by starkly practical and bleakly functional apartment houses, still reflects in its center an architectural legacy of a more formalistic age. The whole of France is dotted now with boxlike and gray-walled concrete structures necessary to the solution of housing problems resulting from the Second World War. But along the smaller roads remain untouched by contemporary modernism such Renaissance chateaux as Chenonceaux sitting astride the river Cher or Chambord with its broad expanse of woods and plain; or, as examples of seventeenth-century propriety, the exquisite chateaux of Cheverny and Vaux-le-Vicomte. And, to climax in stone the age of formalism in France, there rests intact—happily spared from the ravages of the Revolution—for present-day eyes to see the glory of French classicism, Versailles. The great nobles of France have always been builders, frequently in competition with one another in raising their enduring castles; during the sixteenth and seventeenth centuries they had only to follow the lead of two of the most construction-minded of French kings, Francis I and Louis XIV. Not much of Francis I's building interest was centered on Paris itself, though he got close to the city in his work on the chateaux of Saint-Germain-en-Laye, Madrid, and Vincennes. Louis XIV left his imprint on his capital with such creations as the Hôtel des Invalides (with its majestic dome), additions to the Louvre, and the redesigning of the Tuileries gardens.

In spite of the intrusions of modernism, the strict regularity of the noble boulevards and avenues of Paris—with the buildings along each side uniformly seven or eight stories high—is likely to remain intact. An illustration of this attitude might be observed in the architecture surrounding that most impressive of urban squares, the eighteenth-century Place de la Concorde. At its northern extremity are two very correct and matching constructions, the Hôtel Crillon and the Ministère de la Marine, separated symmetrically by an extension of an axis of the square, the rue Royale. Just west of the Hôtel Crillon, and facing the Avenue Gabriel, the new Embassy of the United States was constructed soon after the Second World War—with the proviso (readily accepted by America) that it fit in, as to height and design, with the Hôtel Crillon. A fine example today of early seventeenth-century precision of planning is the Place des Vosges (formerly the Place Royale), the brick-and-stone houses of which still stand in regular alignment as though protecting one another from the strange eccentricities of a more modern world. A contemporary engraving (Figure 14) of the period gives a vivid idea of the Place Royale "as it was supposed to be." Excellent illustrations of uniformity of chimneys and rooflines are to be noted in the buildings of the Place Dauphine (Figure 10), where the theatre was set up for the entree of Louis XIV and Marie-Thérèse; or in the houses on the Pont au Change, the stone bridge (Figure 15) begun in 1639 to replace an earlier one of wood across the Seine. The houses on the bridge are all precisely and formally five stories high, and are in interesting contrast to the earlier and irregular buildings on either side of the bridge.

Much of the story of French formalism is told by the

palace of the Louvre in its long history (Figure 16). Constructed at the beginning of the thirteenth century as a fortified chateau to assist in the defense of Paris against attack along the Seine, the Louvre retained its medieval appearance until the sixteenth century. It was a solid mass of turreted bastions capable of resisting hostile invaders and was strengthened in its military responsibilities by the staunch Tour de Nesle (later the site of one wing of the Institut de France and still later romanticized by Alexandre Dumas in the play named after the tower) on the other side of the river. Francis had plans for modernizing the Louvre after the fashion of his other Renaissance chateaux, and put the project in the hands of the great architect Pierre Lescot, who worked with the fine sculptor Jean Goujon, on the old fortress. Francis died before very much was done, although continued changes were effected by Henry II and Henry III. The Louvre came into the seventeenth century in a rather hybridized condition, half Gothic and half Renaissance. Gunpowder had made it obsolete as a protective fort, and it was not yet altogether satisfactory as a royal dwelling. Catherine de' Medici had made an effort after the death of Henry II in 1559 at improving habitability by building the Tuileries palace some five hundred meters west of the Vieux-Louvre though connected to it by a long gallery parallel to the Seine. Henry IV gave a solid attachment of the gallery to the Tuileries by the erection of the Pavillon de Flore, which still marks the southwestern extremity of the Louvre; the northwest extremity, the Pavillon de Marsan (which continues to balance harmoniously the Pavillon de Flore), was built by Louis XIV.

Louis XIII felt that the interior court of the Vieux-Louvre was too cramped for easy circulation, so he embarked upon a plan to quadruple its size. The result, thanks to his efforts and those of Louis XIV, is the Cour Carrée as it has come down to the twentieth century: a regularized quadrangle that was the seat of the royal family for a large part of the seventeenth century and the scene of many festivals, audiences, and ceremonials. To match the construction of Pierre Lescot in the sixteenth century of the southwest corner of the square, Louis XIII erected the Pavillon de l'Horloge, after the designs of Le Mercier. The classic dignity of Le Mercier's creation fitted in perfectly with the Renaissance structure of Pierre Lescot, and formed a west side which is admittedly an architectural masterpiece. More than thirty years later, Louis XIV continued the work under the direction of the fine designer Le Vau; intervening houses were cleared away and the north and east sides were constructed—which, with an extension of the south side, completely enclosed the Cour Carrée. Louis wished that the main entrance to the Louvre, at the east side, have an imposing and formalistic façade. The plans of a commission composed of Le Vau, Charles Le Brun, and Claude Perrault were put into effect. Perrault, the doctor who was an architect by avocation, was in charge of the operations; it was his idea to create the pompous colonnade of the east wing, as well as appropriate façades of the north and south wings. The embellishment of the Louvre as it appears today was not completed in the seventeenth century, since Louis XIV lost interest in the old palace after he took up his official residence at Versailles in 1680.

After royal abandonment, the Louvre in the eighteenth century was given little official protection and maintenance, and fell into a state of disrepair. Napoleon I, who occupied the palace of the Tuileries, refurbished the Louvre and added a wing (extending to the east) to the Pavillon de Marsan. The present-day Louvre was terminated by Napoleon III: he finished the northern gallery begun by Napoleon I and built the grandiose north and south arms of the Louvre. In 1871 the Commune burned down the Tuileries palace and the whole Louvre almost went up in flames. The destruction of the Tuileries was something of a disguised blessing, however, since it opened up the west end of the enclosed complex and created the magnificently harmonious two-mile vista from the Cour Carrée through the Arc du Carrousel and the Place de la Concorde (putting the Obelisk in the center of the transit sight) to the Arc de Triomphe sitting on the hill at the end of the Champs-Elysées—a formalistic panorama dear to Frenchman and tourist alike. As for the Louvre itself, it sits now on its wide expanse of terrain as a balanced and symmetrical symbol of France's formal past. The additions made by Napoleon I and Napoleon III, though not as distinguished as the sixteenth- and seventeenth-century embellishments, in no sense of the word destroyed its correct harmony as a whole. In addition to being possibly the greatest of repositories of the art of the Western world, the Louvre in its own right is today a visual manifestation of Renaissance and classical formalism.

With the coming of the Renaissance, the term "Gothic" came to be one of reproach both in literature and art. It was a manifest lack of appreciation on the part of the French of the great heritage of the Middle Ages, notably of such monuments as Notre Dame de Paris and Chartres, but it was a mark of the general turning toward Italy and antiquity. Gothic meant at the time "barbaric" or "uncouth," like the Goths. Thus the Pléiade's experimenter in verse forms, Jean-Antoine de Baïf, said: "Therefore I am abandoning Gothism and taking the path of the ancient Greeks and Romans." Even as in literature, the proper architecture by 1550 in France was paganized Italian, as interpreted by the Bolognese Sebastiano Serlio who became Francis I's architect in 1541 and whose treatise on architecture was published in Lyon between 1537 and 1551—a document which went back for its precepts to the *De Architectura* of the Roman Vitruvius. Among other structures, Serlio left his imprint on the Louvre, the Tuileries, and Francis I's renovated hunting lodge, Fontainebleau. For their part, French artists and designers like Androuet du Cerceau and Philibert Delorme, as well as men of letters like Rabelais and Du Bellay, went to Italy to examine the ruins of Rome and bring back to France their measurements and inspiration. Claude Fauchet said in 1581: "Antiquity is so much in favor among men who have even a little sentiment for humanity that there are few people of means, however untutored they may be, who do not desire to make the best possible representation of it: some by books and medals, others by all the bits and pieces of ancient things that they can find." Thus, many "important men" have their cabinets and studies filled with broken segments of antique statues, "heads without noses and ears, busts without arms and legs." Desmarets de Saint-Sorlin almost a century later attacked such a deification of antiquity, and told a story of Michelangelo's breaking an arm off a statue he had made of Bacchus in order to make it "antique" and more acceptable; the operation was so cleverly done that it fooled Raphael. During the proper age of formalism in France things classical and most things Italian were admired; things Gothic were ignored.[1]

Fontainebleau, the "fountain of beautiful water," became in the sixteenth century an Italianized chateau in design and décor. Le Père Dan, who in 1642 catalogued every feature of the construction and decoration of Fontainebleau said of it: "We can truly say, with as much right or more than might be had by those Ancients, that it can be called another Parnassus." In more recent times the setting of Fontainebleau has been described as "Olympus and Parnassus triumphant over the Evangel, a whole pagan people joyfully celebrating the beauty of the body and the

intoxication of living." It is true that, after the architects
had created a building that was balanced and open to vis-
tas of water and gardens, Italian artists like Rosso, Primaticcio, and Niccolò dell' Abbate lavished their talents on
paintings and frescoes of mythological inspiration. The
whole process was symbolized by the sketching (noted
earlier) of a supposed visit of Francis I and his court to the
nymph who presided over the fountain from which the
chateau took its name. Before 1530 Francis I had constructed correct courtyards for approaching his new palace, the
Cour de la Fontaine in 1528, and the Cour du Cheval Blanc
in 1529. Rosso the Florentine came to decorate the great
chateau in 1531 and left his particular mark on the Galerie
François I<sup>er</sup>, which lies adjacent to the Cour de la Fontaine.
This long and imposing gallery had its walls balanced and
embellished by fourteen tableaux, eight feet high and fourteen feet wide, with borders and ornamentations of Francis'
great gilded "F's" and his salamanders that both lived in
and ate fire. Le Père Dan described every one of these
cartouches, most of which went back for their mythological foundations to Herodotus, Apuleius, or Ovid. Dan
thought that Rosso wished to represent the life of the King
in these frescoes, and some of them—like the thirteenth
which shows a triumphal entry and the ninth which has the
centaur Chiron training the young Achilles—might well do
just that. Thirteen of them, in some doubtful conditions
of restoration, remain today to illustrate the paganized formalism of the Renaissance. The figures of Ulysses, Flora,
and Pan came to life again under the brush of Primaticcio,
who arrived at Fontainebleau in 1532 and spent some forty
years on recreating in the palace the spirit of antiquity. He
left his mark especially on the Salle de Bal, which is known
today as the Galerie Henri II, since Henry II carried on the
formalistic plans of his father. Fontainebleau, built by Italian artists and craftsmen with Renaissance training and

supported by the largesse of French kings, gave further evidence of the abandonment of the Gothic. The well-planned paganism in the depiction of Fontainebleau's Greek and Roman deities might have been a shock for those brought up in "the shadow of churches."[2]

The chateau of Chambord, erected for Francis I by ten thousand Italian workmen out of the facile and yielding stone of the Loire Valley, was a spot for royal relaxation for over two centuries (Figure 17). Its main hall had in its ceiling more than three hundred of Francis I's salamanders and its general atmosphere was one of pleasant living, in spite of its pseudo-defensive towers which were in reality gracious points for viewing the countryside rather than crenelated turrets of war.* Rabelais had Chambord (as well as Chantilly and other chateaux in mind) when he evolved his idealized Abbaye de Thélème, which stressed genteel living rather than monastic discipline in Gothic cells. Rabelais' abbaye built in newly renovated antique style did, indeed, rival Chambord and Chantilly in spaciousness: the Abbaye de Thélème, in full expression of Rabelaisian enthusiasm, contained 9332 rooms. Rabelais' Oracle of the Holy Bottle at the end of his book showed even more formalized ornamentation and allegiance to Renaissance and antique concepts of architecture. The oracle was set in proper elegance to make a temple to Bacchus; one of the rooms inside contained an alabaster fountain surrounded by seven antique columns of blue sapphire, hyacinth, diamond, ruby, emerald, agate, and "transparent selenite of the whiteness of beryl." Renaissance and ancient architectural motifs were frequently reflected in the prose and poetry of the period, though not always with the imaginative grandeur of Rabelais; Jean Lemaire de Belges de-

---

* Turrets were attached to many Renaissance chateaux as a suggestion of antiquity of family.

cribed a temple to Venus in 1511, and Clément Marot built a poetic one to Cupid a few years later.[3]

As the age of formalism proceeded into the seventeenth century, Gothic architecture received further condemnation. Even Molière took time to join in the assault with a poem entitled *La gloire du Val-de-Grâce*, published in 1669. It was a series of verses honoring Molière's friend, the painter Pierre Mignard, who had embellished the interior of the dome of Val-de-Grâce (Figure 18), the church erected by Anne of Austria in appreciation of divine termination of her condition of sterility. According to Molière, Val-de-Grâce was an "august construction, a majestic temple, the worthy fruit of twenty years of sumptuous endeavor." By the brush of Mignard the interior of the dome had been fashioned into a "gentle concert, a handsome ensemble," where everything was "seasoned with the salt of our ancient graces, and not with the faded taste of Gothic ornaments: these odious monsters of ignorant centuries which the torrents of barbarism produced, when their currents, inundating almost all the earth, made a mortal war on politeness and, beating down the ramparts of magnificent Rome, moved in their onrush to stifle the fine arts." René Rapin gave support to Molière's opinion when he said in 1674, in comparing an epic with a "grand palace" —they both needed "uniformity of design" and "proportion in their parts"—that "this barbarous flavor of the Gothic" had spread over all the arts in Europe. La Bruyère spoke his mind on the Gothic in 1687 in connection both with writing and building: "We have had to do with literary style what was done with architecture: the Gothic concept, which a barbarous taste introduced for palaces and temples, has been entirely abandoned; the Doric, Ionic, and Corinthian have been brought back." The classic restoration, according to La Bruyère, is now visible in "our porticoes and in our peristyles."[4]

Fénelon, who did not understand too well the purpose of flying buttresses, opposed in his discourse to the French Academy in 1693 what he considered the useless frills of Gothic architecture: "The boldest and most intricate creations in Gothic style are not the best. It is not necessary to include in an edifice any detail destined simply for ornament; but, always aiming at beauty of proportion one should turn into ornamentation all the parts necessary for the support of the edifice." Fénelon was not willing to let the matter rest with this commentary but came back to it in a letter to the French Academy in 1715, not long before he died: "The inventors of the architecture that is called Gothic, and which undoubtedly originated with the Arabs, thought surely that they had surpassed the architects of Greece." But, Greek architecture was balanced in its proportions, while "the Gothic architect lifts on very thin pillars an immense vault that rises to the skies. One would think that everything is going to fall, but it has lasted for several centuries. The stone seems to be cut out of cardboard; everything is open to daylight, everything is up in the air. Is it not natural that the first Gothic architects flattered themselves with having surpassed in their vain refinement the simplicity of the Greeks?" For Fénelon, who lived during the peak of the era of formalism in France, the very features most admired in Gothic structures today, were trivial and unregulated excrescences.[5]

Many objections would have been raised to Gothic architecture during the sixteenth and seventeenth centuries on the basis of its lack of symmetry. Criticism of this type would scarcely seem valid now, but the many projections, the apparently detached arches, and the at times unmatching spires of Gothic cathedrals were displeasing to a formalistic eye. Symmetry was definitely an attribute of classicism; in the words of H. Havard, symmetry "rules the process of building in the classic style." A primary element of symmetry—and one admired by ancient Greek, Roman, and formalistic Frenchman—was the column, which when repeated over and over with exactitude became a harmonious colonnade. Montesquieu in his *Essai sur le goût* of the eighteenth century spoke of the "pleasures of symmetry" and the satisfactions it gave the human spirit; on this point he made a wise comment: "From here evolves a general rule: everywhere that symmetry is useful to the soul and can aid its functions, it is satisfying to it; but wherever symmetry is not needed, it is dull because it takes away variety." For Montesquieu, things that are seen successively should have variety, while those that are viewed as a whole —like a building, or a garden, or a temple—should have symmetry since it pleases the soul to encompass easily the whole object. Thus a building with one wing would be out of balance and displeasing, even as a body with one arm. If the age of formalism in France was the age of the symmetrical, the later eighteenth century will have leanings toward the asymmetrical. However, the most symmetrical and classical structure in Paris, the church of the Madeleine, is considered by some contemporary Frenchmen to look exactly like a box of cigars.[6]

If the formalistic French rejected Gothic architecture as being barbarous and undisciplined, they did the same thing for a lineal descendent of the Gothic, the baroque. What has been said for literature during the period from the sixteenth century into the eighteenth century can in large part be said for art and buildings: in these fields of creativity, too, the French were unreceptive to the effusion and diffusion of the baroque. The Renaissance style, as has already been seen in the chateaux of the first half of the sixteenth century, derived from the Italians; but, when Italian architects in later decades began to add broken façades and irregular oddments, the French were unwilling to go along with such disunity. They preferred structures that were "directly inspired by the antique," as a mark of their native formalism, and left the flamboyance of the baroque to other nations of Europe—to Spain, Italy, and the Low Countries. Even an interpreter of the baroque like Victor L. Tapié tended to agree: "French architecture has often adopted an attitude based on soberness and severity, which one likes to call classic" and which is "without any surcharge of decorations." From this classic essence, he said, "has been evolved the principle of a quality of elegance, in which French good taste attests its sense of measure and self-control." A near deification of the age of French classicism by critics of the nineteenth and early twentieth centuries has caused many later analysts, in a reversed swing of the pendulum, to minimize this formalistic period in art and letters as a mere contrary phase of a "generalized baroque" in Europe. However, it would be hard for any thoughtful Frenchman today to accept such a casual dismissal of the seventeenth-century classical period, "this *fait majeur*" in his cultural history.[7]

Several architectural devices, generally listed in the category of the baroque, had little appeal for sober French tastes. A smooth and unencumbered wall, for example, would in the baroque manner be indented with niches and bits of statuary (a legacy from the Gothic). An entrance façade might have arches and columns on different levels. As for the columns, instead of having the simple majesty of a Greek or Roman original, they might be twisted and convoluted after the manner of the baldaquin of Saint Peter's in Rome. Water in movement, as has been suggested, is supposed to be in its rippling instability completely symptomatic of the baroque; an Ionic column reflected in this changing water would be a baroque column, and a Renaissance façade so mirrored would become a baroque façade. A Renaissance interior might well be a circle, while a baroque interior would tend to be an oval, thus scattering concentration. A simple jet of water rising and falling back in a clean line would belong to the Renaissance, but a plume of spray diffused like a peacock's tail would be baroque. Carved garlands of flowers, fruits, or foliage over an entrance door might be classified as baroque. In any event, none of these structural processes that destroyed unity was very attractive to the formal French. Paris was barely marked architecturally by the baroque, though some of the large town houses built in the Marais quarter during the seventeenth century had a goodly amount of carved decorations at their entrances. Some have seen in the basilica of Notre Dame des Victoires, begun in 1629 under Louis XIII, both ugliness and the baroque. And the façade of Anne of Austria's church of Val-de-Grâce (Figure 18) has been called baroque; but the construction as a whole an "église romaine."[8]

The high priest of the baroque was the seventeenth-century Italian sculptor and designer Bernini, whose ideas were paralleled by those of his great rival, Borromini. If Paris is devoid of many evidences of the baroque, the cities of Italy, especially Rome, still reveal the nonclassical architectural elaborations of Bernini and Borromini; and Quatremère de Quincy, the eighteenth-century critic of buildings and design, thought that Guarini's church in Turin was the essence of the baroque. The contemporary *baroquiste* Jean Rousset has stated that through the creations of Bernini, Borromini, and their allies one "can seize a pure and unarguable definition of the baroque." For Rousset the perfect approach to the baroque would be by way of a Bernini fountain, though the transfer of such an impression to literature would be far from "unarguable." But there would be no argument about the colorful magnificence of Bernini's fountains, one of the finest examples of which is his Fountain of Four Rivers in the Piazza Navona in Rome. The fact that he has blended together four great rivers of the world creates a torrential diffusion; a stone lion drinking comfortably out of one of them adds an unexpected touch of contrast. A delight-fully intimate Bernini fountain is the one of the sinking boat in Rome's Piazza di Spagna. The semi-sunken stone craft (it looks like a rowboat) rests in water that is constantly vi-brating in small waves, partially caused by liquid spoutings from the mouths of two carved faces, one at each end of the boat, enclosed in circles made by the rays of the sun. Under the prow and stern of the boat are carved escutcheons over which stone flies are crawling.[9]

None of these intriguing combinations made much impres-sion on the French, and neither did Bernini despite his repu-tation of being the Michelangelo of his time. It is true that Bernini was invited to France and given almost a royal recep-tion; and he made a bust of Louis XIV in 1665. Yet his major plans for design on French soil ran into French formal-istic conservatism and were never put into effect. His proj-ects for the renovation of the Louvre were grandiose and elaborate, and would undoubtedly have resulted in a most ostentatious palace; but they required the almost total destruc-tion of the historic Louvre, and were therefore rejected. The suggestions of Claude Perrault—the doctor turned archi-tect and disciple of Vitruvius—were then accepted and the result was Perrault's sober and classical colonnade. Bernini was accorded critical admiration, nevertheless, on into the eighteenth century. Quatremère de Quincy gave a full story of his career in Italy and his sojourn in France, which latter detail of history was derived from Charles Perrault, the lit-erary brother of Claude. After the abandonment of the or-nate visions of Bernini, it was decided that "one would follow the plan of Claude Perrault, the author of the famous peri-style of the Louvre." During the period of French formalism baroque concepts of architecture had little chance of success. Only in temporary structures and changing settings would much evidence of them be found. For illustration, the décor of the machine plays of Mazarin—which were set by the

Italian technician Giacomo Torelli—would involve gods coming out of clouds and wavy seas inhabited by dragons. Also, such an entree as that of Louis XIV and Marie-Thérèse in 1660 might have some arches and floats that were ostentatiously baroque. But the permanent structures in Paris, with which the formal Frenchman was destined to spend his life, reflected a classical sobriety.[10]

The showplace of formalistic building outside Paris, which has caused the French of all succeeding centuries (except during the moment of the Revolution) to beam with pride, was Versailles. The chevalier de Méré compared it to the Louvre, in 1676 before Versailles was finished: "The Louvre is larger than Versailles but Versailles is more beautiful, more noble, more satisfying than the Louvre, and indeed reflects more completely that veritable grandeur which is pleasing to persons of good taste." The early beginnings of Versailles around 1670 revealed a touch of the Italianate and the doctrines of Bernini, but Louis XIV really did not want a baroque chateau, so he turned toward the sober and majestic ideas of native designers like Perrault, Le Vau, and Mansart for later construction; to the dignified Charles Le Brun for interior decoration; and to the impeccable André Le Nôtre for the grandiose scheme of the gardens. The result of their endeavors stands today as the very "model of a French palace," despite its near destruction by Revolutionaries in their irritation at the idea of royalty. The Academician Pierre Gaxotte has said recently: "Versailles is one of the noblest places of the world, the most beautiful artistic accomplishment of modern civilization, one of the masterpieces of the genius of France." This could scarcely be called an understatement, but the impressive and formalistic dignity of Versailles makes it valid. The great palace unquestionably symbolizes at the same time the minimizing of baroque art in France and an inborn allegiance to classical reserve. It would be repetitious to enumerate the many features that make up its tranquil majesty. But it is an experience for Frenchman and foreigner alike to stand today in the dusk of the evening by the *bassin* of Latona on the upper terrace, and look toward the darkened and regular façade of the palace stretching out for hundreds of meters. In the midst of the nearly awesome silence a light appears in a window of the second story—this is a ceremonial of sound and light wherein Versailles tells its own history—and the voice of the dying Louis XIV, that most formal of French monarchs, gives advice to his great-grandson (the future Louis XV) concerning the responsibilities of a king.[11]

The buildings inside and outside Paris, during the period of French formalism, in order to enhance their dignity needed to have around them gardens of proper design. A major change took place in the sixteenth century in regard to the relation between house and garden. The fortified chateaux of the Middle Ages were detached from their gardens which were normally situated beyond the ramparts. The terrain for the flowers and plants would frequently be surrounded by a high wall; it will be recalled that in the popular medieval narrative poem, *Le roman de la rose*, the lover had to peer over a wall on a bright May morning to see the superb symbol of love, the rose. In such an enclosure there would be birds and butterflies in the air, and a mixture of fruit trees, herbs and medicinal plants, flowers and shrubs on the ground. There were squares and borders, but vegetables and flowers were not as distinctly separated as would happen later in the sixteenth century; and until around 1500 plants used just for ornamentation were scarcely known. Also, gardens from the sixteenth century on into the eighteenth century emphasized, as might be expected, greater formality of structure. An important feature differentiating a Renaissance garden from its medieval counterpart was its intimate relation to the chateau to which it was attached: the chatelain and his lady could pass easily from a gallery to a terrace to a pleasant promenade in the garden. Francis I liked to walk in the gardens of Fontainebleau after his noonday meal: during this interval he was likely to be in a pleasant mood and accept new ideas (like Guillaume Budé's proposal for the foundation of the Collège de France) or listen to feminine blandishments. And the duke of Buckingham supposedly seemed most attractive to Anne of Austria while they were promenading through a garden.

At the end of the sixteenth century appeared a lengthy tome of some nine hundred pages, Olivier de Serres' *Le théâtre d'agriculture et mesnage des champs*, in which complete instructions were given for the building of a gentleman's house and garden. The work was sufficiently popular to have had six editions by 1646, and must have been something of a manual for its time. The whole of its sixth book, or some two hundred pages, is devoted to gardens and bears the subtitle: "Gardening: herbage and vegetables; herbs and odoriferous flowers; medicinal herbs; fruits; saffran, linen, and hemp." Serres obviously has left out very little, though the "pleasure garden" is a prime object of his attention. The many engravings in his work give a very good concept of what a gentleman's garden should be; its formality of design is indicated on Serres' title page for his sixth book where an engraving (Figure 19) shows an arrangement of the beds and borders in proper balance and equilibrium. Also included in the work are pictures of the gardens of the Tuileries and Saint-Germain-en-Laye, with royal initials sometimes attached. He illustrates what he calls a "squared compartment" and a "bar-long" (oblong) bed (Figure 20 a,b). Serres' conclusion to his instructions for the well-designed and genteel garden is delightful: "These are the ornaments of the pleasure garden, destined for the satisfaction of the sight; pleasing also to the spirit are the sweet and precious odors coming from the infinity of herbs and flowers that one has chosen;

it is to such rewarding labor that an intelligent man lends himself gladly to relieve the serious problems of life." Ideally, a gentleman should lay out his garden in proper form, and then work in it himself.[12]

A garden a bit too extensive to be maintained by one gentleman in his spare time was that of the chateau of Beauregard (Figure 21), built in the region of Loir-et-Cher around the middle of the sixteenth century. It was constructed for Jean du Thier, one of Henry II's secretaries of state, who undoubtedly had a large enough household to keep the place up. Though Beauregard lacked the size and pretentiousness of a royal chateau, it reflects a formal precision of planning and setting. Unless the engraver has drawn too greatly on his imagination (he has said in the upper left-hand corner of the plate that he has shown the "elevation of the building in the direction of the vines"), Beauregard had its trees, walls, and garden arranged in the most regularized fashion. As for the garden, it has been described as being "quite refined." The four "squared compartments" are in two designs and match diagonally—which would give symmetry along with a little variety. The trees that rim the four squares might seem a trifle large, but they are something of a connecting link with the trees carefully planted in quincunx at the rear of the garden. The two colonnades with portals are almost too formalistic a touch for a relatively small chateau like Beauregard; but they do form effective lines of demarcation between the trees in back and the trees and vines at the front. The two colonnades are connected by rather low walls, giving the garden a slight medieval flavoring. The whole garden is somewhat detached from the chateau after the fashion of the Middle Ages and is readily approachable only through one gate in the wall. There is also a medieval touch in the octagonal tower in the courtyard of the chateau (at the center of the engraving). However, Jean du Thier had fewer guardsmen around him than would be found at the Louvre or Fontainebleau, so walls and towers were a protection against night prowlers. The plot for the vegetable garden, separate from the "pleasure garden," can be observed in the rear of the right wing of the chateau—a division more in keeping with the sixteenth and seventeenth centuries than the Middle Ages. Beauregard looks as though it would have been an attractive abode for one of the King's secretaries of state; and its garden is adequately formal in the best spirit of the Renaissance.[13]

It is difficult to examine any aspect of French formalism from the sixteenth on into the eighteenth century without spending some time at the great chateau of Chantilly. The charming Beauregard in comparison is not much more than a neat and well-planned playhouse. As for the gardens of Chantilly in the sixteenth century, during the time of the first occupancy of the chateau by the Montmorency, they were in an incomplete and confused state. However, with the Condé family in possession in the seventeenth and eighteenth centuries Chantilly was continually and formally embellished, as can be seen from Perelle's engraving (Figure 4), one of a series in homage to "monsieur le Prince," the Great Condé. The ample amount of space surrounding the chateau is visible in the Perelle composition, much of which terrain is given over to formalized planting and gardens, and to a lagoon extensive enough for a ship to sail on it (the lagoon was fed by a vigorous stream of water that flowed through the grounds of Chantilly). The formal gardens occupy three primary plots, two of which are in harmonious balance with an arm of the lagoon. These latter two are completely identical in design; the five fountains in each garden all have single jets of water which rise perpendicularly and fall straight back into four circular and one rounded "barlong" basins, without any baroque ovals or aquatic diffusion. Piganiol de la Force, who published a multivolumed *Description historique de la ville de Paris* in 1742, had a great deal to say about Chantilly. On the matter of the chateau's gardens, he remarked: "The gardens are of a greaty beauty and the effects are admirable. A whole volume would be necessary to make an exact description of them." Not much remains today of the formal and grandiose design, imagined by Le Nôtre, of the gardens of Chantilly except some long lines of perspectives, illustrated expecially by two avenues of plane trees called the *Allées des Philosophes*.[14]

The most complete and intact gardens of Le Nôtre for present-day eyes to see are those of Vaux-le-Vicomte, the domain that was built and lost by Fouquet, Louis XIV's disgraced superintendent of finances. Some idea of the architecture of the "maison de Vaux le Vicomte" and a partial view of its gardens may be gained from Perelle's engraving (Figure 5), made, as can be learned from the legend underneath, after Fouquet's fall from favor. A better concept of the extent of the gardens at Vaux-le-Vicomte can be derived from a contemporary aerial photograph which shows them almost down to the lagoon (Figure 6). From this photograph may be determined the harmony and symmetry of Le Nôtre's over-all scheme. Le Vau, Le Brun, and Le Nôtre collaborated to produce this masterpiece of building and terrain; the whole complex of construction was completed in 1661, "with extraordinary promptitude and expenditure." The gardens were among the most majestic that had ever been built in France; and they contained a greater profusion of statuary than had been employed up to that time. As can be seen from the plates, Le Nôtre's plan was rigorously regular, with the jets of water and basins simple and unruffled; but the first two parterres below the broad terrace of the chateau are interlaced with a running filagree of trimmed boxwood to give a touch of variety to regularity. Vaux-le-Vicomte was justly renowned in its own day, and remains a point of pilgrimage for a twentieth-century voyager. There is a lift to the spirit for the wanderer who picks his way through the calm and correct grandeur of Le Nôtre's creation, an expanse that could not be wrapped around with a wall like the plot at Beauregard. Nor are the gardens of Vaux-le-Vicomte so extensive, like Versailles, as to be incomprehensible except in segments. They are a fine example of Aristotle's golden mean, and in their formal perfection are satisfying to the soul.

The startling panorama of Versailles provides a history of French gardening from the seventeenth to the nineteenth century, from Le Nôtre to the royal bosket of Louis XVIII. Worthy of special designation from the formalistic age are the lengthy perspectives (up to five miles) and quiet reflections on liquid surfaces* of Le Nôtre, the pavilions of Mansart, and the "concerting harmony" of the statues laid out in balancing proportions by Le Brun. A twentieth-century commentary on the external terrain runs as follows: "Versailles is the most beautiful, the most lofty, the most complete lesson on gardening that exists in the world." A relatively small detail from the pompous grandeur of Versailles will illustrate its horticultural regularity: namely, the vegetable garden of Louis XIV (Figure 22). As can be seen from the engraving, the *Jardin potager du Roy* was no backyard patch of lettuce to be cultivated by the King when he came home from the office. According to the scale in *toises* (a *toise* was the equivalent of about two yards) at the bottom of the plate, this vegetable garden measured around 300 by 250 yards or something like nine football fields. The harmony of its over-all design, with slight variations in the interior arrangements of some of the squares, is immediately obvious. A full explanation is given on each side of the engraving of the garden's location at Versailles (it was "between the piece of water for the Swiss and the stag park") and the

---

* Le Nôtre had as his collaborator the Italian Fr. Francini who was responsible for the waters of Versailles. The Francini family had been in service to royalty in France since the early sixteenth century.

contents of the various squares. That it is a royal garden is made clear at once since the first numbered indication on the legend is the "entrance of the King," a short tree-lined avenue on the right of the picture. Lower down in the right-hand corner is the "common entrance" next to the gardener's house and that of his assistants. In the center of the plot is the "grand square or garden of *gros légumes*"; and in the center of the grand square is a familiarly formal circular *bassin* from the center of which a jet of water rises straight up and falls straight down (with a slight allowance for windage). It is all quite symmetrical.[15]

In the Jardin potager du Roy all the vegetables, plants, bushes, shrubs, and trees associated with one another according to their natures, sizes, and personal idiosyncracies; and they were all serviced by properly spaced "reservoirs for sprinkling" when the weather was dry. For example, the grand square had its various parterres filled with "cooking herbs and vegetables" and rimmed with trees of correct size and spacing. The smaller squares surrounding the grand square were filled with shrubs and fruit trees of different sizes, "according to the rarity and use of the fruits that they produce." The borders in the garden were lined with dwarf trees and contained "creeping fruits and vegetables* for salads and desserts." As a general policy, the espaliered trees were "exposed to the sun according to the needs of each tree." The eighteenth parterre in the lower left-hand corner of the engraving is made up of "natural and espaliered fig bushes." And the two parterres numbered nineteen (since they are of exactly the same design) are filled with "espaliered peach trees and asparagus beds." The whole wall surrounding the grand square was decorated with espaliered peach trees and pear trees. The Jardin potager du Roy was maintained "with care and according to plan"; there could

*The French on the Perelle engraving is *fruits reptiles et légumes.*

20. A "squared compartment" and a "bar-long" garden

19. Title page of Serres' *Le théâtre d'agri-culture et mesnage des champs*

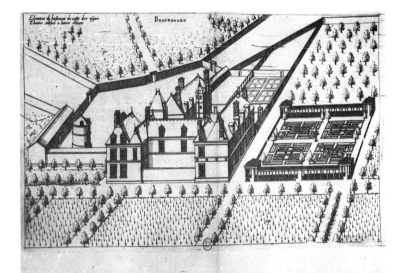

*21.* Garden of Beauregard

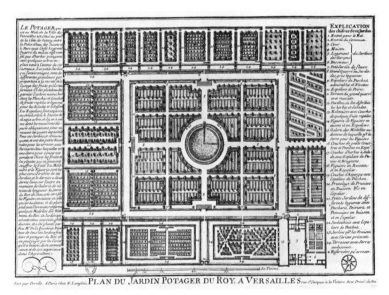

*22.* The vegetable garden of Louis XIV

scarcely have been a more correct collection of fruits and vegetables.

In the present century, the name most naturally associated with a garden in the age of French formalism is that of Le Nôtre. This great and precise designer, who left his mark on Vaux-le-Vicomte, Versailles, and many other seventeenth-century gardens, was not without renown in his own day. One of his most solid admirers was Louis XIV himself. Dangeau told an incident concerning the last days of Le Nôtre who died in 1700 near the age of eighty-eight: "M. Le Nôtre, illustrious in his profession because of his gardens, before his death came to see the King"; Louis XIV received him with pleasure, provided him with a "rolling chair" like his own, and they took a promenade together through the gardens of Versailles. Le Nôtre was accorded further praise in the eighteenth century by the chevalier de Jaucourt, who wrote the article on gardens in the *Encyclopédie*; Jaucourt is not uncertain in his opinions: "The French, so long buried in barbarism, had no inkling of an idea on the decoration of gardens or on gardening before the century of Louis XIV. It is under this prince that this art was in a sense created; it was perfected as for utility by La Quintinie* and as for decorative charm by Le Nôtre." Le Nôtre was a "creative genius" and nothing has been constructed since, according to Jaucourt, like the gardens of the Tuileries (Le Nôtre redesigned them), the terraces of Saint-Germain-en-Laye, the natural porticoes of Marly, or the trellises of Chantilly. André Le Nôtre (1613-1700) grew up in an ambiance of royal gardens, since his father, Jean Le Nôtre, was the chief gardener at the Tuileries under Louis XIV; the Tuileries thus became the first object of the son's creative and regularizing desires. He changed the narrow *allées* of Catherine de' Medici's Tui-

*La Quintinie was the creator of the Jardin potager du Roy at Versailles. Jaucourt gives him credit for discovering the art of pruning trees so that they might grow "fruitfully."

leries and gave the garden both more equilibrium and more aeration, and more of the general appearance that it has at the present time. Le Nôtre, who was an architect as well as planner of gardens, liked "levels" (with steps leading to and from them) and uncluttered spaces. One of his principles was, therefore, not to have a clump of trees too close to a building since a cramped feeling resulted from such a positioning. Possibly the cardinal principle of Le Nôtre in the matter of garden design was to divide the terrain lengthwise in half by a long *allée* with a perspective prolonged to the horizon; and to put a transversal *allée* across the garden, dividing it in half and carrying the eye to a salient point of perspective like a statue or a tree. These concepts are still to be seen at Vaux-le-Vicomte, and, most grandiosely, at Versailles.[16]

A more intimate picture of Le Nôtre's genius would have been the gardens of Clagny, the chateau that Louis XIV had built near Versailles for madame de Montespan after the plans of Mansart. Unfortunately, nothing remains today of this example of Le Nôtre's craftsmanship. As for the chateau itself, Piganiol de la Force called it the "most regularly beautiful in Europe," both in exterior and interior. Madame de Sévigné in a letter to her daughter described the gardens at Clagny, which were evidently finished before the chateau: "The gardens are complete; you know the manner of Le Nôtre. He has left a dark spot of a wood which is very good; it is a little orange grove in large boxes; you walk around in it; there are paths where you are in the shade; and in order to hide the boxes there are palisades on each side shoulder high, all blooming with tuberoses, roses, jasmine, carnations. It is assuredly the most beautiful, the most surprising, the most enchanting novelty that can be imagined. This wood is much admired." Here is Le Nôtre a little more relaxed and less formal, when he is producing a more personal garden for a favorite of the King.[17]

The techniques and materials of what has since been called a formal French garden evolved in the sixteenth and seventeenth centuries; the full pomp came after 1650. The processes of getting adequate water to a garden were improved in the sixteenth century, due in large part to techniques brought in from Italy. At the beautiful chateau of Chenonceaux, the object of contention between Diane de Poitiers and Catherine de' Medici, was probably installed the first jet of water. It is mentioned by Androuet du Cerceau in his two-volume study of "the most excellent buildings in France" (published between 1576 and 1579) as an "invention." The jet of water falling back into a circular basin, as has been observed in several engravings, remained a favorite motif in formalistic French gardens for nearly two centuries—despite such ornate creations as the *bassins* of Neptune and Latona at Versailles. On the matter of growing materials, the sixteenth century did not care for boxwood, though artichokes became a delicacy for vegetable gardens. As for boxwood, Claude Mollet, one of the gardeners at the Tuileries, said in 1652 that in earlier times "the boxwood plant was used very little because few persons of quality wished to have boxwood planted in their gardens." Mollet did much to change this point of view, and advised the use of "big boxwood" and mentioned a more delicate "type of boxwood which is dwarf." In application of these theories, he put a great deal of boxwood into the Tuileries and employed the dwarf variety for complicated designs inside a parterre, a procedure that was followed by Le Nôtre at Vaux-le-Vicomte. As a result of Mollet's ideas the gardens of Saint-Germain-en-Laye were, in their turn, filled with boxwood. And, too, the more formal alignment of trees came in for definite consideration during the seventeenth century: a grand avenue with a double or triple rank of trees, properly pruned, was deemed appropriate to a royal house. All of these formalistic concepts of planting and pruning are still visible on many parts of the French landscape. But as the eighteenth century ran into its second half the formal garden after the manner of Le Nôtre began to fall into disfavor in France.* Even a correctly designed vegetable garden could incur disapproval; the marquis d'Argenson said in 1749 that he had just visited a certain courtier's chateau where there was a superb jardin potager—"and each vegetable worth a sou in the street market must cost more than a crown in a garden built at such great expense."[18]

A pleasant device of formalism and pseudo-ruralism, in between the gardens and the main chateau, was the milk house at Chantilly. It was evidently a popular spot with the lofty ladies who visited the chateau, since in Piganiol de la Force's story of Paris and its environs there is a full description of it. This *laiterie* was something that could have come out of fiction: it had an anteroom "paved and decorated with porcelain," a round table of marble in the main milk room, and the constant tinkling of water from dainty cascades and fountains. The picture of the "charming little edifice" as it is drawn in Piganiol de la Force's book goes in part as follows: "Its plan is circular and it is covered by a dome pierced with round windows. In the interior, running around this pavilion, is set a marble shelf high enough to lean on. A drain is hollowed out along its border to carry away the water from several little cascades falling from porcelain masks, the sound of which is quite agreeable. In the middle of this little salon is a round marble table pierced in the center from where there rises a little spray of water, the noise of which joined to that of the cascades makes a sweet and charming murmur. Often the princesses come down to this spot to drink milk and beat butter." This ornate and formal little rendezvous for royal milkmaids might well have been taken out of some "romance of fiction"; it resembles Rabelais' Oracle of the Holy Bottle. But there was also historical and regal

*The influence of English and Chinese gardens will be taken up in Chapter X, *Formalism Declines*.

precedent for the Chantilly milk house: Charles IX had one at Fontainebleau in 1563 decorated with the paintings of Niccolò dell' Abbate, and Marie Antoinette would have a very stylish one later at the Petit Trianon.[19]

Buildings and gardens during the age of formalism were frequently used in literary comparisons and analogies, even though architecture was placed by such a critic as Charles Batteux a little below poetry and music. Bouhours, it will be recalled, believed that exactitude and regularity in "works of the mind" were comparable to these same qualities in buildings and paintings; in either case, they were qualities necessary to the creation of something "august and grand." Le Moyne said in the very beginning of his *Dissertation du poème épique* that an epic poem should resemble a "great palace,"* and not be like the house of some bourgeois. The dissertation concluded with the parallel being repeated of the epic and great palace; and in the opinion of Le Moyne, just as the architect should place the plan of his building at its entrance, so should the poet preface his epic with the "argument." In a shorter poem called the "Palais de Fortune" Le Moyne described a formless abode belonging to the variable and fickle Lady Fortune. The garden is altogether irregular, "without order and without plan," and constructed according to the dictates of chance. The trees are in total disarray as to shape and line, as though they had been struck by a "whirlwind descended from a cloud." Then the whole garden is invaded without warning by a growth of mushrooms, "formed out of decay," which rises higher than the ill-assorted trees. It was hardly a garden that would have appealed to Le Nôtre. But gardening and poetry had gone hand in hand since the early years of French formalism. In his abbreviated art of poetry of 1565, Ronsard urged the hopeful composer to be laborious in "correcting and trim-

---

*A point made earlier, as has been noted, by René Rapin.

ming your verses" just as the gardener prunes his vine "when he sees it weighed down with useless branches." And Vauquelin de la Fresnaye at the end of the sixteenth century in his *Art poétique* said that poetry is like a garden and should be laid out with symmetry and in proper form.[20]

Thus buildings, gardens, poetry, painting, and the other arts blended together to create the substance of formalism. A salon, with a parquet floor of correct geometrical design and containing sofas properly covered with the tapestry of Beauvais, might be the setting for the reading of a new tragedy. Or a garden, with a few chairs drawn under the shade of some correctly pruned trees, could be the scene of a discussion of Descartes' philosophy. A classical repose pervaded the atmosphere: Poussin and Le Brun were better understood than the spots of color of the Flemish Rubens. The poet and critic Urbain Chevreau paid a visit toward the end of the seventeenth century to the palace of the duc de Richelieu and made the comment: "In whatever direction one may turn, there is seen only marble and porphyry, only statues and busts from ancient Greece and from Italy." In a more personal and intimate vein madame de Sévigné spoke of madame de la Fayette's garden as it was at the end of May in 1672. For madame de Sévigné it was the "prettiest thing in the world," with its abundance of flowers and their fragrances. She spent many evenings in it since madame de la Fayette could not ride in a carriage. They were undoubtedly in the company of the duc de La Rochefoucauld, whose precisely worded but sardonic philosophy would have offered a contrast to the scented air.[21]

A lingering blend of poetry and gardens can be enjoyed by Parisians today in the Jardin des Poètes at the Porte d'Auteuil. This calm and modestly formal nook was dedicated in 1954 by the Société des Poètes, in the midst of the traffic and hubbub around one of the important gates of Paris. Poets who wrote of flowers, from Jean Froissart in the fourteenth century to the comtesse de Noailles (who died in 1933), have some of their verses inscribed on a stone plaque in their own bit of terrain planted with the appropriate type of bloom. The verse from Froissart runs in his phrasing: *Sur toutes flours tient on la rose belle*, "Among all the flowers one clings to the beauty of the rose." Around a curve in the gravelly path (paths of sand and gravel pellets were approved for gardens back in the sixteenth century) is a chiseled portion of Ronsard's famous Anacreontic ode to Cassandra, which compares her fragile beauty to that of the rose.

# ⟨ IX ⟩

# THE GREAT CLASSICISTS

IF AN allegiance to formalism was evident, from the sixteenth into the eighteenth century, in the visual arts, the
plastic arts, and in the processes of everyday living in France,
it was possibly more visible in the writing of the period. And
it was most visible among the great classicists, the *grands
classiques* of the age of Louis XIV; with them the essence of
classicism and the clothing of formalism were combined at
their best. It was a moment in cultural history that was a few
years later catalogued by Voltaire as being the highest of
the four great peaks of civilization in the Western world—
the age of Pericles in Greece, the age of Augustus Caesar in
Rome, the Renaissance, and the age of Louis XIV. Even
when due allowance is made for Voltaire's nationalistic bias,
there can be little argument that the years between, approximately, 1660 and 1690 in France were properly grandiose for
literature and the criticism thereof. The school of 1660—so
called because it was in this year that Louis XIV took active
control of his domain and with it the patronage of arts and
letters—marked the full growth of classical and formalistic
seeding that had been done in the 1500's. The seventeenth
century thus saw the well-pruned fruition of plantings that
had grown somewhat tumultuously earlier in the verse of
Clément Marot or the prose of Rabelais. The Pléiade around

1550 had recommended the grafting of antique shafts onto native French trunks; by the end of the seventeenth century such a blending of ancient and national seed had produced in France hybridized and correctly formed giants like Racine and Bossuet.[1]

It has come to be fashionable in the last twenty-five years to minimize the regularities of the *grands classiques* and to speak of the freedom of French classicism; or to consider the period of Louis XIV a rule-ridden irritant against the broad sweep of untrammeled creativity developing in other countries of Europe. A part of this attitude has been a reaction against the nineteenth-century deification of the great classicists by many critics in France, England, and the United States. The pendulum at the present time has swung too far in the other direction and the tendency to regard the primary French classical age as a "classicizing" section of an uninhibited artistic whole in Europe does an injustice to an era that was splendid in its own right. Many French scholars and critics have today joined their voices to the foreign chorus that has sought to reduce "the importance and autonomy of French classicism." It has been pointed out, and rightly, in recent years that such classicists as Pascal and Molière were not subservient to the rigors of the rules; yet Pascal wrote in a style that was classically unencumbered and the larger plays of Molière in language and precision of characterization fitted smoothly into the mannered ritual of Louis XIV's court. The great classicists —Racine, Boileau, Molière, La Fontaine, and Bossuet, supported by figures like Pascal, La Rochefoucauld, Fénelon, La Bruyère, and madame de Sévigné—in their respect for rules and form remain the great classicists. Their compositions, many of which continue to be the basis of the cultivated Frenchman's education, show that their creative urges were not stifled by the formalistic regulations of their time.[2]

After 1660 there was no dearth of the written word as to

the proper manner of creating poetry or prose. The earlier part of the seventeenth century had belonged primarily to the grammarians and builders of language, who gave limited emphasis to questions of style, poetic theory, and literary genres. However, by 1660 the French language had become a precise instrument capable of both nuances and clarity which needed very little further tinkering on its mechanics of structure. The critics of the school of 1660, therefore, concerned themselves for the most part with a higher level of the problems of literary creativity. It would not be exact to say that such matters as imitation, poetic inspiration, and the proprieties (*bienséances*) were left unmentioned in the sixteenth century: Sebillet spoke of divine frenzy, Du Bellay talked of proper imitation and inspiration (inspiration was not enough by itself for the writing of poetry but needed to be accompanied by hard work), and Vauquelin de la Fresnaye thought that "the proprieties should be carefully guarded in everything." And in the first part of the seventeenth century Jean Chapelain and the abbé d'Aubignac took up the question of verisimilitude (*vraisemblance*). It would be equally incorrect to suggest that criticism with the great classicists ignored completely details of grammar, words, and word order, as has already been indicated in Pascal's comparison of well-placed words with a well-placed ball in a game of jeu de paume. On the other hand, it can be justifiably maintained that the embryo of critical admiration for antiquity, existent in the sixteenth and earlier seventeenth centuries, reached its full maturity during the formal reign of Louis XIV. During the decades following Louis' triumphant entree into Paris in 1660, the formal cirtics of French classicism—men like Boileau, Racine, Bossuet, Bouhours, Rapin, Le Bossu, La Bruyère, and some others—spoke with confidence of what was on their well-disciplined minds.[3]

As a generality the critics among the great classicists

rested their case on the same monumental figures from antiquity that had been cited earlier in the sixteenth century; seventeenth-century appreciation was simply more mature. Homer remained the first captain of the Muses with Vergil as his able lieutenant; both were proper models for epic composition even though the French were singularly inept at writing epics. Aristotle was the "philosopher" who did not have to be called by name, so ultimate had become the authority of his *Poetics* over poetry and artistic creation. The lofty Renaissance position of Plato, who had really done little to defend the privilege of the poet to practice his art, declined as the essence of Aristotelian doctrine came to be better understood. Aristotle, the mudsill on which French formalistic classicism was set, was supported in critical detail by that urbane Roman, Horace, whose art of poetry was the breviary of Boileau. Other titans from ancient Greece and Rome would be brought in regularly by the school of 1660 for substantiation or illustration, as when Boileau suggested that Sophocles "increased the pomp" of tragedy. In the opinion of the critics around the *grands classiques*, those writers in other countries who have not based their works on Aristotle's *Poetics* have inevitably fallen into error, since Aristotle (said René Rapin) "is the only one that should be followed." Rapin would for his part minimize Plato's "fury," an element not submissive to rules and form, in the work of the poet. Bossuet did not have much that was favorable to say about poetry, even that of the ancients; he preferred the formal prose style of Cicero. The two Roman poets least afflicted with conceits and antitheses were, for Bossuet, Vergil and Horace—and only to them did he give his approval. On into the eighteenth century, after the Moderns had won out in their quarrel wth the Ancients and poetry was regarded as unCartesian frivolity, some writers still had respect for the Greeks and Romans. Charles Batteux said in the 1740's that he relied on the principles of imitation in the fine arts as established by the "Greek philosopher," and that these tenets had been brought on down by Horace (especially with his *ut pictura poesis*, "poetry is like a painting") and by the seventeenth-century counterpart of Horace, Boileau.[4]

Nicolas Boileau-Despréaux (1636-1711), formal and dignified in appearance (Figure 23) as well as in his literary style, was indeed the critic of the great classicists and the legislator of the French Parnassus. He was the friend of Molière, La Fontaine, and Racine—the greatest of the classicists—and sought to counsel them on the principles of regularity in their literary compositions as well as in their private lives; he was not too successful in the latter endeavor. Boileau was strategically placed both as to time and habitat in order to be the spokesman for the formality of French classicism: he lived through the golden years of the age of Louis XIV and he spent all his life in Paris and its environs—favored, pensioned, and honored by Louis (as royal historiographer) but not an active participant in the trivialities of life at Court or in the salons. Before his death at Auteuil in 1711 he made a belated effort to refute the arguments of the Moderns in a treatise which he called *Reflections on Longinus*. One of the points he made was that the writings and critical ideas of the ancients did not deserve respect because they were old but because they were good. Such a lone voice was ineffective against the resounding chorus of the Moderns (led by Fontenelle, La Motte-Houdart, and others), which left Boileau well-nigh abandoned as almost the last of the French formalists.

From the time of his first satire in 1660 (which led to the designation of the "school of 1660") until his final argument with the Moderns, Boileau never veered from a rigid and correct literary code which might be summed up as follows: literary creativity is an exact and demanding performance requiring talented practitioners; they can come nearest to perfection by following the rules and examples of the Greek and Roman past. The formalized severity of Boileau's doctrines have come under attack in our own time, and he has been accused of "having understood little of Greek antiquity, and even less of the sense of the Gothic and Christian genius"; and, he was so involved in the "precision of regularity" that he allowed in poetry "neither sufficient suppleness nor extension." All of which is a bit overdone, even though the rigors of Boileau's formalism would be admitted. It might be said in defense of the strict Boilevian program that within its framework there functioned one of France's greatest poets and her greatest writer of tragedy, Jean Racine.[5]

Boileau's critical formulas are to be discovered both in his verse—which he conceded to be difficult for him to write and sometimes as "forced" as that of Chapelain—and in his prose. The official proclamation of his principles was in the rhymed couplets of his *Art poétique* of 1674, though many of his most quoted dicta are in his satires and epistles which appeared both before and after the art of poetry. In all of these compositions Boileau reflected a language that was soberly formal as well as a series of rules that were rigidly unyielding. He fixed the vocabulary of French classicism, with such generic terms as *raison, bon sens, jugement, vérité, vraisemblance, bienséances, nature* (by which he meant human nature), and *goût* (or possibly *bon goût*, "good taste"). Throughout his writings he sought to pay proper homage to the King, as in his "Discours au Roi" of 1665; Boileau conceded along the way in this discourse that in reality he was unable to give suitably lofty praise to Louis XIV, though many feeble poets in their "pompous style" had tried it. In most delightful fashion in his second satire, Boileau, admitting once more his inadequacies as a poet, begged Molière to teach him how to rhyme; it is from this poem that comes the notable comment on a "fault-less model" for versification: if it were only a question on rhyme the facile dramatist Quinault would suffice but "the reason would choose Vergil."[6]

The formalism of Boileau was based on the deep integrity of the man: a poet who possessed the correct skills of his craft would, in Boileau's opinion, be inadequate if he lacked loyalty and moral responsibility. In his fifth satire, dedicated to the marquis de Dangeau, Boileau applied the same measurement to inherited nobility: a title was an empty thing unless its holder had along with it solidity of character. And this meant correct service to the King rather than the mere occupancy of a "superb palace" or the parading around Paris in a "pompous carriage." In the eleventh satire, written to the King's counselor monsieur de Valincour, Boileau praised honor and virtue as opposed to pretense and insincerity; from this poem come the following verses:

> The truth is always master of the lie.
> In order to appear to be a man of honor one must be one,
> And never, whatever he may do, can a man here below
> Be before the eyes of the world what he is not.

Boileau even went so far in his first epistle as to advise the King not to seek conquests but rather the welfare of the people; included in these verses is the somewhat personal admonition that Louis also should take care of poets, since "it is easy for a Caesar Augustus to create a Vergil." The fourth epistle, again dedicated to the King, is more lightly formalistic. Here Boileau took proper recognition of royal victories in the field, but he would prefer that the King not win places with names like Zutphen and Hardervic since they are too hard to fit into commemorative verse. It would be much easier to give poetic attention, in best classical formality, to the "banks of the Scamander" or to the "ashes of Ilium."[7]

Boileau revealed his own dignified loyalty, in this case to Racine, in his notable seventh epistle where he sought to console the playwright for the hostile reception accorded his great tragedy *Phèdre* by a cabal of his enemies. It must be agreed that Racine through his own fickleness of friendship (especially to Molière) deserved many of his difficulties. In any event, Boileau's consolation was based on the fact that proper and formal men like the King, the Great Condé, Colbert, and La Rochefoucauld all approved of *Phèdre;* it should cause no worry if the rabble should proceed to admire "the skill of Pradon," whose *Phèdre et Hippolyte* had momentarily eclipsed Racine's masterpiece. The best of critical judgment would inevitably put *Phèdre* in its properly lofty place. Boileau consistently defended the worthy and the true, even though he thought, like Plato, that the highest aesthetic and ethical qualities would never be discovered in the lower classes. The ninth epistle contains the famous verse, "nothing is beautiful but the true, and only the true is worthy of admiration." A poet thus should not lavish his talents on an ignoble person and seek to raise him to an "august rank." On the other hand, a man of real nobility (like the Great Condé) would require a good poet to portray in formal couplets his proper grandeur. The correct master of versification would on the basis of propriety, as was suggested by Boileau in the tenth epistle, throw out of his work hyperboles, metaphors, and metonymy—these "hideous monsters" that appealed to Pradon and his ilk.[8]

The most important critical document of the formal age of French classicism was Boileau's *Art poétique,* a work that drew a great deal of its substance from Horace and one that was influential in England as well as in France. It was published on July 10, 1674 but circulated in correct literary circles around Paris before this date. Madame de Sévigné wrote to madame de Grignan on December 15, 1673: "I

dined yesterday with monsieur le Duc, monsieur de la
Rochefoucauld, madame de Thianges, madame de la
Fayette . . . at Gourville's. A toast was drunk to you and we
wished you were there; and then we listened to the
*Poétique* of Despréaux which is a masterpiece." On January 12, 1674 madame de Sévigné wrote, after a "very sad"
ball at the palace (evidently the Louvre): "Monsieur de
Pompone invited me for dinner tomorrow with him and
Despréaux, who is going to read his *Poétique*." On January 15, 1674 madame de Sévigné informed her daughter:
"I went then on Saturday to dine with monsieur de Pompone as I had mentioned to you; and afterward until five
o'clock* we were enchanted, transported, and carried away
by the perfections of the verses of the *Poétique* of Despréaux." At least two private readings, one of them almost
six months in advance, were thus held of Boileau's *Art
poétique* before its publication. Only in a precise and formal age would it have been considered "enchanting" to
listen to a treatise on poetic composition, in rigid alexandrines, as after-dinner entertainment.[9]

The *Art poétique* of Boileau laid out no easy road for the
poet; it would be better for him, if he lacked the essential
qualities for creativity, to become a good brick layer
rather than a mediocre versifier. Two basic maxims were
taken from Horace's *Ars poetica*: the necessity of long
and careful hours at work (the *festina lente*, "make haste
slowly," of Horace), and the inevitable polishing and re-
polishing of the product before it was considered finished
(Horace's *labor limae*, "the labor of the file"). Early in the
first canto Boileau advised the poet on the sober guide-
posts of *bon sens* and *raison*: "let good sense always be
blended with rhyme," be submissive to the "restraint of
reason," and "in short, love reason." Baseness should be

*This would mean five o'clock in the afternoon, since dinner at this
time in France would have been a midday meal.

avoided and the low language of the marketplace—"let us leave burlesque to the charlatans of the Pont Neuf." Verses should have a regular and smooth design, without vowels bumping one into the other; that is, there should be no hiatus, a proscription made earlier in the century by the rigid Malherbe. Boileau thought that the "pedantic display" of Ronsard (Boileau is too hard on Ronsard) had been cleared up by Malherbe, who insisted on "clarity" and persuaded the Muses to submit to "dutiful rules." Style should have the quiet dignity of a clear stream, and not be an "unbridled torrent full of gravel flowing over muddy ground"; nothing should be loosely dangling but "put in its proper place." Of the shorter poetic genres the sonnet was to be preferred to an unrestrained "Gothic idyl"; the sonnet was splendid in its rigorously "prescribed form," which Apollo himself had measured as to its "number of lines and its cadence."[10]

Tragedy and the epic were for Boileau the noble forms which he treated in the third canto of his *Art poétique*. He most probably, like Aristotle, considered tragedy artistically superior to the epic; at any rate, he had around him many fine examples of tragedy and a large collection of poor epics (like Chapelain's *La pucelle*) which he thoroughly lambasted. As for tragedy, it demanded a high order of imitation, both of nature and of classic models, and should be set in correctly "pompous verse" without any "vain exhibition of rhetoric." Displays of rhetoric would only put the spectator to sleep if the dramatist did not know how "to please and to move."* Everything should be made clear and fixed at the beginning, and the action of a year not reduced to one day; Boileau strongly supported the unities and disapproved of the lack of restriction that

*Racine said the same thing—the prime aim of tragedy is *de plaire et de toucher* in the preface of his tragedy *Bérénice*. The play was produced in 1670 and the preface added in 1671, some years earlier than Boileau's *Art poétique*.

existed "beyond the Pyrenees." And the audience should not be offered anything that is "unbelievable," since "the truth can at times lack verisimilitude"—and here Boileau makes a distinction between *vérité* and *vraisemblance*. After the religious plays of the Middle Ages, "we have seen the rebirth of Hector, Andromache, and Troy." However, the heroes of antiquity should not be reduced to the size of the sentimental gallants of the frivolous romances; they should be presented on stage with a "strict propriety." As for the epic, it had the privilege of "aggrandizing everything," and indulging in "rich and pompous" descriptions. But if the opening lines are pretentously bombastic, like "I sing of the conqueror of the conquerors of the earth," the continuation may have "the mountain producing only a mouse." It is better to begin modestly as does Vergil's *Aeneid*—"I sing of arms and this noble man" (*Arma virumque cano*)—and later add figures that are "pompous and pleasing." Boileau disapproved strongly of aimless wandering in an epic; the verses therein should have a "methodical order" like those of Homer. If the aspiring writer should be guided by an "unregulated muse" he should not pick up the epic trumpet, an instrument too imposing for his vacillating tones.[11]

For Boileau comedy also had its dignity, even though in its Greek origins it was unrefined. At its best it should reflect nature, or human society; and a writer of comedy should "study the Court, and be acquainted with the city." In its proper form comedy should not contain dirty words (*mots sales*) or low pantomime, and its actors should practice "noble badinage." Boileau, in his pronouncements, obviously had Molière in mind and his masterful portrayal of the people of the century; however, Boileau had already said that in such a farce as Molière's *Les fourberies de Scapin* he could not see "the author of *Le misanthrope*." The *Art poétique* concludes with admonitions to the writer concerning the choice of a good critic (he should be capable of advising in regard to an occasional deviation from "prescribed rules"), the responsibility of the poet to mankind, and a loftily resounding series of verses in praise of Louis XIV, the prime regulator of the whole formalistic stage. Boileau, too, was a regulator of any careless or undisciplined manipulator of verses; and his art of poetry, though hardly as enchanting as madame de Sévigné would imply, is a document with which he could be well pleased.[12]

Boileau had additional remarks to make, in his later prose writings, on proper words in their proper place. He gave an interesting commentary on the simple dignities of formalism in his *Discours sur le style des inscriptions*. A question had arisen concerning the suitable inscriptions to be put on some of Le Brun's paintings of Louis XIV's victories, in the grand gallery of Versailles. Louvois, who had succeeded Colbert as royal superintendent of buildings, asked Boileau's opinion about the language of the legends describing these grandiose canvases. The latter stated categorically that it should be short and simple, since for such a description "the pomp* and multitude of words would have no value." For example, to have a plate on a painting indicating "the crossing of the Rhine" would be much more proper than "the marvelous crossing of the Rhine," which is declamatory and would only reduce the grandeur of the King's actions. Boileau came back to "low words"—something which Homer never used—in the sixth of his *Réflexions sur Longin*. Nothing, according to Boileau, so corrupted "a discourse" as an ignoble vocabulary. Such words as *vache* and *cochon* would never fit into an elevated style (and they still would not fit); "gardeur de boeufs" would be "horrible" in French although βονκόλος ("cow-

---

*Boileau, as a generality, used *pompe* and *pompeux* in an approving sense, but here he is derogatory.

herd") would be acceptable in Greek. Charles Perrault, against whom Boileau's remarks were directed, was not conscious of these linguistic niceties when he put some passages of Homer into French. As a result many of Homer's epithets lost their magnificence when they were translated into Perrault's supposed equivalents.[13]

The formalistic critics of French classicism labored hard at defining the primary generic terms of the movement. A major effort was made to distinguish between *vérité* and *vraisemblance*, or truth and verisimilitude. Earlier in the century a fairly mechanical interpretation was given to verisimilitude, chiefly in connection with the theatre. A tragedy was supposed to have characters that were convincing in their verisimilitude, and it was supposed to be set in a verisimilar spot. Verisimilitude was in many ways an attribute of the dramatic unities, with their automatic restrictions and limitations. The subject of a tragedy was verisimilar, according to the abbé d'Aubignac in his *Pratique du théâtre* of 1647, if the concept on which it was based would be accepted by the audience without proof. This was a practical and workable definition, but it made no distinction between historical truth and idealized truth. The great classicists, and the body of critical theorists around them, were more conscious than previous interpreters of the differences Aristotle drew between the truth of the historian and the higher truth (or verisimilitude) of the poet. The critics of the school of 1660, in their desires for rigorous exactitude, were not always successful in drawing lines of demarcation but they made valiant efforts to do so. René Rapin in some ways restated in 1674 the preclassical beliefs, but then added the fuller Aristotelian principle. For Rapin, the rules—and he meant the dramatic rules—were necessary to give "verisimilitude to the story, for if there is no unity of place, or of time, or of action in the great poems there is no verisimilitude." The noble poem should have a plan, which "is nothing else but the form that the poet gives to his work." If the design is good it will include a "proportion of the parts which makes for perfect harmony." The well-designed plan will allow the poet to mix in correct portions truth and fiction, the marvelous and the verisimilar, so that everything will be in proper balance. The verisimilar, in a repetitious interpretation, was for Rapin "everything that is in conformity with public opinion"; but a few paragraphs later he lifted verisimilitude higher and said it was attached to the "universal principles of things." Factual truth could often be "defective," but verisimilitude, according to Rapin's more Aristotelian conclusion, molded "things as they should be."[14]

Among the great classicists the question of verisimilitude received due consideration in its association with the epic. It will be recalled that Le Moyne said in 1671, as a prelude to his interminable epic on Saint Louis, that the *vraisemblable* was "the foundation of opinion and the basis for belief," and that too great an attachment to the actuality of truth destroyed verisimilitude. Verisimilitude could be combined with the marvelous, which in its turn should be only moderately mixed with "magic." The Reverend Père Le Bossu was esteemed in his day a very great authority on epic composition. His *Traité du poème épique* of 1675, which was much admired by Boileau and later by madame Dacier, took its lead from the Greeks and Romans who had given the examples of art imitating nature and who had "most judiciously assembled and prescribed the rules." Aristotle and Horace had devised the regulations while Homer and Vergil had, by the general "agreement of all centuries," served as the most perfect models of them. The epic was concerned with both the habits and passions of its characters; and should involve an "action *vraisemblablement* imagined." But, Le Bossu maintained in a gesture toward the factual, verisimilitude was expected to be compatible with the truth; the poet thus would not be given full license to exaggeration: he would have the privilege to "imagine" but not to "lie." Le Bossu was much intrigued by verisimilitude and came back to it some two hundred pages later in his treatise. His strict formalism was revealed by the statement that the "principal type of verisimilitude" was that which was "in accord with common belief." Then would arise the question as to whether the common belief would be that of the "people" or of the "savants." On that point Le Bossu, rigorous classicist that he was, would have sided with the intellectuals. Saint Evremond had an interesting comment to make in 1688 on verisimilitude as it was practiced by the poets of antiquity. In his opinion they were "scrupulously" exact as to verisimilitude in their treatment of men, but not in their portrayal of the gods— a procedure that was contrary to "good sense." For Saint Evremond, however, poetry as the "language of the gods" was more likely to be discovered in Lucan than in Homer or Vergil since Lucan was less "hyperbolical."[15]

Verisimilitude received interpretation on into the eighteenth century, particularly by such a continuing classicist as madame Dacier who thought that when the rules of art have been approved for centuries, "it is impossible to please by following a different road." She felt that the marvelous and verisimilar went along together, though the marvelous might be more appropriately used in the epic while a tragedy had to be very carefully based on verisimilitude. Charles Batteux, in the midst of a period that placed little value on the formalistic legacy of the ancients, thought that "the material of the fine arts is not truth but verisimilitude." Juno and Aeneas, therefore, did not actually say the words that Vergil put into their mouths but they could have done so. In the same fashion, Molière did not make of his misanthropist, Alceste, in Le misanthrope a "painting of Alceste" in particular but rather "the history of misanthropy taken as a generality." And, when Charles Le Brun put on canvas the battles of Alexander the Great, he had the basis of history; but he needed also invention and the imagined truth. In like manner L.-S. Mercier approved of verisimilitude, since "the truth does not always have the characteristics of the verisimilar." But by this moment in the nonregular eighteenth century, the voices of Batteux and Mercier were only feeble notes against a surging and dissenting chorus.[16]

Another term given sober precision and formalized defining by the great classicists was *bienséance(s)*; it could be used either in the singular or plural, and meant the amenities or proprieties. It was a difficult word to pin down, since its connotation might involve manners, dramatic representations, or a choice of proper language. The foundation for the ideological background of the word was laid by Horace in his *Ars poetica* when he stated that there are certain scenes that cannot be with propriety shown to an audience and certain characters that cannot, because of their natures and conditions, appear on stage. La Mesnardière said in 1631 that Horace "has left us an art of poetry where the greater part of the *bienséances* which concern the theatre are adroitly touched upon." The term reached its full application and rigid acceptance with the school of 1660 and the courtly regime surrounding it. Objection could thus be raised in 1662 to Molière's *L'école des femmes* which contained some verses about the young heroine's being so ignorant that she thought children were born "through the ears"—all of which shocked the proprieties. That perfect gentleman, the chevalier de Méré, had some thoughts on *bienséance* as it applied to personal behavior: *bienséance* required that one be neither too gay nor too sad but, in applying the Aristotelean or Horatian golden mean, something in between. Méré gave around 1676 a good phrasing to the concept of social bienséance when he said that it came from "doing the proper thing as though it were the natural thing." Anyone who in such manner carried out the demands of decorum would find that he would "live well" in the atmosphere of the Court. For Rapin everything that was contrary to the rules of "time, customs, sentiments, and expression" was opposed to bienséance, "the most universal of all the rules." Many of the earlier sixteenth- and seventeenth-century writers were too rough to appeal to "genteel people"; for illustration, the satirist Mathurin Régnier had "no concept of the amenities." And Fénelon said, in his discussion of the values of rhetoric, that the proprieties should be obeyed in language as well as in one's personal habits.[17]

One of the most intriguing terms of the period of the great classicists was *goût* or *bon goût*, taste or good taste. Taste had most formalistic implications both for literature and for society, but it was a difficult word to define in the 1660's even as it would be today. Voltaire, who deep down in his heart was a classicist though he liked to make money and enjoy the comforts of eighteenth-century modernism, took a look at literary taste in his *Temple du goût*; he was very careful as to those he admitted into his sanctuary and refused entry to Pierre Bayle, the Modern, because Bayle's taste was so bad that he preferred Pradon's *Phèdre et Hippolyte* to Racine's tragic masterpiece, *Phèdre*. During the primary moment of French formalism the chevalier de Méré made a pretty good effort at defining good taste. He called it a "subtle discernment"* that caused a person to choose "excellent things rather than mediocre ones." La Bruyère made a perceptive comment in 1687 when he said that there is a "point of perfection" in art which only an

---

*Voltaire said almost the same thing in his *Dictionnaire philosophique* (1764), article on "Goût," when he stated that taste is a "prompt discernment," which it is a waste of time to discuss with *esprits faux*.

observer of "perfect taste" can recognize since there is such a thing as "bad taste" as well as "good taste."* Urbain Chevreau was given credit by his editor in the late 1600's for writing with "finesse, elegance, and judgment," and combining the "good taste of the moderns with that of the ancients." Fénelon in his famous letter to the French Academy had some remarks to make concerning the addition of new words to the language: they should not be left "to chance, to ignorant vulgarians, or to the caprice of women," but should be inserted into the vocabulary by people of "taste and discernment." Madame Dacier sought to analyze the whole problem of the corruption of taste, which she blamed specifically on either ignorance of or rejection of antiquity. Desmarets de Saint-Sorlin, for example, showed in the earlier seventeenth century considerable "cleverness" and "knowledge" in his play *Les visionnaires*; but in his more recent attacks on Homer he has revealed himself to be completely "without taste." The study of the Greeks and Romans brought "politeness and propriety" and removed "rusticity," but children have ceased to study the ancients and have been misled by the "false taste of the opera and novels." Thus deviation from the "great models" like Homer has depraved "judgment and taste," which might be restored only by a return to antiquity, the period in which the authentic rules were discovered. Some eighteenth-century critics carried on with efforts at analyzing good and bad taste. Mercier, who disliked the ancients, said that the "overblown Seneca, improperly called the tragedian, wrote in servitude and in bad taste." La Harpe, who admired Racine, thought that the great classicist included certain inexactitudes in his tragedies as "sacrifices to good taste." Batteux dealt at some length with the problem; he thought that good taste was

* La Bruyère thought that entertaining should be done in accordance with the "taste" of the guest of honor.

for the arts what intelligence was for the sciences. From a slightly different angle he suggested, with considerable critical insight, that taste like genius was an "innate faculty," and that all the rules had been constructed in an effort to satisfy it. In his excellent approach to a definition Batteux assumed a more formal tone: "Good taste is an habitual admiration for order." The question of *goût* was one of the most ever-present (and evanescent) principles of, and a bit beyond, France's formalistic age.[18]

The other terms that made the formalistic guidelines of the great classicists were *jugement, bon sens, raison,* and *nature*—the last being human nature around Louis XIV's court and not the budding flowers or the buzzing of the bees. All had been mentioned by Boileau but they received further amplification from other commentators on the age of formalism. Bouhours said in 1671 that cleverness of the mind was "inseparable from good sense," which assisted in creating the golden mean between intellectual and corporal pursuits. Rapin minimized Plato's "frenzy" (or "fury") in poetic composition—he thought that Plato had decried poetry because of his "inability to write it"—and said that a "serenity of spirit which makes for *sang-froid* and judgment" was essential. Rapin would agree, in rejecting Plato's limiting "frenzy," with Aristotle that there was "something divine" in a poet's character that gave him a quality of genius. Nevertheless, "genius without judgment" was "extravagant and blind" just as "judgment without genius" was "languishing and cold." Rapin, strict formalist that he was, then went on to claim that the rules were based on reason and good sense, and that there was a necessary "subjugation of genius to the rules of art"; thus poetry at its best would be obedient to "ultimate regularity." Méré was another disciple of "good sense and the strictness of reason," and would object on this basis to the flowery and exaggerated language of the salon poet Voiture. Molière, in the quarrel he became involved in over his *L'école des femmes*, rested his case on the "judgment of the Court"; like Boileau, he advised the "study of the Court" since it was there that nature was to be found at its best. In his *Critique de l'école des femmes*, scene seven, Molière used the character of Dorante as his own spokesman: "Remember if you please, monsieur Lycidas, . . . that the important test for all our plays is the judgment of the Court; that it is the taste of the Court which should be studied in order to discover the art of success; that there is no other place where decisions are so just." Le Bossu concluded his treatise on the epic with an admonition to poets that they were "obliged to keep within the rules of art"; and that later critics of poetry must have *jugement* sharply edged like a ruler in order to measure with exactitude. Bouhours stated in 1675 that language had not lost its tenderness of sentiment, but that now it had become sufficiently formalized to express a passion "reasonably." Fénelon felt that there were requirements of reason and judgment for an orator as well as for a poet: an orator should be an intelligent and rational man, have a "unity of plan," and be guided by "good sense." And even Saint Evremond, whose admiration for antiquity was definitely under control, believed that good sense was the basis of "certain eternal rules."[19]

A matter that agitated the formalistic critics of the great classical age in France was the nature of the tragic or epic hero and heroine. Upsetting opinions could be derived from the criticism of the ancients. Plato had said that Homer portrayed the gods in unseemly fashion, and that Achilles in the *Iliad* was a sulky and peevish character unworthy of admiration. Horace, the favorite mentor of the great classicists, had stated that certain personages— Medea and Philomela would be examples—could not properly be shown on stage. Among the French themselves the argument had gone on throughout the seventeenth century as to whether the figures from antiquity were being depicted too gallantly or too rudely. By common consent, it was agreed that the novels made rough warriors like Cyrus into courtly fops; but some of Racine's opponents blamed him for giving too much harshness to Pyrrhus, the son of Achilles, in *Andromaque*. A very good answer was accorded the problem in the tragedies of Pierre Corneille whose heroes were in general honorable men of Rome; and, according to La Bruyère, more Roman in Corneille's plays than they were in history. By the 1660's the tenets of Aristotle were well-known, including the one from the *Poetics* to the effect that the hero should be neither too good nor too bad. With due seriousness, the formalists of the age of Louis XIV wrestled with the problem of what constituted heroism in a tragic or epic character.[20]

Boileau's ideas on the subject were crisply stated. He was certain, as was said in the third canto of his *Art poétique*, that the "trivialities" of the heroes in the romances should be avoided. Agamemnon in a tragedy or epic should be "proud, superb, self-interested"; on the other hand it would be permissible, in keeping with the Aristotelean theory of the tragic flaw, to depict Achilles with some "small faults." The subject and the characters chosen for representation in a tragedy or epic should be taken from pagan mythology and not from the Christian marvelous, which would create too realistic a picture for an adherent of the Church of Rome. Astaroth, Beelzebub, and Lucifer would be too close to "the terrible mysteries of a Christian's faith" to lend themselves to poetic narrative. For Boileau, the very names of heroic personages like Hector, Andromache, Alexander, and Caesar sounded better and were more capable of aggrandizement in verse than their approximate equivalents among Christian heroes. With dignified formalism, however, he insisted that the matronly Hecabe, the wife of

Troy's slain King Priam, should not be made by any writer of epics to weep with a "bombastic lament."[21]

Le Bossu, in his over-six-hundred-page study of the epic, made an effort to answer the accusation that Homer's heroes were ungenteel and unworthy of imitation. Fine Aristotelian that he was, Le Bossu made the basis of his discussion the question: "whether according to Aristotle a poetic hero should necessarily be an honorable and virtuous man." With Aristotle for backing, he concluded that there was a "moral goodness" and a "poetic goodness" which did not of necessity go hand in hand. Thus "cruel and unjust men" (like Achilles) could be "poetic heroes"; and the major character of an epic poem would be its "hero" just as the dactylic hexameter would be designated as "heroic" meter. Also, a man like Achilles born of the goddess Thetis and the mortal Peleus (or Hercules born of Jupiter and the charming Alcmena) would automatically be "heroic" because of lofty ancestry. This was an argument that the formal Frenchman could understand since he had to deal frequently at the court of Louis XIV with an inherited gentility that was not always admirable in performance. So from Aristotle and Horace (said Le Bossu) came the assurance that there was no absolute requirement for "the principal personage of an epic poem to be a man of honor."* Therefore, the child-slaying Medea and the "brutal" Achilles could be legitimately used as primary figures in tragic and epic compositions. The "fable" that was being told (and Aristotle had said that a family history, even if it were bad, could not be altered) might well demand nonadmirable episodes, though this did not mean that the reader or playgoer was encouraged to imitate such actions. But the poet was expected to remember, even in the recounting of ignoble incidents, that an "essential" quality of art was to be

---

*Le Bossu uses both *honnête homme*, "man of honor" or "gentleman," and *homme de bien*, "man of position" or "man of property," in his treatise. The connotations of these terms have varied with the passing centuries: *honnête homme* today might mean simply "honest man."

"useful." With this point in mind, Le Bossu defended Homer's revelation of bad qualities in the gods; such a picture was "indeed less a pernicious example of adultery or impiety than a very useful admonition that is being given to those who wish to live as people of honor." Le Bossu has aimed the complexities of his criticism at persons who have been reared under proper "customs," in a milieu of the "nobility," and exposed to the rigors of "education."[22]

Fénelon did not join Le Bossu in defending Homer's portrayal of ancient warriors or the pagan deities. For Fénelon the Homeric heroes in no sense of the word resembled "gentlemen," and the activities of the gods in Homer's poems were beneath what would be considered becoming conduct among "honorable" people of the earth. Nobody, in Fénelon's opinion, would wish to have a father like Jupiter of a mother like Juno—the French preferred the Roman Jupiter and Juno as king and queen of the gods to the Greek Zeus and Hera. Madame Dacier endeavored to answer Fénelon, La Motte-Houdart, and others in their disparagement of Homer's gods and heroes. La Motte, according to madame Dacier, had misinterpreted Boileau's supposed defense of the misdeeds of the gods in the Homeric poems: Boileau had simply stated that Homer had used "happily" what the theology of his day had "published on the gods." Homer was not trying to render the *Iliad* more spicy with tales of the foibles of the gods, but had employed these adventures in his poem as a necessary part of the mores of the Greeks. As for the question of heroes of classical mythology, madame Dacier agreed with Le Bossu that they did not have to be "men of honor and virtue." Thus, in keeping with his own character and the customs of ancient times, Achilles could appropriately hurl insults at Agamemnon. In another critical direction, madame Dacier objected strongly to antique personages like Epaphus and Phaëthon quarreling with each other on stage in an opera of Quinault, "because that is entirely opposed to our mores and customs"; also, it was an action that took place in front of an audience and was consequently contrary to the proprieties. A similar dispute in Homer between Glaucus and Diomedes would be quite acceptable because it was described and not seen. Fénelon and La Motte indulged in a sprightly series of letters on Homer, his poems, and his heroes. In one of them Fénelon admitted, in a slight shift of position, that, even if Agamemnon displayed in the *Iliad* a "gross arrogance" and Achilles a "ferocious nature,"* they were better than the heroes of the romances who were "false, simpering, and insipid." There was some feeling, at any rate, during the age of Louis XIV that the Homeric Achilles might seem too attractive to the century in spite of his "vicious" qualities. The heroes of antiquity did at times come into conflict with the measured procedures of French formalism.[23]

The proper and correct age of Louis XIV was concerned not only with poetic rules and epic heroes, but also with the dignity of oratory. La Bruyère, as has been observed, said that "eloquence" had disappeared from the lawcourt because of the pressure of affairs, and that it was no longer "suffered" in the pulpit; nowhere could "pieces of eloquence in a just cadence" be heard except at the Académie Française. When La Bruyére made this pronouncement in 1694, he was so intent on pleasing the Academicians that he forgot one of the greatest ecclesiastical orators of all time, Jacques Bénigne Bossuet (1627-1704), bishop of Meaux, preceptor of the Dauphin, and right-hand man of Louis XIV in matters of religious orthodoxy. Bossuet was one of the most formal and articulate men who ever lived, as can be confirmed by the more

*Le Moyne had said in 1671 in his *Dissertation du poème épique* that "anger" was not a "heroic passion."

than thirty volumes of his collected speeches and writings. He opposed the Protestants, the Jansenists, the quietists (in his quarrel with Fénelon), the professional theatre, and the union of Church and State; he therefore supported Gallicanism, and the concept that Louis XIV was by divine right King of France and in governmental affairs, therefore, the representative of God on earth. And he did it all in some of the most magnificently correct and dignified prose to be found in the French language.[24]

The French had had a great deal to say about oratory ever since they had learned about it in earlier centuries from Cicero, who was their primary model rather than the Athenian Demosthenes. Before the middle of the seventeenth century La Mothe le Vayer, in his study on French eloquence of his time, said in 1637 that there were many attributes of eloquence, but that the "three perfections of an orator are to teach, to please, and to move"—almost an exact phrasing of Racine's and Boileau's later statement concerning the purpose of tragedy.* Also, as early as 1631 La Mesnardière advised care in writing about princes because it should always be remembered that "they preside over men as the lieutenants of God." The idea of both La Mothe le Vayer and La Mesnardière were to find an echo during succeeding decades in the opinions of Bossuet, who pounded out his rigid dicta with an authoritarian air sufficient to discourage opposition.[25]

Bossuet's *Sur le style et la lecture . . . pour former un orateur* appeared in 1669 and 1670 after he had already had some years of experience in preaching to the Court. This association with the Court and his respect therefor is revealed in his first suggestions to a speaker who is learning techniques: "As for style, of first consideration is to talk

*La Mothe le Vayer's phrasing is *de plaire et d'émouvoir* which may have influenced Racine's and Boileau's *de plaire et de toucher*. Rapin, too, said that poetry should *plaire*, but that it should aim also at the "public good."

De Piles pinx.

Portrait de Nicolas Boileau Des Preaux.

Brevet Sculp. 1704.

*Sans peine à la Raison asservissant la Rime,*
*Et mesme en jmitant, toüjours Original ;*
*J'ay sçeu dans mes Ecrits, docte, enjoüé, sublime,*
*Rassembler en moy, Perse, Horace et Juvenal.*

Se vend à Paris rüe S.<sup>t</sup> Jacques à l'Annonciation.

23. Nicolas Boileau

*24.* Panel from Bath at Versailles

well,* which is almost never a problem for those who have been born and reared in the upper stratum of society." For "public discourses," there should be employed "a figured style, an elevated style, an ornamented style; and variety, which is the whole secret of pleasing, and insinuating and moving turns of phrase." Bossuet remarked that he had modeled his own style after the Romans, since he read Latin with facility and Greek was too difficult. The formalistic basis for his oratory was Latin; he said frankly, "I have not read many French books." Cicero, especially in his *De oratore* and the *Orator*, was the prime foundation for "grand eloquence," and continued reading of the Romans would result in a "colorful and well-turned style" in French because the French language has its roots in Latin. Ciceronian prose should be the main point of study since the greater part of Latin poetry would lead only to "conceits, antitheses, big words, little sense, and a frigid beauty." In addition to Latin prose, the prospective orator should be familiar with the Old and New Testaments, especially "the most beautiful spots" rather than the obscure ones. He should also read the Saints of the Church, in particular Saint Augustine who would "elevate the mind to noble and subtle considerations." Bossuet thought that the reading of good literature—and for him good literature had to pass his own rigorous inspection—contributed to the formation of both an orator and a gentleman.[26]

The formal and simple dignity of Bossuet's prose can be seen in the funeral oration for madame Henriette d'Angleterre,** duchesse d'Orléans and wife of Louis XIV's younger brother; the final rites of the youthful (she was twenty-six years old when she died) and attractive princess were held at Saint Denis on August 21, 1670. Bossuet, who like the rest

*Bossuet's wording here, *parler bien*, has been translated literally "to talk well." The essential meaning of it would seem to involve, even as in English, both the manner of speech and the choice of words.
**She was the daughter of Charles I of England.

of the Court was shocked at the sudden death of Madame, chose for his discourse a familiar theme from the first chapter of Ecclesiastes, "Vanity of vanities, and all is vanity." He was thus enabled to make the loss of the young princess a part of the universal sorrow of the world:

"'Nous mourons tous,' disait cette femme dont l'Ecriture a loué la prudence au second Livre des Rois, 'et nous allons sans cesse au tombeau, ainsi que des eaux qui se perdent sans retour.' En effet nous ressemblons tous à des eaux courantes. De quelque superbe distinction que se flattent les hommes, ils ont tous une même origine; et cette origine est petite. Leurs années se poussent successivement comme des flots: ils ne cessent de s'écouler, tant qu'enfin, après avoir fait un peu plus de bruit, et traversé un peu plus de pays les uns que les autres, ils vont tous ensemble se confondre dans un abîme où l'on ne reconnaît plus ni princes, ni rois, ni toutes ces autres qualités superbes qui distinguent les hommes; de même que ces fleuves tant vantés demeurent sans nom et sans gloire, mêlés dans l'océan avec les rivières les plus inconnus."*

The principle of universality was an important one for the great classicists, and here Bossuet has applied it to man's position on earth just as Boileau would have insisted on it

*No translation can do justice to Bossuet's dignified style in this passage, which opens the first division of the *oraison funèbre* to madame Henriette d'Angleterre:

"'We are all dying,'" said this woman whose prudence the Scripture praised in the second Book of Kings, 'and we go unceasingly toward the tomb, even as waters which trickle away not to return.' Indeed we all resemble flowing waters. With whatever superb distinctions men may be flattered, they all have the same origin; and that origin is small. Their years are pushed forward in succession like waves: they do not stop flowing along, until finally, after having made a little more noise and after having covered a little more terrain some than the others, they all go together to mingle in an abyss in which no longer are recognized either princes, or kings, or any of these other lofty rankings by which men are differentiated; they are like these so mighty rivers that end up without a name and without glory, blended in the ocean with rivulets utterly unknown."

in a tragic character or Molière would have illustrated it in a play such as *Le misanthrope*. Bossuet, like his contemporaries who indulged in formalistic criticism, thought that whatever the literary composition might be—tragedy, comedy, or oration—it should have a "formality of plan"; and any inclination toward license should be "restrained by the rules." Also, it should be kept in mind at all times that the ultimate purpose of eloquence was "to enflame men to virtue." Even Racine, said Bossuet in 1694, has "turned away from *Bérénice*"—his tragedy that may have been inspired by Henriette d'Angleterre—and has begun to occupy himself "with subjects more worthy of him." Bossuet, who considered the public theatre a den of iniquity, reserved some of his most formal and pungent prose for attacking it. In a very spirited passage he lamented the lot of the professional actress: "What mother, not necessarily a Christian mother but one with some fragment of gentility, would not prefer to see her daughter in the tomb rather than on the stage? In truth, has a mother brought up her daughter, so tenderly and with so much attention, for this disgrace? Has she kept her night and day so carefully under her wings, so to speak, to put her then out on public display and make of her a temptation for the youth of the land?" Bossuet, the rigid authoritarian with the formidable prose style, did much to discredit the theatre as he saw it at the end of the century of the great classicists.[27]

In regard to pulpit oratory there were other able practitioners of it along with Bossuet during the age of Louis XIV. Madame de Sévigné mentioned frequently the sermons of Bourdaloue: "Le Père Bourdaloue is preaching, and good heavens! Everything that is said about him is below the praise that he deserves." On the question of eloquence in general La Bruyère in his *Caractères* sought to point out certain features that were not necessary to it (this was said by La Bruyère in 1687 before he consigned in 1694 all eloquence to the sessions of the French Academy): these would be a "bombastic style, the piling up of figures of speech, big words, and a rotundity of periods." For real eloquence, said La Bruyère, there should be "proper terms" which would express "noble, vivid, and solid thoughts." According to Fénelon, the orator should construct his speech, in details of proportion and design, as though it were a great palace and a "complete whole." A "veritable order" would be derived from an arrangement in which no phrases could be displaced without upsetting the entire creation—a paraphrase of Aristotle's remarks concerning the ideal structure of tragedy. The orator who came nearest to filling these specifications was the unyieldingly formal Bossuet.[28]

Many poets and writers of prose after 1660 sang in resounding tones of the patron and guide of the formalistic age in France, Louis XIV. Possibly none did it more properly than did Boileau in the fourth and last canto of his *Art poétique*. In earlier periods in France, said Boileau, an artist might go hungry and a poet "depend for his dinner on the success of a sonnet"; and it was a difficult thing to "go promenading on Mount Helicon" on an empty stomach. Under the beneficence of Louis the situation has been changed:

> ... mais enfin cette affreuse disgrace
> Rarement parmi nous afflige le Parnasse.
> Et que craindre en ce siècle, où toujours les beaux-arts
> D'un astre favorable éprouvent les regards,
> Où d'un prince éclairé la sage prévoyance
> Fait partout au mérite ignorer l'indigence?
> Muses, dictez sa gloire à tous vos nourrissons.
> Son nom vaut mieux pour eux que toutes vos leçons.
> Que Corneille, pour lui rallumant son audace,
> Soit encore le Corneille et du Cid et d'Horace;
> Que Racine, enfantant des miracles nouveaux,
> De ses héros sur lui forme tous les tableaux; ...
> Mais quel heureux auteur, dans une autre Enéide,

Aux bords du Rhin tremblant conduira cet Alcide?
Quelle savante lyre, au bruit de ses exploits,
Fera marcher encor les rochers et les bois? . . .
   Auteurs, pour les chanter, redoublez vos transports:
Le sujet ne veut pas de vulgaires efforts.*

Boileau in these lines, though scarcely a "poet in some new *Aeneid*," has done a creditable job of paying pompous homage to his King. As a mark of his admiration for Vergil, Boileau quite cleverly adapted the opening lines of the *Aeneid* to the beginning of his mock-epic, *Le lutrin*, the story of an argument over a reading-stand in the Sainte Chapelle; the first four lines, in pseudo-formal heroics, run:

I sing of combats, and of this terrible prelate
Who, through his long efforts and unconquerable strength,
In an illustrious church revealing his great courage,
At last managed to place a lectern in the choir.

Formalism could take its momentary relaxations.[29]

But the great formalists of the age of Louis XIV were seldom inclined toward trivialities. They believed in the rigors of the rules, in life as well as in literature, because they

---

*Boileau's formal alexandrines—some nine couplets, involving minor authors and place names have been omitted from the original passage—in a literal English translation would run as follows:

   . . . but in truth this terrible disgrace
   Rarely in our own day afflicts Parnassus.
   And what is to be feared in this century, where the fine arts
   Always rest under the gleam of a favorable star;
   Where the wise foresight of an enlightened prince
   Causes merit in no place to endure indigence?
      Muses, let all your nurselings proclaim his glory.
   His name is better than anything you can teach them.
   Let Corneille, for him rekindling his flame,
   Be again the Corneille of *Le Cid* and *Horace*.
   Let Racine, in new miracles of creativity,
   Make him the model of all tragic heroes; . . .
   But what happy poet in some new *Aeneid*,
   Will lead this Hercules to the banks of the trembling Rhine?
   What skillful lyre with the song of his exploits
   Will cause the rocks and the forests to ring? . . .
   Poets, redouble your efforts to sing of his deeds;
   His glory deserves more than a commonplace voice.

thought that through regulations come the ultimate satisfactions. It was dangerous to veer from established tenets in seeking other sources of pleasure. Madame Dacier, in an argument for the Ancient position, asserted that the rules were not to be followed because "Aristotle and Horace stated them, or even because Homer followed them, but because the works based upon them have given pleasure." The rigidity of the rules were a natural part of a gentleman's life at Court; and by extension an argument against Protestantism. As has been said by a contemporary Academician, it was "according to the rules" in the time of Louis XIV for a subject to have the same religious belief as his King in order that the "two obeisances [that is, to God and to King] might be blended and one fortified by the other." In any case, the age of the great classicists in France—a formal age in which there was a "love of unity and symmetry, an innate taste for proportion, a predominance of reason as it sought for the truth"— was an age to which Frenchmen still look back with pride.[30]

# FORMALISM DECLINES

THAT INTENSE commentator on the last years of Louis XIV and the Regency, the duc de Saint Simon, said that all classes in France were glad to watch the end of the Sun-King's regime, and that the only persons to regret his passing in 1715 were his "personal valets." The nobles were pleased to see the conclusion of a reign "under which there had been nothing for them to expect"; Paris, tired of a subjugation and a forced dependence, "breathed in the hope of liberation"; the provinces, having lived under Louis XIV in despair and oblivion, "inhaled the new air and shivered with joy"; and the people, "ruined, beaten down, and desperate, gave thanks to God." Saint Simon, like La Rochefoucauld, was one of the great nobles whose power had been diminished by the absolutism of the monarchy, so his opinions in his colorful *mémoires* could hardly be called unbiased. Other chroniclers took a less harsh view of the last years of the most formalistic of French kings. The tough old soldier, the maréchal de Villars (who was himself sixty years old in 1715 and a veteran campaigner against the English), was more kindly disposed in his estimate of the last days of Louis XIV. Villars said that the old King, despite a loss of appetite and a diet of only a little soup, still enjoyed going out to watch the hunt. According to Villars, two days before Louis XIV died he called into his presence "the first noblemen of the Court" and said: "I recommend to you the young King. He is only five years of age . . . I recommend to you the avoiding of wars: I have waged too many; they have forced me to burden my people and because of them I ask the pardon of God." These words were spoken with "dignity" and "kindness." The marquis de Dangeau (possibly a more accurate reporter than Saint Simon) gave, in his turn, a rather sympathetic description of the last days of Louis XIV, with many details of his piety, the deep concern of his courtiers, and the continued presence at his side of madame de Maintenon. It was Dangeau that chronicled the much-quoted remark (and one used in the present-day sound and light program at Versailles) made by the dying Louis XIV to the little five-year-old who was to be Louis XV: "My son, you are going to be a great king; do not imitate me in the taste I have had for war." Then, said Dangeau, all the princes and princesses of the blood passed by the bed of Louis XIV; to each one of them he spoke a few words of farewell. The primary age of formalism in France was over.[1]

If there were those who sighed with relief and release at the passing of the rigidly correct Louis XIV, there were others who thought that the freewheeling Regency which followed offered little reason for pride. The marquis d'Argenson disapproved heartily of the duc d'Orléans' regime and in 1717 decried a "modern Court" which took delight in "turning into ridicule and treating with arrogant superiority all the accomplishments, manners, and objects of respect of the former Court." According to him, uncontrolled selfishness was rampant everywhere, guided by a "satrapy of the ordinary which has made everything acceptable under bad rules, wicked principles, and general ruination"—and this was the situation as it continued under Louis XV. The price of bread was augumenting "a sou each day," and the people were "fully ready for a revolt." As Louis XV passed through the faubourg of Saint Victor in Paris there was no shouting of "long live the King," but of "we are starving—give us

bread, give us bread"; and this was in September 1740 rather
than in 1789. On October 4, 1740 the King got up very
early in the morning and was by six o'clock with two of his
favorites, madame de Mailly and madame de Vintimille, in
the forest of Fontainebleau to see the rut of the stags, "such
being the pastime of royalty"; unfortunately for the King
and his retinue, there was on this occasion no performance.
In November of 1740 the duc de Richelieu gave a "large
supper party" at his house in Paris "just beyond the barrier
of Vaugirard."* The decorative motif was "in gallant ob-
scenities," and the wainscoting of the public rooms contained in each panel "very immodest figures in bas-relief."
The old duchesse de Brancas wanted to have a good look at
them, so she put on her glasses while the duc de Richelieu
"held a candle and explained them to her." This type of entertainment was to be expected in the milieu of a Court
made up of bored and self-seeking persons, and where there
was "no more dignity and no more order."[2]

The old cardinal Fleury, who was doing a creditable job
as minister of state, came in for criticism in regard to his at-
tempts at formal ceremonials. Fleury, in the best fashion of
royalty, sought to hold at the end of his long day a *petit
coucher*, or an "intimate reception" just before he went to
bed. On December 18, 1731 he retired to his private cham-
bers and then, for a waiting group on the outside: "the door
is opened and you see this old priest taking off his pants
which he folds up carefully; he is handed a rather ordinary
dressing gown, and his nightshirt; he combs for a long time
his four white hairs, he argues, he babbles, he wanders off the
subject, he tells some rather bad jokes, which are mixed in
with sticky and commonplace platitudes, and some news of
the city." In contemporary opinion this was quite a ridiculous procedure; it was a far cry from the ceremonies at-

---

*This would probably be near the Jardin du Luxembourg, in the present
sixth *arrondissement*.

tending royal awakenings and goings to bed—which it was an obvious attempt at imitating—of the previous century. The *levers* and *couchers* of Louis XIV had been among the grand monarch's most impressively formalistic gestures, and he had expected his favored courtiers to be near him when he waked up in the morning and when he wanted to converse a bit before going to sleep; or when he wished to promenade in the gardens of Versailles which had been so properly designed by Le Nôtre. And woe to any nobleman who was supposed to be at these rituals and who was absent without a valid excuse! Saint Simon has described the piercing eye and memory of Louis XIV on these occasions: "He would look to the right and to the left at his *lever*, at his *coucher*, . . . in his gardens of Versailles, where only the courtiers had the privilege of following him; he saw and catalogued everybody, no one escaped him, including those who would have preferred, surely, not to be seen. He put down in his mind the absences of those who were normally at Court. . . . It was a demerit for some (including the most distinguished) not to make a regular sojourn at Court, a demerit for others to appear there rarely, and a certain disgrace for those who never, or almost never, came. When it was a question of something for them, 'I do not know him,' he would reply haughtily. In regard to those who appeared rarely, he would say, 'He is a man that I never see'; and those decrees were irrevocable." Neither Fleury, nor even Louis XV, could come close to the formalistic rigor of the master of the art, the imperious Sun-King.[3]

Louis XV lacked the essence of "magnificence" or a "sense of grandeur," both so natural to Francis I and to Louis XIV. The trivialities of Court amusements frequently reflected the lackadaisical enthusiams of the King himself. In November 1748 the Court was intrigued by a *parade* (a rough type of short play, proper to farce-players or the charlatans of the Pont Neuf), the words of which were written by a sieur de Moncrif, "one of the forty of the French Academy." In it was a chorus of harlots—chastely designated as *p* . . . (for *putains*), a nicety that the French still observe—who chanted in choral pantomime:

> We are young girls
> And we will listen to your talk;
> But when the moment is right
> We will exercise our thighs.

On December 22, 1748 Crébillon's tragedy *Catalina* was presented by the Comédie Française; in a "disdainful century" it received only "mediocre approbation,"* indicative of the "bad taste" of the age. But it was an age of cleverness used to conceal reality, of the bon mot to minimize misfortune: if the Seine flooded, for example, it had "got out of its bed" or had "gone to see the King." The King might not have been in any mood to receive a swollen river, since it was rumored in 1747 that he was pretty well debilitated: in a pre-Kinsey report, it was estimated that he had need for women only twice a week, "although he is just thirty-seven years old." It was a period, however, in which women were not completely cloistered; in the spring of 1750 a famous madame of Paris took out a fine carriage with four lackeys and went on "public promenade with her demoiselles," a performance that could cause one to cry out rightly: "O the mores of this Christian and well-policed state!" Madame de Pompadour was blamed for much of the whole situation, and in June of 1750 the people wanted to show their opposition to her by going to Versailles and "burning down the chateau." Later in 1750 it was claimed that valets and femmes de chambre were running the government, in a Court that was "corrupting" and where dignity and merit went unrewarded. Possibly conditions were symbolized by an in-

---

*Mediocre approbation was undoubtedly sufficient for this poor play of Crébillon.

cident that occurred on December 17, 1749: Louis XV fell off his horse.[4]

The uncertainties of Louis XV's reign, even after due allowance is made for biased reporting on the part of some of its chroniclers, did not make a sufficiently solid base for a continuation of formalism in literature. The newer generation of writers were ready for experimentation and unwilling to be subservient to a series of rules that went back to the Greek and Roman past. Descartes, whose discourse on the method of training the reason (the *Discours de la méthode* of 1637) had not been accepted in the formalistic seventeenth century, came into full bloom in the tradition-violating eighteenth. In following the dictates of Cartesianism (a generic term taken from the Latinizing of Descartes' name), it was unnecessary for a writer to fit into any universality of traditional truth; he had simply to obey the guidelines of individual rationalization and experimentation. In many ways it was a healthy process since the Cartesian method defended the privilege of individual examination and decision. It led to laboratory exactitude based upon mathematical formulas, to the opening of new avenues of science, and to an interest in faraway lands; it diminished imagination and creativity, and doubted the truth of poetry since the poet's work was not subject to test-tube verification. The effect of Descartes on literature was, on the whole, bad. The Cartesians paid no homage, in regard to literary composition, to the formalized regulations that had come down from antiquity. They felt that Descartes was more worthy of emulation than was Aristotle because Descartes combined the intelligence of Aristotle with two thousand additional years of experience and discovery. Invalid as this assumption might be, it formed the basis of the Modern point of view.

The Quarrel of the Ancients and Moderns was essentially nothing new. Horace had said in his *Ars poetica* that it was better to imitate the Greeks of four centuries earlier than the Romans of a preceding generation. And Longinus voiced a century or so after Horace, in his treatise *On the Sublime*, a basic tenet of the Ancients: Homer was worthy of admiration because his epics had been examined for over a thousand years, had been subjected to a variety of criticism, were still considered excellent, and therefore were deserving of imitation. During the period of the developing power of Christianity, through the Middle Ages in France, there was grave doubt as to the values of pagan literature; but the Ancients of the seventeenth century were approximately of the same belief as Longinus. Le Bossu stated in 1675 that the Greeks and Romans had given examples of art imitating nature and that by the "consent of all the centuries" Aristotle and Horace were the masters of the rules, and Homer and Vergil the proper models to follow; and Rapin at about the same time said that the genius of Homer was "universal." Boileau belatedly started his defense of the Ancient position in 1693 with his very appropriately titled *Réflexions sur Longin*, a series of essays aimed specifically at Charles Perrault. Perrault had irritated Boileau with his poem, *Le siècle de Louis le Grand*, read at a session of the French Academy of January 27, 1687—a session given over to offering thanks for improvement in the King's health and one, therefore, that was proper for praising Louis XIV and his regime. Perrault's poem, however, contained some verses which reduced the ancients while exalting the age of Louis:

> The beauties of antiquity have always been venerated,
> But I never thought they were worthy of adoration.
> I look at the ancients without any bending of the knees;
> They are great, it is true, but they are men just like us;
> And one can compare, without fear of injustice,
> The century of LOUIS to that of Augustus.

There was nothing very violent about these words, and farther along Perrault had some good things to say about Homer even though the blind bard had "bored his readers" with lengthy prefaces explaining the deeds of his heroes. To glorify the seventeenth century, Perrault mentioned many of its supposedly great writers: Malherbe, Racan, Voiture, Molière, Rotrou, the "celebrated Corneille," and others—but Boileau and Racine were omitted. Racine treated the whole matter as something of a joke; Boileau, for his part, was much irked and first wrote the epigram that had Apollo wondering how "the Homers and the Vergils" could be insulted in front of the French Academy. The question was taken up more fully and philosophically in the *Réflexions sur Longin*. Boileau was somewhat petty in his derogation of Perrault's lack of knowledge of Greek, but the crux of his argument against Perrault and the Moderns is to be found in the seventh *Réflexion:* "since it is posterity alone that establishes the true value of literary works, one should not, however admirable a modern writer may appear, put him facilely on the level of writers who have been admired for such a great number of centuries, because one is not even sure that his works may pass with any glory into the next century." This, it might be said in commentary, was a meaty and solid argument.[5]

It had little effect; the mighty current of Cartesianism swept along and the Moderns rode on its swelling tide. La Fontaine made a gentle effort at answering Perrault in his well-modulated *Epître à monseigneur l'évêque de Soissons*, which appeared in 1687 after Perrault's poem in praise of Louis XIV. La Fontaine pointed out quite pertinently that imitation and admiration of the ancients did not require subservience, although there were some writers who, "like sheep," were led around by the "shepherd of Mantua" [Vergil]. As for his own case, said La Fontaine, "my imitation is not an enslavement"; and here he gave expression to a sentiment that was basic to the great classicists: the spirit of antiquity should be digestively assimilated without slavish copying. On the other hand, La Fontaine said farther on in his epistle that, in comparison with Homer and Vergil, "our glory is small." But he agreed that in praising the great "gods of Parnassus" he was in 1687 "talking to the rocks." It is true that the insinuating doctrine of the Moderns was already audible in the midst of the school of 1660. As seen earlier, Desmarets de Saint-Sorlin in his *Comparaison de la langue et de la poésie française, avec la grecque et la latine* of 1670 said that it would be a shameful thing for the empire of France, the "noblest in the universe," if it possessed a "language and minds less elevated than the language and minds of the Greeks and Latins." And Saint Evremond, who could at times be on both sides of the Ancient and Modern fence, claimed in 1685 that the "genius of our century is completely opposed to this spirit of fables and false mysteries" to be found in the writings of the ancients. If Homer were alive today he would compose poems "adjusted to the century in which we was writing." As for the criticism from antiquity, said Saint Evremond, "it is necessary to admit that the *Poetics* of Aristotle is an excellent work"; however, there is nothing sufficiently perfect to regulate "all nations and all centuries," especially in view of the fact that Descartes and Gassendi* have discovered truths that Aristotle did not know. Urbain Chevreau gave the sentiment a slightly different focus when he offered the opinion that "without the aid of Athens or of Rome one can be an *honnête homme*."[6]

The major salvo against the Ancients, and one that laid the critical foundation for the destruction of formalism, was fired by Fontenelle, the nephew of that latter-day Roman, Pierre Corneille. Fontenelle's dissertation came out in 1688, and bore the title of *Digression sur les anciens et les modernes*. It contained some rather apt phrasings and convincing arguments for an oncoming age of social upheaval and philosophi-

*Liberal and epicurean philosopher of the first half of the seventeenth century.

cal explanation. Were the trees of former times, asked Fontenelle, taller than those of today? His answer to his own rhetorical question was in the negative; therefore, "we can equal Homer, Plato, and Demosthenes." Nature has had in her hands "a certain paste which is always the same"; she did not create "Plato, Demosthenes, or Homer out of a finer or better prepared clay than that used for our philosophers, our orators, or our poets of today." We are now, thought Fontenelle of men of his own time, the real ancients since we have the knowledge of previous centuries plus our own; now is "the age of virility in which man reasons with more force and more intelligence than ever before." The chief credit for man's improvement in thinking processes was given by Fontenelle to Descartes, "who introduced this new method of reasoning." Fontenelle voiced some theories that were most acceptable in an era of declining formalism, and which were the basis of the Modern point of view: man is progressing toward a moment of higher perfection sometime in the future; and the concepts of the ancients are not automatically superior to the moderns and thus deserving of deification. Such a philosophy removed the necessity of imitating models from the past, and of obedience to the rules that had come down from antiquity. It was destined to make of the eighteenth century a period that was fertile in idealogies and experimentation, but it was destructive of literature. The Cartesian method with rationalistic thoroughness took the sheen off the butterfly's wing: it destroyed poetry. Not until the nineteenth century would the lyric bard feel inclined again to sing his song.[7]

The theses of Fontenelle were supported by Perrault in his *Parallèles des anciens et des modernes*, which began to appear, also, in 1688. The latter stressed the fact that nature is always the same, and could produce a genius in any age. Therefore, it would be perfectly possible for a Vergil to be born in the seventeenth century; if he were, he would write a finer poem than the *Aeneid*, since he would be working under better conditions. Madame Dacier made a good effort for the Ancients in a losing cause. Her *Des causes de la corruption du goût* appeared, as indicated, in 1714 and took its point of critical departure from La Motte's recent verse adaptation of the *Iliad*. Madame Dacier's primary argument was that those who attacked Homer during the last fifty years were "very mediocre men" who knew no Greek and who ignored twenty-five centuries of admiration for the first captain of the Muses. In particular, it was La Motte who had cut twelve books out of the *Iliad* and "maimed the others"; and he had derided the supposedly overlong episodes and boring descriptions of Homer "without ever having read him or knowing his language." La Motte, in the opinion of madame Dacier, was pursuing the theme of an earlier Modern, Desmarets de Saint-Sorlin—a man of some wit but "without any taste" and an unsuccessful composer of epics. Her own prose rendition of the *Iliad* (which had been used by La Motte) she regarded only as a literal and accurate transference into French, with no pretense of equaling "the most finished work that has come from the hand of man." She then pointed out in detail a number of errors in La Motte's compression of the *Iliad*, many of them the result of his veering from the rules and seeking "other means of pleasing," a procedure that was comparable to a mariner's throwing away his compass in order to wander at random over the seas. La Motte showed arrogance in criticizing and seeking to degrade a poet who had lasted over two thousand years; especially in view of the fact that, to madame Dacier's way of thinking, La Motte's own style was feeble and full of preciosity. She chose an illustration of the latter quality from the fourth book of La Motte's version, where Menelaus has been wounded and is upset over Agamemnon's worries about the injury:

> Menelaus made tender by these vivid alarms,
> Regrets his own blood less than his dear brother's tears.

Madame Dacier rightly called this couplet *outré* and *recherché;* all that Menelaus said to Agamemnon was, according to her: "Don't worry, my brother, and don't disturb the Greeks—my wound is not serious." A part of the decline of formalism was a saccharinelike lack of restraint; La Motte showed it again in his sentimental tragedy *Inès de Castro*.[8]

La Motte and Fénelon, in 1713 and 1714, exchanged a series of letters on Homer and the ancients; this was during the period that La Motte's version of the *Iliad* was beginning to appear. It was a pleasant interchange of ideas, though the essential conflict between the Ancients and Moderns was visible in it. Fénelon (who was a nonvigorous Ancient) wrote, on September 19, 1713, that he feared that La Motte's poetry lacked the "total harmony of Greek and Roman verses" but there was hope that he would manage to become a "new Homer" anyway. La Motte replied, on December 14, 1713, that he had read five or six books of his adaptation—which had omitted large portions of the *Iliad* because of the "many faults mixed in with the great beauties"—to the Académie Française and those members who knew the original poem best "congratulated me." On the question of versification, Fénelon agreed in two letters of January 1714 that there was a real problem with the French heroic couplet (the alexandrine), which has a "rather fatiguing monotony"; the dull regularity of French verse was a standard theme of Fénelon: in his famous letter to the French Academy (slightly later than this correspondence) he maintained that in the poetry of his day there was always "a substantive nominative leading its adjective around by the hand." The Greeks and Romans had an easier time in not having to bother with rhyme. In any event, Fénelon thought that the ancients could not be disdained since they would always be our "masters"—but this did not mean that one had to admire "blindly everything that came from antiquity." In the last of his letters (December 18, 1714) La Motte suggested that he would pay a visit to Fénelon and they would talk about Homer: his paganism, the "grossness of his century," and the "defects of philosophy" therein. La Motte admitted that possibly he might be persuaded to give in to Fénelon's arguments on the other side (which he never did). There were further efforts made at reconciling the differences between the Ancients and the Moderns. Fénelon, for his part, had had a soothing effect before his death in 1715. In the cultivated salon of the marquise de Lambert—La Motte and Fontenelle were habitués—the hostess herself sought to smooth out the conflict between La Motte and madame Dacier. In the early part of 1716 monsieur de Valincour (who occupied Racine's seat in the French Academy and also his post of royal historiographer) invited several of the antagonists, including madame Dacier and La Motte, to his house in Paris for a placating dinner. Everyone behaved in well-mannered fashion, and a toast was drunk to the health of Homer; but the future was bright for the Moderns who recognized no rule or formalized tradition from the past.[9]

There were few defenders of poetry in the eighteenth century except the abbé du Bos, who wrote a critical study in 1719 called *Réflexions sur la poésie et la peinture;* and Voltaire. Voltaire, the inevitable classicist and paradoxical modernist—he believed both in liberty and measured regularity —used poetry more as an instrument than as a fine art. He could make of it a didactic bludgeon or mold it into strict alexandrines for his tragedies; he was probably the best poet of a nonpoetic age, even though he lacked the creative spark of a Ronsard or a Victor Hugo. Voltaire had an early admiration for Shakespeare, after his return from England in 1729; yet, essential formalist that he was, Voltaire at the same time said that the so-called tragedies of Shakespeare were written by a man "without any knowledge of the rules and without the slightest sparkle of good taste." Voltaire's was a lonely voice in an encompassing world of the Moderns. On the other side of the critical ledger, L.-S. Mercier insisted: "methods, rules, and arts of poetry have spoiled and are spoiling every day the most inventive minds." For Mercier Shakespeare was an "independent and proud genius," who spread out his scenes in unrestricted diffusion, while Boileau was a "cold man" capable of "stifling the zest of a poet." Boileau's "minutiae of rules" have seized upon poetry and "dampened its fire." It might be indicated that Mercier went across the Channel to choose one of the greatest of dramatists as a model for his rule-breaking: he might have found at home another great dramatist as a model for rule-conforming—Jean Racine. At any rate, in a moment of non-formalism the French admired those literatures that were unencumbered by the rules; and in the eighteenth century, according to the abbé Raynal, "French folly is now English tragedy." The Moderns had won.[10]

The decline of formalism in eighteenth-century France was discernible in the visual arts even as it was in literary theory and composition. Paris continued to grow as architects, sculptors, and painters plied their skills; the external impressiveness of the city increased as it became more modern. But there was a softening in the rigors of the arts, and Boucher and Fragonard had more delicate colors in their palettes than did Nicholas Poussin and Le Brun. The gods and heroes of mythology were still the subjects of paintings, but the approach was gentler; and the model was likely to be some pink-and-white eighteenth-century beauty (which made the desiccated madame de Pompadour difficult as a subject) or some silken courtier. In the words of one of today's critics, "Jupiter, Juno, and Mars were quietly dethroned [in painting] by Venus, Eros, Amphitrite, Bacchus, and Aurora with their corteges of cupids, nymphs, fauns, and tritons"—and the setting might be in the water, or a forest, or in a misty cloud. Jupiter was not completely abandoned, according to Raynal: the King had commissioned some pictures for the chateau of Choisy; the fourth one was Boucher's *Jupiter changé en taureau,** which had elegance but was too much dominated by the "color of pink."[11]

Houses and the manner of living in eighteenth-century Paris had less formalistic pomp and a greater feeling of intimacy than their earlier equivalents. Town houses—like the *hôtels* Biron, Matignon, and Elysée—were more comfortable if less rigid in design and appointments than such dwellings in the period of Louis XIV. There were bathrooms in them and comfort stations "in the English fashion." As for bathrooms, a panel from Louis XV's at Versailles (Figure 24) illustrates the tone of informality and relaxation of his regime as well as of his ablutions. The four naiads in the picture are dipping in and out of the pleasant water with graceful unconcern, although one of them is wrapping herself modestly in a drapery that somehow got entangled in the untrimmed tropical tree. The whole scene has a slightly unrigid and asymmetrical lack of balance. The familiar mood of the panel is further enhanced by the border of cattails which could easily have come out of anybody's pond just a short way down the road. It was a type of décor that would have irritated the formal instincts of Louis XIV, but his great-grandson probably relished every curving line.[12]

One of the strong influences in breaking down the formalistic installations of both chateau and town house was the advent of *chinoiseries*, which meant literally in the eighteenth century "things from China," instead of its contemporary connotation of "sly tricks." Importations from China and the Far East became so much in vogue late in the seventeenth century that Louis XIV issued an edict in 1709 against such

*Jupiter visited the maiden Europa in the form of a bull; it was a favorite subject with artists as far back as the sixteenth century.

purchases; it had little effect against the growing fad. The art and decoration from China emphasized asymmetry and convolution in lacquers and woods, all of which fascinated the French as they carried on their resistance to formalism. H. Havard has given a good analysis of the whole procedure: "The disdain of symmetry which marks creations from the Far East, the twisted forms of the frames which surround them, their irregular lines so different from our balanced contours, all this charming phantasmagoria which violates so sharply our classical correctness, must have first astonished then attracted the eyes of our designers and disposed their minds to brilliant audacities." In view of the developing mode, the renewal of the 1709 edict, done several times as the century progressed, was a futile gesture. Among those who were most intoxicated by the arts and crafts of the Far East was that favorite of the King's favorites, madame de Pompadour.[13]

As the seventeenth century ended, a chest of drawers at Versailles might be expected to be in *marqueterie de Boulle*, or in the marquetry of André Charles Boulle, the favored cabinetmaker of Louis XIV and the master of properly designed inlays of tortoise shell, copper, ivory, mother-of-pearl, and other materials. In the time of Louis XV a chest of drawers in a royal or noble household could well be in wood from the Far East, fancy and asymmetrical, and finished in Chinese lacquer. Or a secretary in the eighteenth century might be done in bronze and Chinese lacquer,* ornate but informally convoluted. There was a growing enthusiasm for Chinese *magots*, those grotesque figures in varicolored porcelain; and, as an added fashion note, sphinxes were adorned with hats and coiffures imitative of the ladies of Louis XV's court. Tapestries of French and Flemish design continued to hang on the walls of a chateau and block out the wintry

---

*Pictures of many of these articles mentioned here may be seen in H. Havard's *Dictionnaire de l'ameublement*.

drafts (partially), but they were softened by draperies in Chinese silk. It was all a part of an exotic interest in faraway lands (which included the importation of mahogany from around 1750), and a resistance to the rigors of a formalistic past; even Voltaire was intrigued by it, so he wrote a tragedy called *L'orphelin de la Chine*.

The Far Eastern and the national combined in the eighteenth century to relax the rigidity of living in France. The seventeenth-century *alcôve*—which, as has already been seen, was a part of the décor in such a proper salon as that of madame de Rambouillet—developed in the time of Louis XV into a *niche*. This was an intimate spot equipped with a sofa, and given over to amorous colloquy. The sofa was not likely to be a Louis XIV *canapé* covered with a formal piece of Beauvais tapestry, but rather a soft and comfortable ottoman brought in from the Orient "by a voluptuous society." Bathtubs began to be made of lead or copper with an attached heating mechanism, a legitimate alleviation of the arctic rigors of Louis XIV's tub made of marble. Half-baths came into style, and *bains de siège*, or "chair baths," with possibly a back woven after a sketch of Boucher. Carafes began to be used at table (where they have remained down to this day), replacing the more formal high-spouted silver or crystal *aiguières* of earlier centuries. On the matter of food during the period of Louis XV, it has been said that "the art of cooking during his reign made no progress"; but there was an addition to the diet of dishes that were supposed to have aphrodisiac qualities. Madame de Pompadour probably consumed very few of these concoctions in view of her reputation for frigidity. She did espouse, however, any tendency toward the novel or bizarre; in her collection of birdcages were several with very high domes, and one with an eating trough of silver.[14]

Among the most visible manifestations of declining for-

malism in eighteenth-century France was the changing concept of a garden. The imposing and regular creations of Le
Nôtre and his disciples were considered too precise in a society that was seeking release from regulation; there were
preferences for "English gardens" and "Chinese gardens,"
with varying interpretations as to what constituted these two
horticultural endeavors. The chevalier de Jaucourt in 1765
was opposed to many features of the movement, and blamed
the general popularity of things Oriental for it. In our attitude toward "decoration," he said, we have a "ridiculous
and trivial taste"; as a result of this depreciation of taste, the
designs of the age of Louis XIV have lost favor and been
replaced by imported novelties: "The grand and straight allées (now) appear to us as being stupid; the palisades, cold
and regular; we like to make use of twisting allées, parterres
curved in outline, and wooded areas cut up into pompons.
Baskets of flowers, faded at the end of a few days, have replaced durable beds; everywhere are seen vases of terra cotta,
Chinese magots, and malformations* which prove quite
clearly that frivolity has extended its domain over all our
productions of this nature." Madame de Pompadour, who
was again blamed for deviations from standards in the eighteenth century, was supposed to have liked a garden with
"twisting allées."[15]

The English garden, as a symbol of the natural and unrestricted forces of the earth, had many proponents in Louis
XV's France. The English concept—or, at least, the French
understanding of this concept—fitted into the efforts at
pseudo-ruralism of the Court as well as into the back-to-
nature theories of a philosopher like Jean-Jacques Rousseau.
Jaucourt spoke favorably of the simplicity of an English
garden, and felt that it was an attempted expression of man's
original state in the Garden of Eden. He even went through
the process, with some degree of seriousness, of finding the

---

*Bambochades has been translated as "malformations"; bamboche means
an "ill-formed person."

Biblical garden in a specific spot of "sacred geography"; the world of scholars, according to Jaucourt, had looked without success for the "position of this country." He then included a passage in English on the original and natural paradise as described by John Milton. Milton's description in his *Paradise Lost* of the Garden of Eden was translated into French by Louis Racine in 1755, and may have accentuated in France the idea of an English garden. Mercier thought that English gardens were superior to French gardens just as the tragedy of Shakespeare was superior to French tragedy; in both cases the English forms were less inhibited by the rules. He spoke his mind on the matter with no lack of certainty: "Our tragedies resemble quite closely our gardens, which are handsome but symmetrical, have little variety, and are magnificently sad. The English design a garden wherein the attitude of nature is more nearly imitated and in which it is more pleasant to walk; one finds again in an English garden all of nature's caprices, her situations, and her disorder." The English themselves were not entranced by the architectural regularity of the classical French garden and began in the early eighteenth century to construct gardens wherein the "picturesqueness of nature was substituted for symmetrical and balanced combinations." Kew Gardens— six miles from the center of London and a favorite spot in the eighteenth century of George III—would be an example of horticultural models sought in the forests, and the abandonment of earlier regularized gardens like Hampton Court.[16]

Rousseau, in the fourth part of *La nouvelle Héloïse*, the eleventh letter, gave a full description of a natural garden through the medium of his interlocutor, Saint-Preux. It was a quiet, cool, flowered, tree-shaded, well-watered spot populated with every kind of tree and shrub. Saint-Preux marveled at the fine work of nature, and was told at this point by his host that "nature has done the work but under my direction." Anyway, there was no formality of plan, and roses and strawberry bushes (among dozens of other flowers and fruits) grew in the garden comfortably "without order, without symmetry." A natural moss covered the paths, and the secret of making it flourish had been "sent over from England." It would have been a sad situation, in the mind of Saint-Preux (or Rousseau), if a "well-paid architect" had been called in to "spoil nature" with precisely cut allées and pruned trees in this simple garden. If Rousseau disapproved of a classic and formal garden, he was equally opposed to one decorated with "porcelain flowers, magots, trellises, sand of all colors, and vases full of nothing." Rousseau's tomb on the grounds of the chateau of Ermenonville should have pleased him, since it was in a rather unspoiled and natural setting.[17]

The stately and correct gardens after the fashion of Le Nôtre were not replaced solely by the simple naturalness of English design; there was also the influence of the Orient. The irregularity of Chinese gardens had been learned about toward the end of the seventeenth century both from official reports and from missionaries returning to France. The Emperor's garden in Peking was described in the eighteenth century as having in it hills and valleys, a tortuous stream and a winding path, pavilions, bridges, waterfalls, and misshapen trees. The informal garden that gained favor over the classical garden in Louis XV's time might, therefore, be designated as Anglo-Chinese. English naturalness in horticulture soon blended with the exoticism of the Orient and other distant places; and decadent classicism, English simplicity, and the exotic flavor of distant lands produced some weird combinations in French gardens of the eighteenth century. One was created at Soisy-sous-Etioles which had in it an "Egyptian dance-hall" and a "Gothic orangery." And the duc de Penthièvre (whose tastes must have been a trifle florid) had constructed at his chateau at Armainvilliers* a garden which had as part of its décor a Turkish

*These chateaux were near Paris, in the modern *départements* of Seine-et-Oise and Seine-et-Marne, respectively.

pavilion, a Turkish bridge, a Gothic bathroom, and a Gothic gaming-room—all with a Chinese pavilion and a Chinese salon near by. At Chantilly, in the woods of Sylvia (which contains the conservatively formal house of Sylvia, the secret abode of the poet Théophile de Viau, in the seventeenth century) was built in 1771 a "Chinese kiosk" which was covered with red, yellow, and blue paint. It was all enough to make Le Nôtre and Mansart turn over in their graves. Nevertheless, as has been suggested by a present-day analyst of the history of French gardens, "gardens reflect the mores of their times"; thus it was to be expected that in them during the eighteenth century would be manifest the "enthronement of individuality in opposition to the spirit of discipline."[18]

An interesting and amusing feature of the declining years of formalism in France was the argument over pedantry; nobody, whether he was a formal classicist or emancipated individualist, wanted to be a pedant. Molière had already satirized the vice of pedantry in several of his plays. But the rule-breaking freethinkers following the age of Louis XIV would have liked to make a formalist and a pedant the same breed of dog. Charles Perrault in his poem of 1694, *Apologie des femmes*, gave a picture of a pedant (Boileau was the undeserving model), a dirty fellow who lived apart from the society of women:

> If he joins to his talents a love for antique debris,
> If he finds that in our time nothing worthy is done,
> And if he gives to every good modern a kick in the teeth,
> Of these assembled gifts you have the making of a pedant,
> The most pretentious as well as the most filthy
> Of all the animals that crawl over the earth.

Boileau sought to give his definition of a pedant in the third of his *Réflexions sur Longin*, which came out after Perrault's poem. A pedant, in Boileau's opinion, was not a "college-trained savant, stuffed with Greek and Latin" and "blind in his admiration of ancient authors"; a real pedant would be a man "full of himself who, with mediocre intelligence, makes bold decisions on everything" and "who boasts continually of having made new discoveries." And, along the way, such a man would decry antiquity without having the linguistic equipment to have learned anything about it. It is scarcely necessary to indicate that Boileau's words fell on infertile soil; the eighteenth century was perfectly willing to believe that pedantry and formalism were synonymous terms.[19]

So, in the experimental and unregulated age of Louis XV, formalism declined; but it did not completely disappear from the French artistic and intellectual landscape—it merely went partially underground. No cultivated Frenchman of the present era could conceive of an existence without a periodic renewing of his formal spirit in the stately verses of Corneille or Racine at the Comedie Française. A slightly different illustration of this spirit might be noted in a number of *Paris-Match* of the summer of 1965 wherein there is a description of the *jardin à la mode*, the "fashionable garden" for the alert Parisian. It is the *jardin-decorum*, which should have the following specifications in keeping with the "new tendency": parterres with borders of trimmed boxwood "as in the grounds of the chateaux of the Loire"; stone benches, preferably "old"; bowers and boskets; steps and balustrades; basins and fountains done in "classic" fashion; shafts of columns, which are "incomparable for poeticizing a garden"; orange (or laurel) trees in pots; vases and statues, "ancient and well-chosen."[20]

Around the middle of the eighteenth century, the abbé Raynal stated that "the Frenchman is a being altogether difficult to define."[21] In something of a paraphrase of Molière, it might be said that the more a Frenchman changes the more he remains his own formal self.

NOTES

BIBLIOGRAPHY

INDEX

# NOTES

## CHAPTER I. THE GENERAL PICTURE

1. See Pierre Fabri, *Le grand et vrai art de pleine rhétorique*, ed. A. Héron (3 vols.; Rouen, 1889-1890), I, 9.

2. For Ronsard's comments on the Italians and Spaniards, see Pierre de Ronsard, *Oeuvres complètes.* . . . ed. Paul Laumonier (8 vols.; Paris, 1914-1919), VII, 5, 53, 92.

3. See Jules de la Mesnardière, *La poétique* (Paris, 1639), VII, 122, for opinions on the various nationalities; and T, V for the opinion on Lope de Vega. This is a one-volume edition, with the strange pagination as indicated.

4. Gilles Ménage in his *Observations sur la langue française* (Paris, 1672), "Epistre" of dedication, said to the chevalier de Méré: "En effet, Monsieur, depuis l'établissement de l'Académie Française, nostre langue n'est pas seulement la plus belle et la plus riche de toutes les langues vivantes, elle est encore la plus sage et la plus modeste"—and by the conquests of "notre Roi, elle est aujourd'huy l'étude principale de tous les estrangers."

5. In his *Entretiens d'Ariste et d'Eugène* (Paris, 1671), pp. 37-40, Le Père Francisque Bouhours expounds his opinions through the mouths of his interlocutors. The quotation on foreigners' learning French reads in the original: "On parle déjà François dans toutes les Cours de l'Europe. Tous les étrangers qui ont de l'esprit se piquent de sçavoir le François: ceux qui haïssent le plus nôtre nation aiment nôtre langue." The idea that French may be contaminated by some German visitor comes from Bouhours' *Doutes sur la langue française* (Paris, 1674), p. 85.

6. See Le Père René Rapin, *Réflexions sur la poétique d'Aristote* (Paris, 1674), p. 35, for the Italians and the Spanish. A bit farther on in this work, part two, pp. 69 ff., Rapin speaks of the English: "Les Anglois nos voisins aiment le sang dans leurs jeux, par la qualité de leur tempérament."

7. L'Abbe Raynal in his *Nouvelles littéraires* of *Correspondance littéraire* par Grimm, Diderot, Raynal, *et al.* . . . ed. Maurice Tourneux (16 vols.; Paris, 1877), I, 72, says: "Vous connaissez, Madame, le théâtre anglais; il est sans moeurs, sans décence, sans règles; les insulaires sont naturellement si sombres, si tristes, si mélancoliques, que

les scènes les plus fortes, les plus hardies, les plus outrées, ne le sont jamais trop pour les distraire ou pour les toucher." Raynal continues here with further attacks on the English. Later on in this volume, pp. 133 ff., he takes up the weaknesses of the Spanish.

8. The general references in these last two paragraphs to Du Bellay's *Défense* are too well known to require exact citation. Homer was frequently called during the sixteenth century *le premier capitaine des Muses*. Thomas Sebillet in his *Art póetique françoys* of 1548, ed. Félix Gaiffe (Paris, 1910) says in ch. III, "le poëte naist, l'orateur se fait"—an opinion voiced by many during the period. Sebillet's remarks on the *cygnes* and their *plumes* also derive from this chapter. Fouquelin's ideas come from his *Rhétorique françoise* (Paris, 1557), pp. 3-4. Louis Meigret's *Trętté de la grammęre françoęze* (Paris, 1550) was written in reformed spelling. In his advice to the readers, he says: "Or ęt il que notre lang' et aojourdhuy si ęnrięhie par la profession ę experięnce de langes Latin' e Grecque, q'il n'et poīt d'art, ne sięnçe si diffięil' ę subtile . . . dont ęlle ne puysse tręter amplement ę elegamment."

9. For these points, see Joachim du Bellay, *La deffence et illustration de la langue françoyse*, ed. Em. Person (Versailles, 1878), p. 56— bk. I, ch. 3; Jacques Peletier du Mans, *L'art poétique*, ed. André Boulanger (Paris, 1930), pp. 116 ff.; Pierre de Laudun d'Aigaliers, *L'art poétique français*, ed. Joseph Dedieu (Toulouse, 1909), bk. IV, ch. 4; Vauquelin de la Fresnaye, *L'art poétique* . . . ed. Georges Pelissier (Paris, 1885), bk. I, vs. 277 ff. and bk. II, vs. 89 ff.

10. See Pierre de Deimier, *L'académie de l'art poétique* (Paris, 1610), p. 9; François de la Mothe le Vayer, *Considérations sur l'éloquence françoise de ce tems* (Paris, 1637), pp. 104, 115 ff., 188; La Mesnardière, *La poétique*, preliminary *Discours*.

11. Bouhours, *Doutes*, p. 53; Rapin, *Réflexions*, in the *Avertissement*.

12. L'Abbé Charles Batteux, *Les beaux arts réduits à un même principe* (Paris, 1746), in his *Avant-propos*.

13. Etienne Dolet, *La manière de bien traduire d'une langue en aultre* (Lyons, 1540), p. 14.

14. The *Quintil Horatian* of Barthélemy Aneau, which was once attributed to Charles Fontaine, is included in Person's edition of Du Bellay's *Deffence*, pp. 187-212—see pp. 194-196 for the points involved here, and the preface of Aneau's *Toutes les emblèmes de M. André Alciat* (Lyons, 1558).

15. Desmarets de Saint-Sorlin, *La défense de la poésie et de la langue françoise* (Paris, 1675), preface and p. 23, in an epistle answering *poètes latins*.

16. Pierre Gaxotte, *Histoire des Français* (2 vols.; Paris, 1951), II, 32 ff.; P. Le Moyne, *Les oeuvres poétiques* (Paris, 1671), p. 330.

17. Bouhours, *Entretiens*, p. 153.

## CHAPTER II. LANGUAGE AND STYLE

1. Barthélemy Aneau, *Quintil*, p. 198, discusses the "neuf instruments" of human speech. Claude Fauchet, *Recueil de l'origine de la langue et poésie françoise* (Paris, 1581), p. 43 said: "les langues se renforçent à mesure que les princes qui en usent s'agrandissent."

2. See Fabri, *Rhétorique*, I, 27-28, for the three manners of speech; I, 30, for proper address to a king: "Sire, vous estes nostre souverain roy tresredoubté par le monde universel"; I, 32, for praise and vituperation of woman; I, 21, for order and precedence.

3. For all this material on the "bons orateurs françoys," Horace, Pindar, etc., see Aneau's *Quintil*, pp. 199, 192; for "splendeur des mots," etc., see E. Dolet, *La manière*, p. 15; for accents in French, see L. Meigret, *Le trętté*, pp. 132 ff.

4. Antoine Fouquelin, *La rhétorique françoise* (Paris, 1557), p. 51 verso, discusses the training of a child by a grammarian; and pp. 17 ff., the parts of speech. Frère Jean mentions the "couleurs de rhétorique" in Rabelais' *Gargantua*, ch. XXXIX, at the end of the chapter.

5. For all these details see La Mothe le Vayer, *Considérations*, pp. 14-67.

6. *Ibid.*, pp. 90 ff. For eloquent French (not "stormy," etc.), see the chevalier de Méré, *Oeuvres complètes* (3 vols.; Paris, 1930), I, 60.

7. See Fauchet, *Recueil*, ch. VII; La Mothe le Vayer, *Considérations*, pp. 83 ff., for rhyme in prose and Isocrates; Ménage, *Observations*, p. 163; Scipion Dupleix, *Liberté de la langue françoise dans sa pureté* (Paris, 1651), p. 543; Bouhours, *Doutes*, p. 267.

8. Ronsard, *Oeuvres*, VII, 49-51; Laudun d'Aigaliers, *L'art poétique*, pp. 76-77.

9. Verlaine in his poem *Art Poétique* spoke of the emptiness of rhyme; he also wanted to seize "eloquence" and "twist its neck."

10. Peletier du Mans, *L'art poétique*, p. 148; Vauquelin de la Fresnaye, *L'art poétique*, bk. I, vs. 457 ff., 512; Deimier, *L'académie*, pp. 289, 20 ff.; La Mesnardière, *La poétique*, p. 401, said that rhyme was a "beauté subsidiaire" and an "espèce de fard"; Gilles Ménage, *Les origines de la langue françoise* (Paris, 1650), p. 25.

11. Jacques de la Taille, *La manière de faire des vers en françois, comme en Grec et en Latin* (Paris, 1573). This little treatise contains only twenty-two folios.

12. J.-A. Baïf, *Euvres en rime* . . . ed. Ch. Marty-Laveaux (in *La Pléiade Françoise*, 5 vols.; Paris, 1890), V, 297 ff.; Jean Passerat, *Les poésies françaises* . . . ed. Prosper Blanchemain (2 vols.; Paris, 1880), I, 76; Deimier, *L'académie*, p. 38, for the "douceur de la langue françoise"; Rapin, *Réflexions*, pp. 94 ff., for syllabic count; Batteux, *Les beaux arts*, pp. 179 ff., for long and short syllables, and cadence.

13. Aneau, *Quintil,* pp. 193, 207 (for strophe and antistrophe); Ronsard, *Oeuvres,* VII, 42.

14. The "fils de vache" was Aneau's accusation, *Quintil,* p. 200; Du Bellay, *Deffence,* pp. 141, 100 (for *lumière* and *excellence*), 127; Ronsard, *Oeuvres,* VII, 76 ff., 54 ff. (on imitating the Greeks and Romans).

15. Ronsard, *Oeuvres,* III, 3-4, for Jamin's statement, and III, 11, for the beginning of *La Franciade:*

> Muse, l'honneur des sommets de Parnasse,
> Guide ma langue et me chante la race
> Des Rois François yssus de Francion
> Enfant d'Hector Troyen de nation, . . .

The disgorging of the "Argives soudars" from the horse (III, 12-13) goes as follows:

> Là forcenoyent deux tygres sans merci
> Le grand Atride et le petit aussi
> Ioyeux de sang: le carnacier Tydide,
> Et le superbe héritier d'Eacide:
> Là l'Ithaquois chargé du grand bouclair
> Qui ne fut sien brillant comme un éclair . . .

For the Muses and Pegasus, see Vauquelin de la Fresnaye, *L'art poétique,* II, vs. 1-20, and III, vs. 447-448.

16. Deimier, *L'académie,* pp. 7, 164, 399 ff.—all against Du Bartas.

17. For the anagram of Arthénice, see François de Malherbe, *Oeuvres poétiques . . .* preceded by Racan's *Vie de Malherbe,* ed. Louis Moland (Paris, 1874), pp. 29-30. Most of the stories on Malherbe that have come down were told by his disciple, Racan.

18. Deimier, *L'académie,* p. 159, for Provençal and Gascon usage; Claude Faure de Vaugelas, *Remarques sur la langue françoise* (3rd ed.; Paris, 1655), preface; Dupleix, *Liberté,* p. 508, for the mistakes made by "les nations éloignées de la Cour"; Bouhours, *Remarques,* p. 97, for provincial pronunciations.

19. Vaugelas said in the preface to his *Remarques* that *usage* is "la façon de parler de la plus saine partie de la Cour, conformément à la façon d'escrire de la plus saine partie des auteurs du temps." Other details quoted here from Vaugelas come from this preface. Dupleix in general was opposed to Vaugelas; for specific points cited in this chapter, see Dupleix, *Liberté,* pp. 24-25, 529 ff.

20. Méré, *Oeuvres,* II, 75, 104 (for the "manières de la Cour"); Bouhours, *Doutes,* preliminary letter (for the difficulties of a provincial).

21. Fabri in *Rhétorique,* I, 280, complained of "quattre vingts et douze"; Ronsard, *Oeuvres,* VII, 91-92; Vauquelin de la Fresnaye, *L'art poétique,* II, vs. 531, speaks of "l'ornement de la langue pollie."

22. Much of this criticism is found in Vaugelas' preface to his *Remarques;* the specific words are scattered through the *Remarques,* pp. 23-488.

23. For *poitrine* and *face,* see Vaugelas, *Remarques,* p. 60; Dupleix, *Liberté,* p. 13; Ménage, *Observations,* pp. 187 ff.

24. See Dupleix, *Liberté,* epistle to Perrault, pp. 11 (on style), 24-25 (on women as arbiters of language), and *passim* for individual words; for Ménage's words and his opinions thereon, see his *Observations, passim.*

25. Most of Bouhours' ideas on words are scattered through his *Remarques—renaissance* is on p. 408; *sériosité* is in the *Doutes,* p. 46.

26. Bouhours, *Doutes,* p. 144. Bouhours was not beguiled by Dupleix.

27. Du Bellay, *Deffence,* p. 71; Sebillet, *Art poétique,* bk. I, ch. 3; Ronsard, *Oeuvres,* VII, 97, 88 (for "la splendeur des armes frappée de la clarté de soleil"), 87 (for transpositions); Peletier du Mans, *L'art poétique,* pp. 126 ff.

28. Fauchet, *Recueil,* V, 48-49; Vauquelin de la Fresnaye, *L'art poétique,* I, vs. 595-596: "De nostre Cathelane ou langue Provençalle/ La langue d'Italie et d'Espagne est vassalle: . . ." Vauquelin praised Garnier in *L'art poétique,* II, vs. 1055-1056. Laudun d'Aigaliers, *L'art poétique,* bk. IV, ch. 5, praises clarity.

29. Deimier, *L'académie,* pp. 488 ff.; Malherbe, *Oeuvres,* pp. 11, 33; Vaugelas, *Remarques,* pp. 567 ff.

30. Vauquelin de la Fresnaye, *L'art poétique,* II, vs. 1005-1007; Deimier, *L'académie,* p. 273; Bouhours, *Entretiens,* pp. 40-43.

31. Fouquelin's rhetoric was dedicated "à une Princesse née, et selon la commune espérance divinement prédestinée, non seulement pour l'amplification et avancemēt de notre langue mais aussi pour l'illustration et l'honneur de toute science." In his *Rhétorique,* p. 4 verso, he praises Ronsard's figures of speech.

32. A portion of the original of Dupleix' preface to his *Liberté* runs as follows: "Je ne doubte pas que ceux qui considéront que depuis cinquante ans j'ay donné au iour divers ouvrages d'excellent, haut et sérieux argument, ne trouveront estrange qu'aujourd'huy je produise et estale des observations sur la Langue Françoise, qui ne sont que des bagatelles de grammaire. Car quelle apparence a-t'il qu'un esprit qui a tissu avec un labeur obstiné l'Histoire des Gaules et de France depuis le Déluge jusqu'à présent et la fondation de Rome jusqu'à l'Empire de Charlemagne, . . ."

33. La Mesnardière, *La poétique,* pp. 245, 249-250 (for the "femme médiocre"), 353 (for the Prix d'Eloquence), 129 (for the excerpt from *Alinde*):

Par quel art, Justes Dieux, une Femme, une Amante
Se peut-elle éxenter d'un mal qu'elle fomente!

Et comment un mortel peut-il estre vainqueur
D'un serpent immortel qui renaist dans son coeur?

34. Le Père Le Moyne, *Les oeuvres poétiques* (Paris, 1671), in his *Dissertation du poème épique*, which prefaced his *Saint Louis*.

35. Méré, *Oeuvres*, I, 47 (for "bon sens" and "longue expérience"), 71 (for "le coeur a son langage"), 99 ff. (for Voiture), 104 (for "grandes choses" and "les petites"); II, 61, 102 (for the "manières de la Cour"), 122 ff.

36. Desmarets de Saint-Sorlin, *La comparison de la langue et de la poésie françoyse, avec la grecque et la latine* (Paris, 1670), pp. 7, 18; Bouhours, *Entretiens*, p. 227 (Ronsard and Voiture); Bouhours, *Doutes*, pp. 198, 230 (*exactitude*), 241-242 (Voiture and *contentement*); Bouhours, *Remarques*, in the "*Avertissement*" says: "L'exactitude bien entendue est dans les ouvrages d'esprit, comme dans les bastiments et dans les tableaux je ne sais quoy de propre et de régulier, qui s'accorde bien avec quelque chose de grand et d'auguste." Other ideas of Bouhours on perfection, the rules, polishing, etc. come from this preface. For Rapin's concepts, see his *Réflexions*, pp. 80 (for Ronsard, Du Bartas, Théophile, Malherbe), 94 (order in poetry).

37. Urbain Chevreau, *Oeuvres meslées* (La Haye, 1697), pp. 1-2; Batteux, *Les beaux arts*, pp. 114, 124 ("le bon goût est un amour habituel de l'ordre"). Buffon's famous *Discours sur le style* begins: "Le style n'est que l'ordre et le mouvement qu'on met dans ses pensées."

## CHAPTER III. THE QUESTION OF THE BAROQUE

1. All of these earlier concepts of the baroque can be noted in the cited sources. Victor L. Tapié in his *Le baroque* (Paris, 1961) refers to several of them.

2. Marcel Arland in his edition of the *Oeuvre poétique* of Jean de Sponde (Paris, 1945), p. xi, says that Alan Boase has been particularly interested in "nos poètes 'baroques' du XVIe et du XVIIe siècles." For the designation of Jean Rousset as "maître-pilote en Baroquie," see Marcel Raymond, *Baroque et Renaissance poétique* (Paris, 1955), p. 9.

3. Jean Rousset in *La littérature de l'âge baroque en France* (Paris 1953), p. 8, says that attributes of the baroque are "le changement, l'inconstance, le trompe l'oeil et la parure, le spectacle funèbre, la vie fugitive et le monde en instabilité." Circe, water in movement, and such things, are also in Rousset's work, pp. 8, 157, and *passim*. Raymond, *Baroque*, speaks of the image of death in poetry (p. 23), and of "panpsychisme, pandynamisme, et panthéisme" (p. 22). Imbrie Buffum, in his *Studies in the Baroque from Montaigne to Rotrou* (New Haven, 1957), has a good deal to say about magic, disguise,

exaggeration, and similar matters. Buffum earlier examined the stylistic qualities of the baroque in his *Agrippa d'Aubigné's "Les Tragiques": A Study of the Baroque Style of Poetry* (New Haven, 1951).

4. See Helmut Hatzfeld, "Use and Misuse of 'Baroque' as a Critical Term in Literary History," *University of Toronto Quarterly*, 31: 180-200 (1962).

5. Rousset in *La littérature*, p. 8, says that the baroque movement extended from around 1580 to 1670, or from Montaigne to Bernini. Raymond, *Baroque*, p. 18, states that the period between 1550 and 1650 in France "est celui d'un état de culture, ou plutôt d'une crise de la culture, où des oeuvres de contenu ou de forme baroque ont pu prendre naissance." Lionel Gossman, *Men and Masks: A Study of Molière* (Baltimore, 1963), p. 195, put Racine in the baroque age. For Hatzfeld's opinions on the baroque and mannerism, see p. 192 of his article cited in Note 4.

6. For these ideas, see Eugenio d'Ors, *Du baroque* (Paris, 1935), and Henri Focillon, *La vie des formes* (Paris, 1934); Tapié, *Le baroque*, p. 12, says the baroque "a chanté la gloire, la force, la joie, la liberté, la conquête de Dieu par la foi et le sacrifice lucidement accepté."

7. See Pierre Gaxotte, *Histoire des Français* (2 vols.; Paris, 1951), I, 96, *passim*; Raymond, *Baroque*, pp. 10, *passim*.

8. Many of these opinions are shared by Rousset, Raymond, and Tapié.

9. Some of the original lines of Malherbe's *"Les Larmes de Saint Pierre"* run as follows:

> Que m'est demeuré pour conseil et pour armes,
> Que d'écouler ma vie en un fleuve de larmes
> Et la chassant de moi l'envoyer au tombeau? . . .
>
> Mon regret est si grand, et ma faute si grande,
> Qu'une mer éternelle à mes yeux je demande
> Pour pleurer à jamais le péché que j'ai fait.

Ode VIII, " *Pour le Roi*," begins:

> Ceux à qui la chaleur ne bout plus dans les veines
> En vain dans les combats ont des soins diligents:
> Mars est comme l'amour: ses travaux et ses peines
> Veulent des jeunes gens.

For these excerpts, see Malherbe, *Oeuvres poétiques*, ed. Louis Moland (Paris, 1874), pp. 48, 257.

10. The first four lines from Agrippa d'Aubigné in his French are:

> Terre, qui sur ton dos porte à peine nos peines,
> Change en cendre et en os tant de fertiles plaines,

En bourbe nos gazons, nos plaisirs en horreurs,
En soulfre nos guerets, en charogne nos fleurs.

Corneille's alexandrines from *Médée* are:

Soleil, qui vois l'affront qu'on va faire à ta race,
Donne-moi tes chevaux à conduire à ta place;
Accorde cette grâce à mon désir bouillant;
Je veux choir sur Corinthe avec ton char brûlant: . .

11. For all this material, see Urbain Chevreau, *Oeuvres meslées* (La Haye, 1697), pp. 245 ff.

12. See Du Bellay, *La deffence*, p. 149; Ronsard, *Oeuvres*, VII, 82; Aneau, *Quintil*, p. 149.

13. Rapin, *Réflexions*, p. 92; Bouhours, *Entretiens*, pp. 48, 51, 69, 263 (for the *devises*), 389.

14. Batteux, *Les beaux arts*, dedication, and pp. 2, 167.

15. Deimier, *L'Académie*, pp. 7, 399; La Mesnardière, *Poétique*, QQQ; Saint-Sorlin, *Défense*, p. 27; Ménage, *Les origines*, p. 25; Bouhours, *Remarques*, p. 145; Rapin, *Réflexions*, pp. 80, 82, 230; Chevreau, *Oeuvres*, p. 147.

16. See Jean de Sponde, *Oeuvre poétique;* the first quatrain of the fourth love sonnet runs in French as follows:

En vain mille beautez à mes yeux se présentent,
Mes yeux leur sont ouvers et mon courage clos,
Une seule beauté s'enflamme dans mes os
Et mes os de ce feu seulement se contentent.

And the second sonnet on death begins:

Mais si faut-il mourir, et la vie orgueilleuse,
Qui brave de la mort, sentira ses fureurs,
Les soleils haleront ces journaliers fleurs,
Et le temps crevera ceste ampoule venteuse.

17. For all this material, see J. B. Chassignet, *Sonnets franc-comtois*, ed. Théodore Courtaux (Paris, 1892).

18. See Saint-Amant, *Oeuvres poétiques* . . . ed. Léon Vérane (Paris, 1930). The poem, *"Solitude,"* begins:

Que j'aime à voir la décadence
De ces vieux chasteaux ruinez,
Contre qui les ans mutinez,
Ont déployé leur insolence!

For other details, see Jean de Bussières, *Les descriptions poétiques* (Lyons, 1649), and Martial de Brives, *Les oeuvres poétiques* (Lyons, 1653), p. 20.

## CHAPTER IV. THE FRENCH ACADEMY

1. Much of this is taken from the introductory material of Robert de Bonnières' edition of Saint Evremond's *Les Académiciens* (Paris, 1879). Agrippa d'Aubigné's remarks on the Académie du Palais come from his *Histoire universelle*. Du Boulay, *Historia Universitatis Parisiensis* (Paris, 1715-1773), VI, 115-116, speaks of the musical sessions on Sunday mornings.

2. Le Père Le Moyne, *Oeuvres poétiques*, p. 330, calls Richelieu the "grand Armand, l'honneur de notre histoire." Fénelon's remarks are in his *Discours . . de reception à l'Académie*, p. 277 of the Delplanque edition, and La Bruyère's are in his *Discours à l'Académie*, pp. 412 ff. of the cited edition. The story of the homage to Richelieu at his death comes from Pellisson et d'Olivet, *Histoire de l'Académie Française . . .* ed. Ch. L. Livet (2 vols.; Paris, 1858), I, 130 ff. Pellisson's work appeared in 1652 and contained the important early history of the Academy. His statements have been used freely in this chapter. Olivet continued the history past 1700.

3. For the reunions at Conrart's house, see Pellisson, *Histoire*, I, 8, and I, 7, for the letter to Richelieu. The statutes and letters of the Académie, recopied in many places, are listed officially in L. Aucoc, *L'Institut de France. Lois, statuts et règlements, 1635-1889* (Paris, 1889). Pellisson, *Histoire*, I, 134, said that in 1637, "le nombre de quarante n'était pas encore rempli."

4. See Pellisson, *Histoire*, I, 102-105, for Chapelain's ideas on the dictionary.

5. *Pellisson, Histoire*, I, 106 ff.—for Boisrobert, Vaugelas, and the "quarante personnes des plus intelligentes." A couplet from Boisrobert's doggerel runs as follows: "Et le destin m'aurait fort obligé/ S'il m'avait dit: 'Tu vivras jusqu'au G.'"

6. Fénelon, *Lettre*, pp. 81 ff., Delplanque edition.

7. Article 13 of the statutes reads: "Si un des Académiciens fait quelque acte indigne d'un homme d'honneur, il sera interdit ou destitué, selon l'importance de la faute."

8. Furetière's supposed *privilège* allowed him to print "un dictionnaire universel contenant généralement tous les mots français tant vieux que modernes." Much of the story of Furetière's conflict over the dictionaries is to be found in his *Recueil des Factums. . .* ed. Charles Assélineau (2 vols.; Paris, 1859), the first part.

9. From Furetière's second *Factum*, in the *Recueil*, I, 183, comes the description of the Academy committee meeting: "Celui qui crie le plus haut, c'est celui qui a raison; chacun fait une longue harangue sur la moindre bagatelle. Le second répète comme un écho tout ce que le premier a dit, et le plus souvent ils parlent trois ou quatre ensemble. Quand un Bureau est composé de cinq ou six personnes, il y en a un qui lit, un qui opine, deux qui causent, un qui dort, et un

qui s'amuse à lire quelque Dictionnaire qui est sur la table. Quand la parole vient au second, il faut lui relire l'article à cause de sa distraction dans la première lecture. Voilà le moyen d'avancer l'ouvrage. Il ne se passe pas deux lignes qu'on ne fasse de longues digressions; que chacun ne débite un conte plaisant, ou quelque nouvelle, ou qu'on ne parle des affaires d'Etat et de réformer le gouvernement." From Furetière's *L'apothéose du dictionnaire de l'Académie, et son expulsion de la région céleste* (La Haye, 1696) comes the dedicatory epigram:

> Je suis ce gros Dictionnaire,
> Qui fut un demi-siècle au ventre de ma mère,
> Quand je naquis j'avois de la barbe, et des dents:
> Ce qu'on ne doit trouver fort extraordinaire,
> Attendu que j'avois l'âge de cinquante ans

10. Furetière, *Apothéose*, p. 42 for *amour;* p. 48 for the article; p. 77 for *huictante*. The discussion of the accusative is in Furetière, *L'enterrement du dictionnaire de l'Académie* (n.p., 1697), pp. 176-177.

11. Furetière, *L'enterrement*, pp. 151-152, for attacks on the dedication of the Academy's dictionary; 310, for *compisser;* 153, for *cariatide;* 40, for *capitaine*. See Furetière, *Apothéose*, p. 97, for *puce*.

12. The verses quoted from *Les Académiciens* run in the original speeches of Godeau as follows:

> Eh quoi! chers nourrissons des Filles de Mémoire,
> Qui sur les temps futurs obtiendrez la victoire;
> Beaux mignons de Pallas, vrais favoris des dieux;
> Vous n'êtes pas encore arrivés en ces lieux!
> . . . . . . . . . . . . . . . .
> Manquai-je en quelque endroit à garder la césure?
> Y peut-on remarquer une seule hiature?
> Suis-je pas scrupuleux à bien choisir les mots?
> Ne fais-je pas parler chacun fort a propos?
> Le *decorum* latin, en français *bienséance*,
> N'est si bien observé nulle part, que je pense.

13. The story of the nurses is told by Pellisson and repeated in summary in Bonnières' edition of *Les Académiciens*, p. xliii. For *car, muscadin*, and *malarde*, see Pellisson, *Histoire*, I, 52, 118 ff.

14. See Pellisson, *Histoire*, I, 94, for Corneille's letter; p. 118, for the Académie's being satisfied with "l'ordre de la pièce en général"; p. 121, for Malherbe and the question of vacations. See the marquis d'Argenson, *Journal et mémoires . . .* ed. E. J. B. Rathery (9 vols.; Paris, 1859-1867), II, 36 for the Académie's work on *patton*, or *pâton*.

15. For these points, see Vaugelas, *Remarques*, epistle of dedication; Dupleix, *Liberté*, pp. 6, 20; Bouhours, *Remarques*, p. 343; Fénelon,

*Lettre,* p. 96; J.-A. de La Harpe, *Eloge de Racine* (Amsterdam, 1772), p. 3.

16. From madame Dacier, *Des causes de la corruption du goust* (Paris, 1714), pp. 32-33, comes the statement that it is quite a *fatalité* "que ce soit de L'Académie Française, de ce corps si célèbre, qui doit être le rempart de la langue, des lettres, et du bon goust que sont sortis depuis cinquante ans toutes les méchantes critiques qu'on a faites contre Homère." This same passage contains her favorable comment on Boileau and her husband.

17. Bossuet's *Discours de réception à l'Académie* can be found in many editions of his works; it is handily available in Gustave Lanson's *Extraits des oeuvres diverses* of Bossuet (Paris, 1899), pp. 22 ff. The discourses of Fénelon and La Bruyère have been previously mentioned.

18. Argenson, *Journal,* I, 163; the duc de Luynes, *Mémoires* (17 vols.; Paris, 1860-1865), X, 142.

19. Le maréchal de Villars, *Mémoires,* in the *Nouvelle Collection des Mémoires pour servir a l'Histoire de France,* ed. M. M. Michaud et Poujalat (vol. IX; Paris, 1839), pp. 235, 287 ff.

## CHAPTER V. RIGORS OF THE THEATRE

1. All the material in these early paragraphs is standard, and can be found in such studies as Eugène Rigal, *Le théâtre français avant la période classique* (Paris, 1901); H. C. Lancaster, *A History of French Dramatic Literature in the Seventeenth Century. Part I: the Pre-classical Period* (2 vols.; Baltimore, 1929); S. Wilma Deierkauf-Holsboer, "La vie d'Alexandre Hardy," in the *Proceedings of the American Historical Society* (vol. 91; Philadelphia, 1947). I have also drawn on my own book, *The Early Public Theatre in France* (Cambridge, Mass., 1960).

2. Many of these documents are to be seen in Bernard Weinberg, *Critical Prefaces of the Renaissance* (Evanston, Ill., 1950). For the Ronsard opinion, see the Laumonier edition of his works, III, 79. Vauquelin de la Fresnaye in his *Art poétique,* bk. II, vs. 253-260, said:

> Or comme eux l'Heroic suivant le droit sentier,
> Doit son oeuvre comprendre au cours d'un an entier:
> Le Tragic, le Comic, dedans une journée
> Comprend ce que fait l'autre au cours de son année:
> Le Théâtre iamais ne doit estre rempli
> D'un argument plus long qu'un iour accompli:
> Et doit une Iliade, en sa haute entreprise
> Estre au cercle d'un an, ou guères plus, comprise.

3. See Pierre de Laudun, *L'art poétique français,* bk. V, ch. IX.

4. Chapelain's *Lettre sur la règle des vingt-quatre heures* was writ-

ten to Antoine Godeau, the later Academician and bishop of Grasse, on November 29, 1630. It can be consulted conveniently in Jean Chapelain, *Opuscules critiques*, ed. Alfred C. Hunter (Paris, 1936), pp. 113-126.

5. Corneille's opinions are scattered through his *Examens* and his *Trois discours*. D'Aubignac's *Pratique du théâtre* can be easily consulted in Pierre Martino's edition (Alger-Paris, 1927).

6. Much of this material involving D'Aubignac and others may be seen in Charles Arnaud, *Théories dramatiques du dix-septième siècle* (Paris, 1888). Boileau in the third *chant* of his *Art poétique*, vs. 28 ff. made his famous pronouncement:

> Un rimeur, sans péril, delà les Pirénees,
> Sur la scène en un jour, renferme des années
>
> . . . . . . . . . . . . . . . . . . .
> Qu'en lieu, qu'en un jour, un fait seul accompli
> Tienne jusqu'a à la fin le théâtre rempli.

For these details involving the epic and tragedy see Le Bossu, *Traité du poème épique* (Paris, 1675), I, 11; II, 140, 265 ff.; III, 379.

7. Le Bossu, *Traité*, II, 268 ff., for the duration of the *Iliad;* madame Dacier, *Des causes de la corruption du goust* (Paris, 1714), p. 73.

8. See J.-A. de La Harpe, *Eloge de Racine* (Amsterdam, Paris, 1772), pp. 8-9 for the "déclamateurs barbares"; and L.-S. Mercier, *Du théâtre ou nouvel essai sur l'art dramatique* (Amsterdam, 1773), pp. xiv, 26, 96-97, 144-145, 278, 307.

9. La Taille's comments on tragedy come from his *L'art de la tragédie*. Diderot called the personages of tragedy emptily regal in his novel, *Les bijoux indiscrets*. Voltaire in his *Lettre anglaise*, "Sur la tragédie," described Shakespeare's plays as "farces monstrueuses." Pierre Gaxotte in his *Histoire de Français*, II, 122, compares Hardy to Shakespeare; on p. 123 he says: "Il n'y a pas dans l'histoire des littératures d'autre tragédie que la grecque et la française."

10. Peletier du Mans, *L'art poétique*, p. 190; Vauquelin, *L'art poétique*, vs. 181-182; La Mesnardière, *La poétique*, "Discours" (for the *pompeux et sublime* in tragedy), p. X. ch. III, ch. VII.

11. Boileau said that the writer of tragedy should know how "de plaire et de toucher," in the third *chant* of his *Art Poétique*, vs. 25; Racine said the primary aim of tragedy is "de plaire et de toucher," in the preface of his play *Bérénice*. For Rapin's ideas, see his *Réflexions*, *Avertissement* and ch. X. Saint Evremond's opinions are to be found in his *De la tragédie ancienne et moderne* of 1672.

12. Fénelon criticized Corneille and Racine in his *Projet d'un traité sur la tragédie*, a division of his *Lettre à l'Académie*—pp. 180 ff. of the cited edition.

13. See Mercier, *Du théâtre*, p. 30, for the heroes of tragedy: "tous les héros marchèrent à grands pas, levèrent leurs têtes ornées d'un

panache flottant, furent roides et tendus; ils parlèrent, ou plûtôt ils mugirent par la sarbacane du poète"; pp. 296-297 for the alexandriñe.

14. Gabriel Guéret told the story of Montfleury's death in *Le Parnasse réformé;* it can be seen in Guéret's *Les auteurs en belle humeur* (Amsterdam, 1723). Molière has a valet give, in *Les précieuses ridicules,* his supposed play to the actors of the Hôtel de Bourgogne because the others "ne savent pas faire ronfler les vers."

15. Madame de Motteville in her *Mémoires (Nouvelle Collection de Mémoires,* ed. Michaud et Poujoulat; Paris, 1838), X, 69, speaks of Anne of Austria's going "à la comédie" and of Corneille's "belles pièces." The marquis de Dangeau in his *Journal de la cour de Louis XIV* (London, 1770), p. 151, tells of the King's refusing to allow the Bible to be used in a performance of the *Bourgeois gentilhomme* "dans sa chambre."

16. This performance of *Iphigénie* is described in Les Frères Parfaict, *Histoire du théâtre français* (12 vols.; Paris, 1745-1749), 11, 360; for *Esther* at Saint Cyr, see Dangeau, *Journal,* p. 53.

17. For this story, see the *Lettres de madame de Sévigné,* ed. M. Monmerqué (14 vols.; Paris, 1925), II, 33 ff. The incident took place during the last two weeks of December 1670.

18. See the maréchal de Villars, *Mémoires,* IX, 296. For madame de Pompadour's interest in theatre, see D'Argenson's *Journal et Mémoires.* VI, 77, 145-146 (for "La marquise amuse le roi tant qu'il n'a pas un moment à réfléchir"), and V, 331; and the duc de Luynes' *Mémoires,* X, 45, 99, 190. D'Argenson said that the new Opéra was a monument "au règne du mauvais goût et à la disparition du beau, du noble, du simple, du magnifique" (*Journal,* VI, 4).

19. La Harpe's analysis of the *parterre* is in his *Eloge de Racine,* p. 3, which begins: "Les représentations dramatiques n'auront de la décence et de la dignité, les jugements publics n'auront une expression marquée et incontestable, que quand tous les spectateurs seront assis."

20. Destouches made this statement on criticism in his play, *Le glorieux,* act 2, sc. 5: "La critique est aisée mais l'art est difficile." Peletier du Mans, *L'art poétique,* p. 193, said Jodelle's *Cléopâtre* would bring "honneur à la langue française," while Vauquelin's ideas on Garnier are in his *Art poétique,* bk. II, vs. 1055-1056.

21. Pellisson, *Histoire,* I, 87 ff., describes the quarrel around *Le Cid.* The *Sentiments* of Chapelain are in the cited edition of his works, pp. 153-197. Boileau's verses, from his ninth *Satire,* run as follows: "En vain contre le *Cid* un ministre se ligue:/Tout Paris pour Chimène a les yeux de Rodrigue." La Bruyère's comments are in his *Des ouvrages de l'esprit,* p. 13 of the cited edition.

22. See Vauquelin's *Art poétique,* bk. III, vs. 80 ff.; Desmarets de Saint-Sorlin, *Comparison,* p. 33; Boileau, *Art poétique, passim;* Rapin, *Réflexions,* pp. 216-217; Fénelon, *Projet d'un traité sur la comédie,* pp.

201 ff. of the cited edition; Bossuet, *Maximes et réflexions sur la comédie* (Paris, 1881), p. 27.

23. For these details, see Boileau's seventh *Epître*, dedicated to Racine; Bossuet, *Sur le style et la lecture*, p. 15, in his *Extraits;* La Bruyère, *Des ouvrages*, pp. 22-24; Raynal, *Nouvelles littéraires*, p. 136; La Harpe, *Eloges*, pp. 50 ff.

## CHAPTER VI. MANNERS AND SOCIAL RITUAL

1. For this description of the party at Versailles, see the *Lettres de madame de Sévigné*, IV, 543 ff.

2. See madame de Sévigné, *Lettres*, III, 203, for madame de Lafayette's opinion of Chantilly; II, 172, for "monsieur le Prince's" entertainment of the King; II, 187 ff., for Vatel's death.

3. Letters 54-67 in the cited edition of madame de Sévigné are concerned with Fouquet's trial and sentence to exile.

4. Dangeau, *Journal*, pp. 5-6, tells of the trip to Marly that was postponed; the story of the *boutiques* at Marly is on p. 27; see Villars, *Mémoires*, p. 136, for the waters at Marly.

5. Villars, *Mémoires*, pp. 303-304, 338, for hunting at Chantilly and Rambouillet. D'Argenson, *Journal*, I, 128, said of Chantilly, "cette maison de Condé est magasin de factions et d'avarice"; in I, 281, he describes madame de Mailly's visit to Fontainebleau; in II, 137, D'Argenson gave the following picture of life in the chateaux: "Au voyage de la Muette que fait le roi actuellement, la partie est gaillarde et indépendante. On a invité les dames qui en sont ordinairement et auxquelles on est accoutumé. On dîne à Madrid chez Mademoiselle; on soupe à la Muette; dans l'après-midi à Bagatelle chez la maréchale d'Estrées; on a passé joyeusement le temps, on y fait l'amour, si vous voulez; tout est bien réglé." D'Argenson throughout his memoirs has a good deal to say about the lack of bread and the people's suffering.

6. See D'Argenson, *Journal*, II, 72-73; the duc de Luynes, *Mémoires*, X, 5, for the fruits and harangue at Fontainebleau.

7. Faret's manual was called *L'honneste homme ou l'art de plaire à la Cour*. La Bruyère in his *Caractères* has a division entitled *De la Cour*, from which I have detached excerpts. It is here that La Bruyère says: "La cour est comme un édifice bâti de marbre; je veux dire qu'elle est composée d'hommes fort durs, mais fort polis."

8. For this story on the duke of Buckingham, see the chevalier de Méré, *Oeuvres*, II, 131-132.

9. Méré, *Oeuvres*, II, 75; Le Moyne, *Oeuvres*, p. 316; D'Argenson, *Journal*, I, 22: "une cour moderne se pique de tourner en ridicule et de traiter avec supériorité indiscrète tout ouvrage, manières et respects de l'ancienne cour." For the King's doffing of his hat, and the courtiers wearing theirs, see Dangeau, *Journal*, pp. 33, 103.

10. Villars, *Mémoires*, pp. 237-238, was much upset about the Parle-

ment de Paris' taking no action on the question of doffing hats to the peers of France.

11. D'Argenson, *Journal*, V, 73—madame de Pompadour "une maîtresse de si bas lieu"—and VI, 77, for Pompadour's apartment; Luynes, *Mémoires*, X, 173—"madame de Pompadour connaît le Roi"; D'Argenson, *Journal*, II, 261 (for the hounds), and III, 161 (for the paternosters). See Villars, *Mémoires*, p. 316, for the King and Queen in bed; and Luynes, *Mémoires*, X, 333, for the ladies of the Court seeking culture.

12. Madame de Sévigné, *Lettres*, II, 307, for madame de Chaulnes' party; III, 11, for the midnight feast; and II, 72, for the fire where the Venetian ambassador appeared "en robe de chambre et en perruque and conserva fort bien la gravité de la Sérénissime."

13. Madame de Sévigné, *Lettres*, II, 143 ff.; III, 346—"car ce rouge, c'est la loi et les prophètes: c'est sur ce rouge que roule tout le Christianisme"; III, 349, for the lady who was too fancily dressed.

14. See madame de Sévigné, *Lettres*, III, 204 ff., for the ladies in Holland. The episode of the quarrel between the ladies at the fireworks is in Villars, *Mémoires*, pp. 281-282.

15. L.-S. Mercier tells of the prostitutes and a lady's two toilettes in his *Tableau de Paris* (Paris, 1853), pp. 90 ff., 257. See madame de Sévigné's *Lettres*, II, 173, for her son's being disgusted with women, whom he described as "des tetons, des cuisses, et des panerées de baisers."

16. In his essay *Des Femmes* from his *Caractères*, La Bruyère says: "On regarde une femme savante comme on fait une belle arme: elle est ciselée artistement, d'une polissure admirable, et d'un travail fort recherché; c'est une pièce de cabinet que l'on montre aux curieux, qui n'est pas d'usage."

17. Robert de Bonnières in his edition of Saint Evremond's *Les Académiciens*, p. xxi, spoke of the Hôtel de Rambouillet as a place where one learned refinement and how "on doit déférer aux dames et comment les sexes se règlent."

18. The *alcôve* is described by H. Havard, *Dictionnaire de l'ameublement et de la décoration depuis le XIIIe siècle à nos jours* (4 vols.; Paris, 1894), I, 45 ff. According to Somaise, for the *précieuses*, "laquais, mouchez la chandelle" became "inutile, ôtez le superflu de cet ardent"; and "souffler le feu" was "exciter cet élément combustible"; "il pleut" was "le troisième élément tombe"; and "les pieds" would be "les chers souffrants." La Bruyère in *De la societé et de la conversation* told a man that his desire for *esprit* was the reason "de votre pompeux galimatias, de vos phrases embrouillées, et de vos grands mots qui ne signifient rien." Gaxotte, *Histoire*, II, 123, said that the Hôtel de Rambouillet taught everyone to speak "en honnête homme."

19. Georges Mongrédien, *La vie de société au XVIIe et XVIIIe*

*siècles* (Paris, 1950), pp. 137 ff., speaks of the *Cyrus* and *Clélie* as "manuels de civilité galante." Saint Evremond, *Critique littéraire*, pp. 240-246, talks about conversing with women.

20. Havard in his *Dictionnaire* lists many of the instruments used for eating and drinking from the sixteenth to the eighteenth century.

21. Pantagruel and Panurge visit the land of the Gastrolastres in the fourth book of Rabelais' *Cinq livres*. Robert Mandrou, *Introduction à la France moderne* (Paris, 1961), pp. 15 ff., mentions the types of diet in the sixteenth and seventeenth centuries.

22. Many of these details, including some quoted material, have been taken from Paul Dupays, *Gastronomie historique de l'art culinaire* (Paris, 1953).

23. See Ph.-E. de Coulanges, *Recueil de chansons choisies* (Paris, 1694), for these excerpts on manners. The advice to fathers of families runs in the original:

> Pour bien élever vos enfants,
> N'épargnez précepteur ni mie;
> Mais jusques à ce qu'ils soient grands,
> Faites les taire en compagnie,
> Car rien ne donne tant d'ennuy
> Que d'écouter l'enfant d'autruy.   (p. 51)

Coulanges' poor dinner is in "Sur un disner":

> Figues et melons, des choux pour tout potage,
> Pour toute entrée un peu de boeuf salé,
> Pour tout rôti, des perdreaux de bon âge,
> Un jambon, des cerneaux, du fromage,
>      Du vin frais, et de la liberté.   (p. 194)

Boileau derided the pseudo-formal dinner at considerable length in his third *Satire;* many details have been omitted. Mercier, *Tableau*, p. 186, mentions the less formal dinners of his day, and the fact that demoiselles no longer have to sing at dessert.

24. The couplet from Amiens is in Mandrou, *Introduction*, p. 24: "Gaudeamus, faisons grande chère, / Buvons le vin, laissons la bière." Coulanges, *Recueil*, p. 62, gives advice to coffee-drinkers in a poem, "Pour les preneurs de caffé." For madame de Sévigné's ideas on chocolate, see her *Lettres*, II, 164, 399.

25. Tallemant des Réaux, *Les historiettes* (8 vols.; Paris, 1932-1934), III, 23, speaks of Voiture's preferences. For Anne of Austria's gambling, see madame de Motteville, *Mémoires*, p. 13; madame de Sévigné's *Lettres*, II, 113, for Cessac's dismissal from Court, and II, 546, for madame de Grignan's gambling losses. Le Moyne, *Oeuvres*, pp. 333 ff., takes up moderation in gambling in a poem, "Du jeu," which begins: "De tous les règlements à prendre sur le jeu, / Le premier, Doralis, est de jouer fort peu." See Dangeau, *Journal*, p. 85

(for the "jeu prodigieux"), and p. 98 (for "madame la Duchesse's" losses); D'Argenson, *Journal*, I, 33, 86 (for the story of the orange); Villars, *Mémoires*, p. 290 and pp. 321-322 (for the King's gambling at Marly).

26. D'Argenson, *Journal*, II, 92-94; Luynes, *Mémoires*, X, 8, for the new building at Fontainebleau.

27. Madame de Sévigné, *Lettres*, III, 239 (for the "petit chien de village"), III, 107 (for the "chiennes de punaises"), III, 7 (on Canada). The details on the bathtub, *chaise percée*, and such things are in Havard's *Dictionnaire*. Mercier, *Tableau*, p. 183, made this concluding statement on the tone of Paris.

## CHAPTER VII. ENTREES AND CEREMONIALS

1. Royal entrees and ceremonials were treated early by D. Godefroy, *Le cérémonial français* (Paris, 1649); a more recent consideration of the matter is that of Josèphe Chartrou, *Les entrées solennelles et triomphales à la Renaissance, 1484-1551* (Paris, 1928), from which I have used details on Charles VIII and Louis XII. For some of Francis I's movements over Italy and France, see Auguste Bailly, *François Ier, restaurateur des lettres et des arts* (Paris, 1954), pp. 74 ff., 82 ff., 99 ff.

2. The 1548 entree of Henry II into Lyons was mentioned by various contemporary observers. I have used here, in particular, a pamphlet entitled *La magnifica et triumphale entrata del christianiss. Re de Francia Henrico secondo . . fatta nella nobile & antique citta di Lyone . . . alli 21 di Septemb. 1548* (Lyons, 1549). Ronsard's poem is in the Laumonier edition of his works, II, 684. See Jean Passerat, *Les poésies françaises*, ed. Prosper Blanchemain (2 vols.; Paris, 1880), II, 11, for the sonnet on Charles IX's entree; the poem includes the quatrain:

> L'appareil est superbe, & la magnificence
> Que dressent tant d'ouvriers, & tant de bons esprits:
> Si crain-ie, ô citoyens, que ne soyés repris
> D'avoir faict pour l'entrée une vaine despence.

Passerat's epitaph on Catherine de' Medici is in II, 185, of this edition. Havard, *Dictionnaire*, III, 577, comments on the intricate *machines* in the *Ballet comique de la reine*.

3. The story of the founding of the Order of the Holy Spirit was told by N. Tommasseo, *Relations des ambassadeurs vénitiens sur les affaires de France au XVIe siècle* (2 vols.; Paris, 1838), II, 403 ff. Henry IV's entree into Metz in 1603 is described in Abr. Fabert, *Voyage du Roy à Metz* (Metz, 1603). The illustrative engravings are taken from this volume.

4. The report of Louis XIV's arrival in 1660 in Paris bore the

lengthy title of *L'entrée triomphale de leurs majestez Louis XIV Roy de France et de Navarre et Marie Thérèse d'Autriche son espouse, dans la ville de Paris capitale de leurs royaumes, au retour de la signature de la paix générale de leur heureux mariage, enrichie de plusieurs figures, des harangues et de diverses pièces considérables pour l'histoire* (Paris, 1662). The descriptions of Mazarin and the chancelier Séguier are on pp. 21 ff.

5. See *Entrée, passim;* madame de Motteville, *Mémoires,* p. 499. For madame de Motteville's earlier remark on the new Queen—"sa gorge nous parut bien faite et assez grasse, mais son habit était horrible"—see p. 491.

6. All these details are in the *Entrée;* Boisrobert's verses run as follows:

> Venez, o Reyne triomphante!
> Et recevoir des voeux, et nous donner des lois.
> Venez, régner sur les coeurs des Françoes;
> Et perdez sans regret le beau tiltre d'Infante,
> Entre les bras du plus beau des Roys.

> Voyez dans sa pompe éclatante
> Cet époux si fameux par tant de grands exploits,
> Qui vient borner sa gloire à votre chois.

7. See *Entrée, passim;* the marquis de Villars, *Mémoires,* p. 297.

8. The full title of Pierre du Chastel's story of Francis I's funeral is *Le trespas, obsèques, et enterrement de tres hault, trespuissant, et tresmagnanime François par la grâce de Dieu Roy de France, treschrestien, premier de ce nom, prince clément, père des ars et sciences. Les deux sermons funèbres prononcez esdictes obsèques, l'ung a Notre Dame de Paris, l'autre a Sainct Desnys en France* (Paris, 1547). The document consists of forty-nine folios; this first material is taken from folios 2 ff. Later treatments of royal funerals in the Renaissance include V.-L. Saulnier, "L'oraison funèbre au XVIe siècle," *Bibliothèque d'Humanisme et Renaissance,* X: 124-157 (1948); and Ralph E. Giesey, *The Royal Funeral Ceremony in Renaissance France* (Geneva, 1960).

9. See Du Chastel, *Le trespas,* folios 2, 3.

10. Du Chastel, *Le trespas,* folio 3, verso; and Giesey, *Royal Funeral Ceremony, passim.*

11. Du Chastel, *Le trespas,* folios 4 ff.

12. Du Chastel, *Le trespas,* folios 8 ff.; and Giesey, *Royal Funeral Ceremony, passim.*

13. Du Chastel, *Le trespas,* folios 31-32, in the final paragraph of his first sermon said: "O royaume de France chrétien et catholique, destitué de la glorieuse et fructueuse vie, paré et orné de la mémorable mort de ce grand Roy, peuple, nobles, et iustice de France,

desquels il a continué l'amour et la mémoire jusqu'à la mort: ministres de l'église catholique, qu'il a tenuz et défendus en l'authorité de l'ordre hiérarchique de l'Eglise militante: ne devez vous avoir perpétuelle mémoire et prier continuellement pour lui?"

14. See Du Chastel, *Le trespas*, folios 40 ff. (for the second sermon) and folio 14 (for the ritual of interment and the breaking of the baton); Giesey, *Royal Funeral Ceremony, passim*.

15. Madame de Motteville, *Mémoires*, p. 45, describes the death of Louis XIII and the casual attitude toward it.

16. The couplet against Mazarin (quoted by madame de Motteville, *Mémoires*, p. 507) goes as follows: "Ci gît l'Eminence deuxième: / Dieu nous garde de la troisième." The verses quoted from V. du Val (in the *Pompe funèbre . . . de Iule Mazarini*) begin:

> Au comble de la gloire on a veu des ministres
> Dont la fin fut sujete à des revers sinistres:
> Colosses orgueilleux, qui tombent sous le faix
> Et laissent en mourant leurs desseins imparfaits; . . .

17. See A. Furetière, *Nouvelle allégorique des derniers troubles arrivez au royaume d'Eloquence* (Paris, 1658).

18. See Dangeau, *Journal*, pp. 29-30 (for the Siamese ambassadors), 150-151 (for the page with the frozen arm), and 89 (for the King's reviewing his troops). For the details on the royal wedding and Louis XV's going to the Channel, see D'Argenson, *Journal*, II, 240, VI, 35.

19. L.-S. Mercier, *Tableau de Paris*, pp. 83-84.

## CHAPTER VIII. BUILDINGS AND GARDENS

1. Claude Fauchet, *Recueil*, letter of dedication to Henry III; it begins: "L'antiquité est tellement recommandée à l'endroict des hommes, qui ont le moindre sentiment d'humanité, qu'il se trouve peu de gens aisez, quelques ignorans qu'ils soyent, qui ne désirent se la réprésenter à leur possible: les uns par les livres et médailles, les autres par toutes telles pièces qu'ils en peuvent recouvrer." See Desmarets de Saint-Sorlin, *La comparison*, pp. 27 ff., for the statue with the broken arm.

2. For much of this material on Fontainebleau, see Le Père Dan, *Le trésor des merveilles de la maison royale de Fontainebleau . . .* (Paris, 1642). The comment on "un autre Parnasse" is on p. 19. Pierre Gaxotte, *Histoire*, I, 508, speaks of "l'Olympe et le Parnasse triomphant de l'Evangile," at Fontainebleau. Louis Gillet in G. Hanotaux' *Histoire de la nation française*, XI, 282, speaks of the paganism of Fontainebleau being a change "pour ce public jusqu'alors élevé à l'ombre des églises."

3. The description of the Abbaye de Thélème is in Rabelais' *Gargantua*, beginning with ch. LII; the Oracle de la Dive Bouteille is

described in the *Quint Livre*, starting with ch. XXXIV—the seven columns are in ch. XLII.

4. Molière's poem, *La gloire du Val-de-Grâce*, can be found (among other places) in his *Oeuvres complètes*, ed. Louis Moland (Paris, 1864), VII, 353 ff. The longer quoted excerpt, on p. 356, reads:

> Assaisonné du sel de nos grâces antiques,
> Et non du fade goût des ornements gothiques:
> Ces monstres odieux des siècles ignorants,
> Que de la barbarie ont produits les torrents,
> Quand leur cours, inondant presque toute la terre,
> Fit de la politesse une mortelle guerre,
> Et, de la grande Rome abattant les remparts,
> Vint, avec son empire, étouffer les beaux-arts.

See René Rapin, *Réflexions*, p. 147, for the comparison of an epic poem to a *grand palais*. La Bruyère attacks the Gothic in his *Caractères*, pp. 7-8 (in *Des ouvrages de l'esprit*).

5. For Fénelon's opinion on the Gothic, see his *Lettre à l'Académie*, pp. 269 ff., and 279 (his *Discours*).

6. Havard's ideas on *symétrie* are in his *Dictionnaire*, IV, 1176 ff. Montesquieu's statements are in his "Essai sur le goût," *Oeuvres complètes*, (2 vols.; Paris, 1956-1958), II, 1247. As for the Madeleine's looking like a box of cigars, Frantz Funck-Brentano, *La Renaissance* (Paris, 1935), p. 247, said that on a gray day "le morne édifice ne figure plus à nos yeux qu'une grande boîte à cigares."

7. See Victor L. Tapié, *Le baroque*, p. 27 ("directement inspirées de l'antique"); pp. 50-51 ("l'architecture française a souvent adopté un parti pris de froideur et de sévérité"); pp. 74 ff., *passim*.

8. Tapié, *Le baroque*, p. 80, calls Val-de-Grâce "une église romaine."

9. In *La littérature*, p. 8, Jean Rousset says that in the architecture of Bernini, Borromini, and Pietro da Cortona "on peut attendre une définition indiscutable du Baroque," which can be transferred to "des ouvrages non plastiques."

10. See A.-C. Quatremère de Quincy, *Encyclopédie méthodique* (3 vols.; Paris, 1788-1825), I, 275.

11. For these points, see Méré, *Oeuvres*, II, 22 (for the comparison of the Louvre and Versailles); Gaxotte, *Histoire*, II, 147, says: "Le dernier Versailles, celui de Mansart et de Le Brun, est le modèle de palais français, . . . un des plus nobles lieux du monde, la plus belle réussite artistique du monde moderne, un des chefs-d'oeuvre du génie français."

12. The 1646 edition of Serres' *Théâtre d'agriculture* is particularly valuable because of its wealth of plates.

13. Ernest de Ganay, *Les jardins de France et leur décor* (Paris, 1949), p. 39, says that Beauregard was a garden "assez raffiné."

14. A collection of the engravings of Gabriel Perelle (1603-1677), entitled *Les places, portes, fontaines, églises et maisons de Paris*, was published in Paris after his death, by N. Langlois. The book contains also some plates of Nicolas Perelle. For Chantilly, see Piganiol de la Force, *Description historique de la ville de Paris et de ses environs* (12 vols.; Paris, 1765, first ed. 1742), IX, 80 ff.

15. For the estimate of the gardens of Versailles, see Ganay, *Les jardins*, pp. 86 ff. It is he who uses the term, "harmonie concertante," concerning the statues.

16. The chevalier de Jaucourt praises Le Nôtre and La Quintinie in Diderot's famous *Encyclopédie* (Neufchastel, 1765), VIII, 459.

17. On Clagny, see Piganiol de la Force, *Description*, IX, 141; madame de Sévigné, *Lettres*, IV, 21, described the gardens of Clagny: "les jardins sont faits: vous connaissez la manière de Le Nôtre; il a laissé un petit bois sombre qui fait fort bien; il y a un petit bois d'orangers dans de grandes caisses; on s'y promène."

18. Androuet du Cerceau's notable work bore the title of *Les plus excellents bastiments de France* (2 vols.; Paris, 1576-1579). Claude Mollet's work was called *Théâtre des plans* [plants] *et jardinages* (Paris, 1652). I have used some material of his as quoted by Ganay. The marquis d'Argenson, *Journal*, VI, 58, objected to the expensive vegetables produced in the courtier's *jardin potager*.

19. This description of the *laiterie* of Chantilly is in the *Additions et Corrections* of Piganiol de la Force's *Description*, IX, 518-519. Some later admirer of the milk house thought it had been neglected; the longer quotation which I have excerpted begins: "Son plan est circulaire, et sa couverture en dôme, percée par des yeux de boeufs. Dans l'intérieur, au pourtour de ce pavillon, règne une tablette de marbre à hauteur d'appui. Une rigole est creusée sur ses bords, pour recevoir l'eau de plusieurs petites cascades."

20. Le Père Bouhours, *Remarques*, in the "Avertissement"; Le Père Le Moyne, *Oeuvres*, in the lengthy "Dissertation" and Lettre IX (*Palais de Fortune*), p. 266; Ronsard, *Oeuvres*, VII, 44; Vauquelin de la Fresnaye, *Art poétique*, p. 2.

21. Chevreau, *Oeuvres*, p. 136; madame de Sévigné, *Lettres*, III, 92.


## CHAPTER IX. THE GREAT CLASSICISTS

1. Voltaire's statement concerning the four great cultural ages of the Western world is in the introduction to his *Siècle de Louis XIV*.

2. Tapié, *Le baroque*, pp. 74 ff., in a well-balanced analysis speaks of the present-day tendency to consider "le classicisme français pour un secteur d'un baroque général" and thus reduce "l'importance et l'autonomie du classicisme."

3. Vauquelin de la Fresnaye in his *Art poétique*, bk. II, vs. 330,

said that a poet "la bienséance en tout doit soigneusement garder."

4. See Boileau, *Art poétique*, third canto, vs. 76, where Sophocles "accrut encore la pompe" of tragedy; René Rapin, *Réflexions*, the "Avertissement," for "Aristote . . . est le seul qu'on doit suivre," and ch. V for comparisons of Plato and Aristotle ("sérénité d'esprit qui fait le sang-froid et le jugement"); Bossuet, *Sur le style et la lecture*, for Cicero and the Roman poets; Batteux, *Les beaux arts*, "Avant propos."

5. Doubts about Boileau's critical breadth have been expressed by many commentators on him during the last fifty years or so. The particular excerpts quoted here were made by Georges Pellissier in his edition of Boileau's *Oeuvres poétiques* (Paris, 1891).

6. Boileau attacked Chapelain in many of his verses, especially in the fourth *Satire;* from the second *Satire* comes the much-quoted line, "La raison dit Virgile et la rime Quinault."

7. The quoted lines from Boileau's eleventh *Satire* run as follows:

Du mensonge toujours le vrai demeure maître.
Pour paraître honnête homme en un mot il faut l'être
Et jamais, quoi qu'il fasse, un mortel ici-bas
Ne peut aux yeux du monde être ce qu'il n'est pas.

8. The ninth *Epître*, written to the marquis de Seignelay in 1675, contains the famous verse (vs. 43), "Rien n'est beau que le vrai, le vrai seul est aimable."

9. Madame de Sevigné's comments on Boileau's *Art poétique* are to be found in the cited edition of her *Lettres*, III, 315-316, 369.

10. Most of this material comes from the first *Chant* of Boileau's *Art poétique;* the idyll and the sonnet are taken up in the second *Chant*.

11. Much of the meat of Boileau's *Art poétique* is in the third *Chant* where he treats the noble genres of tragedy and the epic. Vs. 272, "Je chante le vainqueur des vainqueurs de la terre," is delightful satire.

12. The third *Chant* of the *Art poétique* concludes with a discussion of comedy; the fourth *Chant* returns to some general advice for the poet, and ends with some well-worded praise of Louis XIV.

13. This material may be seen easily in Boileau, *Oeuvres poétiques* . . . ed. Ch. Gidel (Paris, n.d.).

14. See Rapin, *Réflexions*, pp. 27 ("vraisemblance dans la fiction"), 39 ff. (for *forme, proportion*, etc.), 52 (for continuing definitions of *vraisemblance*).

15. For these points, see Le Moyne, *Oeuvres, Dissertation du poème épique* (the *vraisemblable* is "le fondement de l'opinion et l'objet de la créance"); Le Bossu, *Traité*, pp. 2-3 ("le plus judicieusement ramassé et prescrit les règles"), 18 ("action feinte vraisemblablement)", 96, 327 ff. (for *vraisemblance* again); Saint Evremond, *Du*

*merveilleux qui se trouve dans les poèmes des anciens* (in his *Critique littéraire*), pp. 71-74.

16. Madame Dacier, *Des causes*, pp. 76-77, 98; Batteux, *Les beaux arts*, pp. 13 ff. ("la matière des beaux arts n'est pas le vrai, mais seulement le vraisemblable"), 25-26 (on Molière), 28 (on Le Brun); Mercier, *Du théâtre*, pp. 144-145.

17. La Mesnardière, *La poétique*, p. FF; Méré, *Oeuvres*, II, 10 ff. ("bienséance vient de ce que nous faisons comme il faut ce qui nous est naturel"), 29; Rapin, *Réflexions*, pp. 108, 230 ff. (on Régnier).

18. Méré, *Oeuvres*, II, 128-129; La Bruyère, *Les Caractères* ("*Des ouvrages de l'esprit*"), p. 7; Chevreau, *Oeuvres meslées*, "Avertissement"; Fenelon, *Lettre*, p. 95; madame Dacier, *Des causes*, pp. 5 (on Desmarets de Saint-Sorlin), 9, 26 (*faux goût* of opera and novels), 393; Mercier, *Du théâtre*, p. 24 ("le boursoufflé Sénèque, imprapre-ment appelé le tragique, eut le style du mauvais goût et de la servi-tude"); La Harpe, *Éloge*, p. 21; Batteux, *Les beaux arts*, "Avant-propos," pp. 53 ff., 124 ("le bon goût est un amour habituel de l'ordre").

19. See Bouhours, *Entretiens*, p. 193 ("le vrai bel esprit. . . est inséparable du bon sens"); Rapin, *Réflexions*, ch. V (poetic *fureur*, etc.), ch. 1 ("jugement san génie," etc.), pp. 37 ("l'assujettissement du génie aux règles d'art"), 114 ("la dernière régularité"); Méré, *Oeuvres*, "Discours de la justice"; Molière, *Critique de l'école des femmes*, sc. 7: "Sachez, s'il vous plaît, monsieur Lycidas. . .que la grande épreuve de toutes nos comédies, c'est le jugement de la Cour"; Le Bossu, *Traité*, bk. VI, "Des sentiments"; Bouhours, *Re-marques*, pp. 190 ff.; Fénelon, *Lettre*, p. 124; Saint Evremond, *Critique*, "Sur les poèmes des anciens," pp. 66 ff.

20. These are basic critical tenets, needing no individual citations.

21. All of these points and many others can be confirmed in the third *Chant* of Boileau's *Art poétique*.

22. See Le Bossu, *Traité*, IV, 35 ff. Le Bossu treats this whole problem of the hero at considerable length.

23. Fénelon, *Lettre*, p. 254; madame Dacier, *Des causes*, pp. 108, 115 ff. (heroes do not have to be "gens de bien et vertueux"), 183 ff. (on Quinault, etc.); La Motte et Fénelon, *Lettres sur Homère et sur les anciens. . .* ed. M. l'abbé P. Bauron (Paris, Lyons, 1897), pp. 171 ff.

24. La Bruyère, *Oeuvres* (3 vols.; Paris, 1818), II, 261 ff.

25. La Mothe le Vayer, *Considérations*, pp. 67 ff. ("les trois per-fections d'un orateur sont d'enseigner, de plaire, et d'émouvoir"); La Mesnardière, *La poétique*, p. 102 (princes "président aux hommes comme lieutenants de Dieu").

26. Bossuet's *Sur le style et la lecture. . .pour former un orateur* can be conveniently consulted in Bossuet, *Extraits des oeuvres di-verses. . .* ed. Gustave Lanson (Paris, 1899), pp. 13 ff.

27. The other ideas of Bossuet mentioned here, and the quotation

on the sad lot of actresses, are to be located in his *Maximes et réflexions sur la comédie. . .* ed. A. Gazier (Paris, 1881).

28. Madame de Sévigné, *Lettres*, II, 102; La Bryuère, *Caractères*, pp. 7-8, 13 24 ff.

29. Boileau's *Le lutrin* has for its opening lines:

> Je chante les combats, et ce prélat terrible,
> Qui par ses longs travaux, et sa force invincible,
> Dans une illustre église exerçant son grand coeur,
> Fit placer à la fin un lutrin dans le choeur.

30. Madame Dacier, *Des causes*, pp. 75-76 (for the ancients and the rules); Pierre Gaxotte, *Histoire*, II, 168, said, in speaking of Louis XIV's reign: "Partout, il etait de règle que le sujet eût la religion de son prince pour que les deux obéissances fussent confondues et fortifiées l'une par l'autre"; the final quotation is taken from Georges Pellissier's edition of Boileau's *Oeuvres poétiques*, p. 28. Even though Pellissier disapproves of Boileau's rigidity, he calls the seventeenth century in France a "troisième antiquité" with the attributes here indicated.

## CHAPTER X. FORMALISM DECLINES

1. See Saint Simon, *Mémoires* . . . ed. Chéruel et Ad. Regnier fils (22 vols.; Paris, 1883-1907), XII, 186 ff. Villars, *Mémoires*, IX, 237; Dangeau, *Journal*, pp. 159 ff.

2. For these details, see D'Argenson, *Journal*, I, 22; II, 218 (for the "satrapie de roture qui a tout mis en forme, en mauvaises règles, en méchants principes et en ruine"); III, 171 (for the increasing price of bread), 188 (for the stags in rut), 234-235 (for the duc de Richelieu's supper party, where there were panels containing "des figures fort immodestes en bas-relief").

3. On the cardinal Fleury's ridiculous *petit coucher*, D'Argenson said, *Journal*, I, 113: "puis on ouvre, et vous voyez ce vieux prêtre qui ôte sa culotte, qu'il plie proprement; on lui passe une assez médiocre robe de chambre, on lui passe sa chemise; il peigne longtemps ses quatre cheveux blancs"; for Louis XIV's receptions and attitude toward his courtiers, see Saint Simon, *Mémoires*, XII, 70 ff.

4. Auguste Bailly, *François Ier*, pp. 138, 265, speaks of Francis I's *magnificence* and *sens de la grandeur;* the same descriptive terms would apply to Louis XIV. For the *parade*, see D'Argenson, *Journal*, V, 292; the quoted verses run:

> Nous autres jeunesses
> Nous écoutons vos raisons;
> Mais dans la belle saison
> Nous nous en battons les fesses.

Other details mentioned here are in D'Argenson, *Journal,* V, 331; III, 249 (for the *pointes*); V, 76 (for Louis XV's debilitation); VI, 182 (for the famous madame and her carriage), and VI, 211-213 (for the proposed burning of Versailles). See the duc de Luynes, *Mémoires,* X, 55, for Louis XV's fall from the horse.

5. See Le Bossu, *Traité,* pp. 2-3; Rapin, *Réflexions,* ch. IV. Perrault's original verses run as follows:

> La belle antiquité fut toujours vénérable,
> Mais je ne crus jamais qu'elle fût adorable.
> Je vois les anciens sans plier les genoux;
> Ils sont grands, il est vrai, mais hommes comme nous;
> Et l'on peut comparer, sans crainte d'être injuste,
> Le siècle de LOUIS au beau siècle d'Auguste.

Boileau said in his seventh *Réflexion:* "puisque c'est la posterité seule qui met la véritable prix aux ouvrages, il ne faut pas, quelque admirable que vous paraisse un écrivain moderne, le mettre aisément en parallèle avec ces écrivains admirés durant un si grand nombre de siècles, puis-qu'il n'est pas même sûr que ses ouvrages passent avec gloire au siècle suivant."

6. Desmarets de Saint-Sorlin, *Comparison,* introductory *Epître*; Saint Evremond, *Critique,* pp. 58-67, 106-118; Chevreau, *Oeuvres,* pp. 161-162.

7. For these quoted excerpts from the *Digression,* see Fontenelle, *Oeuvres* (11 vols.; Paris, 1761-1767), IV, 170-200.

8. See madame Dacier, *Des causes,* pp. 3 ("des hommes tres médiocres"), 5 (for Desmarets de Saint-Sorlin), 3-6 (for La Motte's maiming Homer without knowing Greek), 76 ("autres moyens de plaire" and mariner's compass), 479 (for Menelaus' wound.)

9. This series of *Lettres sur Homère et sur les anciens,* between La Motte and Fénelon, may be found at the end of Fénelon's *Lettre sur les occupations de l'Académie Française . . .* ed. l'abbé Bauron (5th ed.; Paris, Lyons, 1897).

10. Voltaire's comments on Shakespeare are in his *Lettres anglaises,* from the letter "Sur la tragédie." For other details in this paragraph, see Mercier, *Du théâtre,* pp. xiii-xiv, 256, 278; Raynal, *Nouvelles,* p. 72 ("leur [i.e., the French] folie est maintenant pour la tragédie anglaise").

11. Gaxotte, *Histoire,* II, 218 (for the softening of the gods); Raynal, *Nouvelles,* p. 92 (for the too dominant "couleur de rose").

12. See Gaxotte, *Histoire,* II, 221 (for "le lieu de commodité à l'anglaise," etc.).

13. H. Havard, *Dictionnaire,* I, 839, says: "Le mépris de la symétrie qui distingue les oeuvres de l'Extrême Orient, les formes contournées des cadres qui les enveloppent, leurs lignes irrégulières, si différentes de nos contours pondérés, toute cette fantasmagorie char-

mante, qui tranche si vivement avec la correction classique, ont dû étonner d'abord, puis séduire l'oeil de nos dessinateurs et disposer leurs esprits à des brillantes audaces."

14. See Havard, *Dictionnaire*, III, 1325 (for *ottomane*); Paul Dupays, *Gastronomie historique*, p. 60 (for cuisine under Louis XV).

15. For Jaucourt's remarks on "un goût ridicule" in eighteenth-century gardens, see the *Encyclopédie*, VIII, 460: "Les grandes allées droites nous paraissent stupides; les palissades, froides et uniformes; nous aimons à pratiquer des allées tortueuses, des parterres chantournés, et des bosquets coupés en pompons; . . . Les corbeilles de fleurs, fanées au bout de quelques jours, ont pris la place de quelques parterres durables; l'on voit partout des vases de terre cuite, des magots chinois, des bambochades . . . qui nous prouvent assez claire-ment que la frivolité a étendu son empire sur toutes nos productions en ce genre."

16. Jaucourt continues the above discourse and favors English gardens for their simplicity. See Mercier, *Du théâtre*, pp. 96-97, for his praise of English gardens; Havard, *Dictionnaire*, III, 90 ff. (for substitution of "le pittoresque de la nature aux combinaisons sy-métriques et pondérées").

17. This letter from *La nouvelle Héloïse* may be seen in the *Oeuvres complètes de J. J. Rousseau* (37 vols.; Paris, 1793), V, 147 ff. The note, pp. 167-168, shows Rousseau's fear of the disappearance of naturalness from gardens: "Je suis persuadé que le temps approche où l'on ne voudra plus dans les jardins rien de ce qui se trouve dans la campagne; on n'y souffrira plus ni plantes, ni arbrisseaux; on n'y voudra que des fleurs de porcelaine, des magots, des treillages, du sable de toutes couleurs, et de beaux vases pleins de rien."

18. Much of this material has been treated by Ganay, *Les jardins*, pp. 176 ff., and Georges Gromont, *L'art des jardins* (2 vols.; Paris, 1953). It was Ganay who said (*Les jardins*, p. 187) that "les jardins reflètent les moeurs de leur temps," and thus in the eighteenth cen-tury, "l'avènement de l'individualité opposée à l'esprit de discipline." Some of the exotic descriptions are to be seen in Havard's *Diction-naire* as quoted above. Other examples of exoticism in French gardens of the eighteenth century will be found in Jean-Charles Krafft, *Plans des plus beaux jardins pittoresques de France, d'Angleterre et d'Alle-magne* (2 vols.; Paris, 1809-1810).

19. Perrault's verses in the original run as follows:

> S'il joint a ses talents l'amour de l'antiquaille,
> S'il trouve qu'en nos jours on ne fait rien qui vaille,
> Et qu'à tout bon moderne il donne un coup de dent,
> De ces dons rassemblés se forme le pédant,
> Le plus fastidieux, comme le plus immonde
> De tous les animaux qui rampent dans le monde.

These verses are included in the Ch. Gidel edition of Boileau's *Oeuvres*. Boileau also attacked pedantry in his fourth *Satire*.

20. All the short quotations in this paragraph are taken from the *Paris-Match* description.

21. Raynal, *Nouvelles littéraires*, p. 76: "Le Français est un être tout à fait difficile à définir."

# BIBLIOGRAPHY

(This is a selected bibliography of material referred to either in the main body of the book or in the notes.)

Aneau, Barthélemy. *Toutes les emblèmes de M. André Alciat de nouveau trāslatez en françoys vers pour vers.* Lyons: Chez Guillaume Rouille, 1558.

—— *Quintil Horatian,* in Em. Person's edition of Du Bellay's *Deffence et illustration...(see* Du Bellay).

Argenson, Le marquis d'. *Journal et mémoires...* ed. E. J. B. Rathery. Société de l'Histoire de France. 9 vols. Paris: Chez Mme Ve Jules Renouard, 1859-1867.

Aubignac, Abbé d'. *La pratique du théâtre....* ed. Pierre Martino. Algiers, Paris: Charbonel et Champion, 1927.

Baïf, J.-A. *Euvres en rime...* ed. Ch. Marty-Laveaux. La Pléiade Française. 5 vols. Paris: Lemerre, 1890.

Bailly, Auguste. *François Iᵉʳ, restaurateur des lettres et des arts.* Paris: Arthème Fayard, 1954.

Batiffol, Louis. *Le siècle de la Renaissance.* 10th ed. Paris: Hachette, n.d.

Batteux, Charles. *Les beaux arts réduits à un même principe.* Paris: Chez Durand, 1746.

Boileau. *Oeuvres poétiques...* ed. Georges Pellissier. Paris: Delagrave, 1891.

—— *Oeuvres poétiques...* ed. Ch. Gidel. Paris: Garnier, n.d.

Bossuet. *Extraits des oeuvres diverses...* ed. Gustave Lanson. Paris: Delagrave, 1899.

—— *Maximes et réflexions sur la comédie, précédées de la lettre au P. Caffaro...* ed. A. Gazier. Paris: Lib. Clas. Eugène Belin, 1881.

Bouhours, Le Père Francisque. *Les entretiens d'Ariste et d'Eugène.* Paris: Chez Sébastien Mabre-Cramoisy, 1671.

—— *Remarques nouvelles sur la langue françoise.* Paris: Chez Sébastien Mabre-Cramoisy, 1675.

—— *Doutes sur la langue françoise proposez à Messieurs de l'Académie françoise par un gentilhomme de province.* Paris: Chez Sébastien Mabre-Cramoisy, 1674.

Boulenger, Jacques. *Le grand siècle.* 10th ed., rev. Paris: Hachette, n.d.

Buffum, Imbrie. *Studies in the Baroque from Montaigne to Rotrou.* New Haven: Yale University Press, 1957.

Bussières, Jean de. *Les descriptions poétiques.* Lyons: Chez Jean Bapt. Devenet, 1649.

Chassignet, J.-B. *Sonnets franc-comtois inédits.* . . ed. Théodore Courtaux. Paris: Cabinet de l'Historiographe, 1892.

Chevreau, Urbain. *Oeuvres meslées.* La Haye: Chez Adrian Moetjens, 1697.

Coulanges, Ph.-E. de. *Recueil de chansons choisies.* Paris: Simon Bernard, 1694.

Dacier, madame. *Des causes de la corruption du goust.* Paris: Aux Dépends Rigaud, 1714.

Dan, le Père. *Le trésor des merveilles de la maison royale de Fontainebleau, contenant la description de son antiquité, de sa fondation, de ses bastimens, de ses rares peintures, tableaux, emblèmes et devises: des ses jardins, de ses fontaines, et autres singularitez.* . . Paris: Chez Sébastien Cramoisy, 1642.

Dangeau, le marquis de. *Journal de la cour de Louis XIV, depuis 1684 jusqu'à 1715* . . . London, 1770.

Deimier, Pierre de. *L'académie de l'art poétique.* Paris: Chez Jean de Bordeaux, 1610.

Desmarets de Saint-Sorlin. *La comparaison de la langue et de la poésie françoise, avec la grecque et la latine.* Paris: Chez Thomas Jolly, 1670.

——— *La défense de la poésie et de la langue françoise.* Paris: Chez Nicholas de Gras. 1675.

Du Bellay, Joachim. *La deffence et illustration de la langue françoyse* . . . suivie du *Quintil Horatian.* . . ed. Em. Person. Versailles, Paris 1878.

Du Chastel, Pierre. *Le trespas, obsèques, et enterrement de tres hault, trèspuissant, et trèsmagnanime François par la grâce de Dieu Roy de France, trèschrestien, premier de ce nom, prince clément, père des ars et sciences. Les deux sermons funèbres prononcez esdictes obsèques, l'ung à Nostre Dame de Paris, l'autre à Sainct Denys en France.* Paris: De l'imprimerie de Rob. Estienne Imprimeur du Roy, [1547].

Dupays, Paul. *Gastronomie historique de l'art culinaire.* Paris: Editions de la Critique, 1953.

Dupleix, Scipion. *Liberté de la langue françoise dans sa pureté.* Paris: Denys Bechet, 1651.

Duplessis, Georges. *Costumes historiques des XVIe, XVIIe et XVIIIe siècles.* 2 vols. Paris: Librairie d'Architecture de A. Lévy, 1867.

*Encyclopédie, ou Dictionnaire raisonné des sciences, des arts et des métiers.* 17 vols. Neufchastel: Samuel Faulch, 1765.

*Entrée triomphale de leurs majestez Louis XIV Roy de France et de Navarre et Marie Thérèse d'Autriche son espouse, dans la ville de Paris capitale de leurs royaumes, au retour de la signature de la paix générale de leur heureux mariage, enrichie de plusieurs figures,*

*des harangues et de diverses pièces considérables pour l'histoire.*
Paris: Pierre le Petit, 1662.

Fabri, Pierre. *Le grand et vrai art de pleine rhétorique.* . . ed. A.
Héron. 3 vols. Rouen: A. L'Estringant, 1889-1890.

Fauchet, Claude. *Recueil de l'origine de la langue et poésie françoise*
. . . *plus les noms et sommaire des oeuvres de CXXVII poètes
françois.* Paris: Par Mamert Patisson imprimeur du Roy, 1581.

Fénelon. *Lettre à l'Académie.* . . ed. l'abbé Albert Delplanque. Paris:
L. de Gigord, 1911.

Fontenelle, Bernard de. *Oeuvres.* 11 vols. Paris, 1761-1767.

Fouquelin, Antoine de. *La rhétorique françoise.* . . 2nd ed. Paris:
André Wechel, 1557.

Funck-Brentano, Frantz. *La Renaissance.* Paris: Fayard, 1935.

Furetière, A. *Nouvelle allégorique ou histoire des derniers troubles
arrivez au royaume d'Eloquence.* 2nd ed. Paris: Pierre Lamy, 1658.

—— *L'apothéose du dictionnaire de l'Académie, et son expulsion de
la région céleste.* La Haye: Chez Arnout Leers, 1696.

—— *L'enterrement du dictionnaire de l'Académie.* n.p. 1697.

—— *Recueil des factums.* . . ed. Charles Assélineau. 2 vols. Paris:
Poulet-Malassis et De Broise, 1859.

Ganay, Ernest de. *Les jardins de France et leur décor.* Paris: Larousse,
1949.

Gaxotte, Pierre. *Histoire des Français.* 2 vols. Paris: Flammarion, 1951.

Giesey, Ralph E. *The Royal Funeral Ceremony in Renaissance
France.* Travaux d'Humanisme et Renaissance, XXXVII. Geneva:
E. Droz, 1960.

Godefroy, D. *Le cérémonial français.* Paris, 1649.

Gossman, Lionel. *Men and Masks: A Study of Molière.* Baltimore:
The Johns Hopkins Press, 1963.

Gromont, Georges. *L'art des jardins.* 2 vols. 2ième éd. Paris: Vincent,
Fréal et Cie, 1953.

Hatzfeld, Helmut. "Use and Misuse of 'Baroque' as a Critical Term in
Literary History." *Univ. of Toronto Quarterly,* 31:180-200 (1962).

Havard, H. *Dictionnaire de l'ameublement et de la décoration depuis
le XIIIe siècle à nos jours.* 4 vols. Paris: Librairies-Imprimeries Ré-
unies, 1894.

Krafft, Jean-Charles. *Plans des plus beaux jardins pittoresques de
France, d'Angleterre et d'Allemagne.* 2 vols. Paris: Imprimerie de
Levrault et de C. Pougens, 1809-1810.

La Bruyère, Jean de. *Oeuvres.* 3 vols. Paris: Chez Antoine-Augustin
Renouard, 1818.

—— *Les caractères.* . .suivis. . .du *Discours à l'Académie.* Société
de Saint-Augustin. Lille: Desclée de Brouwer et Cie., 1884.

La Fontaine, Jean de. *Fables.* . .avec notes et commentaires. Lille: L.
Fort, 1837.

La Harpe, J.-A. de. *Eloge de Racine*. Amsterdam, Paris: Chez Lacombe, 1772.

*La magnifica e triumphale entrata del christianiss. Re di Francia Henrico secondo. . .fatta nella nobile ed antiqua città di Lyone. . .alli 21 di septemb. 1548*. Lyons: Gulielmo Rouillio, 1549.

La Mesnardière, Jules de. *La poétique*. Paris: Chez Antoine de Sommaville, 1639.

La Mothe le Vayer, François de. *Considérations sur l'éloquence françoise de ce tems*. Paris: Chez Sébastien Cramoisy, 1637.

La Motte et Fénelon. *Lettres sur Homère et sur les anciens* (included with Fénelon's *Lettre* to the Académie Française). . .ed. M. l'abbé Bauron. 5th ed. Paris, Lyons: Dehomme et Briguet, 1897.

La Taille, Jacques de. *La manière de faire des vers en françois comme en grec et en latin*. Paris: Fréderic Morel Imprimeur du Roy, 1573.

Laudun d'Aigaliers, Pierre. *L'art poétique français, édition critique*. . . ed. Joseph Dedieu. Toulouse: Au Siège des Facultés libres, 1909.

Le Bossu, le R. P. *Traité du poème épique*. Paris: Chez Michel le Petit, 1675.

Le Moyne, le Père. *Les oeuvres poétiques*. Paris: Chez Louis Billaine, 1671.

Luynes, Charles-Philippe d'Albert, duc de. *Mémoires du duc de Luynes sur la cour de Louis XV (1735-1758)* . . . ed. MM. L. Dussieux et Eud. Soulié. 17 vols. Paris: Firmin-Didot, 1860-1865.

Malherbe, François de. *Oeuvres poétiques de Malherbe précédées de la vie de Malherbe par Racan* . . . ed. M. Louis Moland. Paris: Garnier Frères, 1874.

Mambrun, le Père Pierre, S.J. *Dissertatio peripatetica de epico carmine*. Paris, 1652.

Mandrou, Robert. *Introduction à la France moderne, 1500-1640*. Paris: Albin Michel, 1961.

Martial de Brives, R.P. *Les oeuvres poétiques*. Lyons: Chez François La Bottière, 1653.

Meigret, Louis. *Le tretté de la grammere françoeze*. Paris: Chés Chrestien Weschsel, 1550.

Ménage, Gilles. *Les origines de la langue françoise*. Paris: Chez Augustin Courbé, 1650.

—— *Observations sur la langue françoise*. Paris: Claude Barbin, 1672.

Mercier, L.-S. *Du théâtre ou nouvel essai sur l'art dramatique*. Amsterdam: Chez E. van Harrevelt, 1773.

Méré, le chevalier de. *Oeuvres complètes*. . . ed. Charles H. Boudhors. 3 vols. Paris: Fernand Roches, 1930.

Molière. *Oeuvres* . . . ed. M. Louis Moland. 7 vols. Paris: Garnier Frères, 1863-1864.

Mollet, Claude. *Théâtre des plans et jardinages*. Paris, 1652.

Mongrédien, Georges. *La vie de société aux XVIIe et XVIIIe siècles* Paris: Hachette, 1950.

Montesquieu. *Oeuvres complètes,* ed. Roger Callois. Bibliothèque de la Pléiade. 2 vols. Paris: Nouvelle Revue Française, 1956-1958.

Motteville, madame de. *Mémoires. Nouvelle Collection de Mémoires pour servir à l'Histoire de France.* . .ed. MM. Michaud et Poujoulat. Vol. X. Paris, 1838.

Parfaict, les Frères. *Histoire du théâtre français depuis son origine jusqu'à présent.* 12 vols. Paris: Lemercier et Saillant, 1745-1749.

Pascal, Blaise. *Pensées et opuscules philosophiques,* . . . ed. Fernand Flutre. Paris: Hachette, 1927.

Passerat, Jean. *Les poésies françaises.* . .ed. Prosper Blanchemain. 2 vols. Paris: Lemerre, 1880.

Peletier du Mans, Jacques. *L'art poétique.* . .ed. André Boulanger. Paris: Les Belles Lettres, 1930.

Pellisson et d'Olivet. *Histoire de l'Académie Française.* . .ed. M. Ch.-L. Livet. 2 vols. Paris: Didier et Cie., 1858.

Perelle, Gabriel. *Les places, portes, fontaines, églises et maisons de Paris.* . .Paris: Chez N. Langlois, *circa* 1680. (This is a volume of engravings done by Gabriel and Nicolas Perelle.)

Piganiol de la Force, J.-A. *Description historique de la ville de Paris et de ses environs.* 12 vols. Paris: Chez G. Desprez. 1765.

*Pompe funèbre ou éloges de Iule Mazarini, cardinal, duc, et premier ministre.* . . Poème héroique. Paris: Chez Sébastien Martin, 1665. (This is a series of verses—signed on the last page, V. du Val.)

*Pompes funèbres . . . de l'archiduc Albert VII.* Brussels, 1623. (This is a large volume in-folio of various aspects of Albert VII's funeral; plates of other funerals are also included.)

Quatremère de Quincy, A.-C. *Encyclopédie méthodique.* 3 vols Paris: Pankoucke, 1788-1825.

Rapin, le Père René, S.J. *Réflexions sur la poétique d'Aristote et sur les ouvrages des poètes anciens et modernes.* Paris: Chez François Muguet, 1674.

Raymond, Marcel. *Baroque et Renaissance poétique.* Paris: José Corti, 1955.

Raynal, l'Abbé. *Nouvelles littéraires (1747-1755),* in vol. I of *Correspondance littéraire* . . . by Grimm, Diderot, Raynal, *et al.,* ed. Maurice Tourneux. 16 vols. Paris: Garnier Frères, 1877.

Ronsard, Pierre de. *Oeuvres complètes.* . .ed. Paul Laumonier. 7 vols. Paris: Lemerre, 1914-1919.

Rousset, Jean. *La littérature de l'âge baroque en France.* Paris: José Corti, 1953.

Saint-Amant. *Oeuvres poétiques.* . .ed. Léon Vérane. Paris: Garnier Frères, 1930.

Saint Evremond. *Critique littéraire.* . .ed. Maurice Wilmotte. Paris Bossard, 1921.

—— *Les Académiciens*. . . ed. Robert de Bonnières. Paris: Charavay Frères, 1879.

Saint Simon, Louis de Rouvroy, duc de. *Mémoires*. . . ed. A. de Boislisle, *et al*. Grands Ecrivains de la France. 42 vols. Paris: Hachette, 1879-1928.

—— *Mémoires*. . . ed. MM. Chéruel et Ad. Regnier fils. 2nd ed. 22 vols. Paris; Hachette, 1883-1907.

Sebillet, Thomas. *Art poétique françoys* . . . ed. Félix Gaiffe. Paris: Société nouvelle de Libraire et d'Edition, 1910.

Serres, Olivier de. *Le théâtre d'agriculture et mesnage des champs*. . . Rouen: Chez Jean Berthelin, 1646.

Sévigné, madame de. *Lettres de madame de Sévigné, de sa famille et de ses amis* . . . ed. M. Monmerqué. Grands Ecrivains de la France. 14 vols. Paris: Hachette, 1866 (new ed., 1925).

Sponde, Jean de. *Oeuvre poétique*. . . ed. Marcel Arland. Paris: Ed. Stock, 1945.

Tapié, Victor-L. *Le baroque*. Paris: Presses Universitaires Françaises, 1961.

Vaugelas, Claude Faure de. *Remarques sur la langue françoise utiles à ceux qui veulent bien parler et bien escrire*. 3rd ed. Paris: Chez Augustin Courbé, 1655.

Vauquelin de la Fresnaye. *L'art poétique* . . . ed. Georges Pellissier. Paris: Garnier Frères, 1885.

Villars, le maréchal de. *Mémoires. Nouvelle Collection des Mémoires pour servir à l'Histoire de France*. . . ed. MM. Michaud et Poujoulat. Vol. IX. Paris: Chez l'Editeur, 1839.

*Voyage du Roy à Metz* . . . by Abr. Fabert. Metz, 1603. (This is a description, with illustrative plates, of Henry IV's entree into Metz.)

Weinberg, Bernard. *Critical Prefaces of the Renaissance*. Evanston: Northwestern University Press, 1960.

Wiley, W. L. *The Gentleman of Renaissance France*. Cambridge: Harvard University Press, 1954.

# INDEX